The Overall Development of Chile. Mario Zañartu, S.J., and John J. Kennedy, eds.

The Catholic Church Today: Western Europe. M. A. Fitzsimons, ed.

Contemporary Catholicism in the United States. Philip Gleason, ed.

The Major Works of Peter Chaadaev. Raymond T. McNally.

A Russian European: Paul Miliukov in Russian Politics. Thomas Riha.

A Search for Stability: U. S. Diplomacy Toward Nicaragua, 1925–1933. William Kamman.

Freedom and Authority in the West. George N. Shuster, ed.

Theory and Practice: History of a Concept from Aristotle to Marx. Nicholas Lobkowicz.

Coexistence: Communism and Its Practice in Bologna, 1945–1965. Robert H. Evans.

Marx and the Western World. Nicholas Lobkowicz, ed.

Argentina's Foreign Policy 1930–1962. Alberto A. Conil Paz and Gustavo E. Ferrari.

Italy after Fascism, A Political History, 1943–1965. Giuseppe Mammarella.

The Volunteer Army and Allied Intervention in South Russia 1917–1921. George A. Brinkley.

Peru and the United States, 1900–1962. James C. Carey.

Empire by Treaty: Britain and the Middle East in the Twentieth Century. M. A. Fitzsimons.

The USSR and the UN's Economic and Social Activities. Harold Karan Jacobson.

Chile and the United States: 1880–1962. Fredrick B. Pike.

INTERNATIONAL STUDIES OF THE

COMMITTEE ON INTERNATIONAL RELATIONS

UNIVERSITY OF NOTRE DAME

Revolution and Church

STUDIES IN
CHRISTIAN DEMOCRACY
VOLUME IV

Revolution

and

Church

The Early History of Christian Democracy,
1789–1901

HANS MAIER

Translated by
EMILY M. SCHOSSBERGER

 UNIVERSITY OF NOTRE DAME PRESS
NOTRE DAME   LONDON

Croire que les sociétés démocratiques sont naturellement hostiles à la religion est commettre une grande erreur: rien dans le christianisme, ni même dans le catholicisme, n'est absolument contraire à l'esprit de ces sociétés, et plusieurs choses y sont trés favorables.

Tocqueville

La Révolution fera le tour du monde, comme l'a dit Mirabeau, mais ayant derrière elle l'Eglise catholique.

Lacordaire

Immo neque illud per se reprehenditur, participem plus minus esse populum rei publicae: quod ipsum certis in temporibus certisque legibus potest non solum ad utilitatem, sed etiam ad officium pertinere civium.

Leo XIII

CONTENTS

PREFACE TO THE AMERICAN EDITION

Christian Democratic parties are phenomena of the twentieth century. After the Second World War they began to make their appearance in several European as well as Latin American countries. Yet the idea of Christian Democracy is much older: it goes back to the disputes between Catholic followers and opponents of the French Revolution that mirror the struggles between the church and modern democratic ideas in the span between 1789 and 1900.

The early history of the idea of Christian Democracy is little known. The intention of this edition is to present it in the English language. Anglo-Saxon readers know the history of the Christian Democratic parties from the books of Einaudi-Goguel and Fogarty, which present history from the party point of view. This book attempts to place the origins and development of the Christian democratic idea within a wider context by sharing the spotlight with theology and the history of political ideas, as well as with a consideration of church policy of the nineteenth century. An analysis of writers like Lamennais, Buchez, Ozanam, and De Mun and of the personality of Leo XIII is also undertaken.

Though based on a historical approach, our presentation leads directly into the current problems of church and society. In the disputes between the church and the French Revolution is contained not only the problem of a "theology of revolution" but also the possibility of a fruitful cooperation between the church and democracy, an approach fought for by the pioneering Christian Democrats of the nineteenth century, but one often not even understood by the church.

Special thanks are due to Miss Emily Schossberger of the University of Notre Dame Press, whose constant work and counseling, as well as translation, made the publication of this book possible. To her, and all those who have contributed to her work, go my special thanks.

Munich   Hans Maier
March, 1969

1: CHRISTIAN DEMOCRACY:
PAST AND PRESENT

CHRISTIAN DEMOCRACY IN EUROPEAN POLITICS

Of European political parties the Christian Democratic ones constitute a comparatively late arrival, gaining wide acceptance only after World War II. The MRP (*Mouvement Républicain Populaire*) appeared in France toward the close of 1944; it was a novelty in French party history, "the offspring of tradition and accident," as Jacques Fauvet put it.[1] A year earlier the *Democrazia Cristiana* (DC) had emerged in liberated Italy, a left-wing Catholic party based on the old *Partito Popolare Italiano* and destined under De Gasperi to play the leading role in Italian postwar politics. Germany followed in 1945 with the *Christlich-demokratischen und Christlich-sozialen Union* (CDU/CSU).[2]

---

[1] J. Fauvet, *De Thorez à de Gaulle. Les forces politiques en France* (2d ed., Paris, 1951), p. 168. According to L. Biton, *La Démocratie chrétienne dans la politique française* (Angers, 1954), p. 65, the real origin of the MRP lies in the talks which took place in Paris during the last days of October and the beginning of November, 1943, between Dru, Gilibert, Bidault, and Colin.

[2] From the rapidly increasing literature see, concerning France: F. Goguel, "Christian Democracy in France," in M. Einaudi and F. Goguel, *Christian Democracy in Italy and France* (University of Notre Dame Press, 1952). Concerning Italy: M. Einaudi, "Christian Democracy in Italy," in the above-cited volume by Einaudi-Goguel; L. Somma, *De Gasperi o Gronchi* (Rome, 1953); G. Tupini, *I Democratici Cristiani* (Milan, 1954); F. Magri, *La Democrazia Cri-*

These new organizations were joined after the war by the older, smaller Christian Democratic organizations of Belgium, Holland, Luxemburg, and Austria, suppressed by the Nazis during the war or immediately after *Anschluss*. In Eastern Europe, too, several small Christian Democratic parties raised their heads but survived only briefly. They were either proscribed or were merged in the "national blocs" of their respective countries.[3]

Westward the spread of Christian Democracy was checked in countries of Protestant or Catholic-monarchistic traditions; neither England, Spain, nor Portugal saw the development of a Christian Democratic party. Christian Democracy's main region of development was Central and Western Europe approximately midway between the purely Catholic and the purely Protestant zones, an area bisected by the axis Flanders-Venice.[4]

The Christian Democratic parties of Western Europe had long anticipated their hour of emergence. Nonetheless, they were surprised by their success after the war. Nearly overnight some Christian Democratic leaders, who were sometimes completely unprepared for them, obtained key positions. Within this rather

stiana in Italia 1897–1954 (Milan, 1954). Concerning Germany: L. Schwering, *Vorgeschichte und Entstehung der CDU* (Cologne, 1952); H. G. Wieck, *Die Entstehung der CDU und die Wiedergründung des Zentrums im Jahre 1945* (Düsseldorf, 1953); E. Deuerlein, *CDU/CSU 1945–1957, Beiträge zur Zeitgeschichte* (Cologne 1957); A. J. Heidenheimer, *Adenauer and the CDU* (The Hague, 1960); A. Schardt, *Wohin steuert die CDU* (Osnabrück, 1961); H. Bertsch, *CDU/CSU demaskiert* (East Berlin, 1961). Synopses: M. Vaussard, *Histoire de la Démocratie chrétienne (France, Belgique, Italie)* (Paris, 1956); M. P. Fogarty, *Christian Democracy in Western Europe, 1820–1953* (Notre Dame, 1958); H. Hirten (ed.), *Christliche Parteien in Europa* (Osnabrück, 1964). Cf. my book review in: *Civitas. Jahrbuch für christliche Gesellschaftsordnung*, Vol. III (1964).

[3] For a survey, see Z. M. Ossowski, J. Pecháček, and W. Juhasz in *Church and Society*, ed. by J. Moody (New York, 1953).

[4] On the geographical spread of Christian Democracy in Europe, see Fogarty, *op. cit.*, pp. 7–10.

general development the meteoric rise of the French *Démocratie chrétienne*, until then virtually unnoticed, understandably drew the greatest attention. It suddenly seemed that the French Catholic left, long distrusted by the church and suspect as "*rouges-chrétiens*," were about to triumph in the classical land of secularism and initiate by their example a new wave of supranational party formation, the wave of Christian Democracy now to succeed the earlier liberal and socialist movements. This first impression was misleading. The ties among Christian Democratic parties were to remain much looser than those among liberal and socialist parties. The prerequisites of closer collaboration (a common organizational bureau, common statutes, regular international congresses) clearly were absent. In spite of some few steps in the direction of unity, the preconditions are still lacking. The Nouvelles Equipes Internationales (NEI) is but a loose confederation, since 1947, of the Christian Democratic parties of Western Europe (seat in Paris). The Christian Democratic Union of Central Europe (CDUCE), founded by immigrants from Eastern Europe and comprising the Christian Democratic parties of Poland, Lithuania, Latvia, Hungary, Yugoslavia, and Czechoslovakia, has somewhat stronger ties.

But the lack has not hampered the effectiveness of the new political movement. Without having taken the form of an international, Christian Democracy has, nonetheless, maintained itself in the countries where it came to prominence after the war. The total voting support for Christian Democratic parties remained constant between 1945 and 1960 with only negligible fluctuations. France is an exception. There the Popular Republicans, very successful in the elections of 1945 and 1946, had lost so many votes even before the triumph of Gaullism that it more and more assumed the character of a merely regional party with an area of influence restricted to the pronouncedly Catholic regions—Alsace-Lorraine, Vendée, Brétagne. A similar decrease, although on a smaller scale, has been visible in Italy since the "apertura a sinistra" and the elections of 1962.[5] A downward trend has only recently been observed in some countries. Nor can there be any doubt of the importance of the role played by Christian Democracy in Europe's postwar politics. One need only point to the contribution of European Christian Democratic parties in the creation of the German, Italian, and French social laws, or to the deeply influential European policies of Schuman, De Gasperi, and Adenauer. This great accomplishment, the only one to which Europe, torn after the war by leadership struggles, has been able to rise, would alone be sufficient to assure the movement the interest of the politicians and historians of the future.

What are Christian Democratic parties? An observer is hampered by the variety of their structures. Christian Democracy is organized in the most varied ways, reaches most disparate environments, and recruits members from many layers of society. The parties rise above a tangled network of organizations of pre- and extrapolitical kinds: religious, youth, and lay; corporate and professional associations; Christian labor unions and the older Christian political parties, which are indeed the actual historical models of Christian Democracy.[6] For postwar Christian Democracy has not sprung suddenly from nowhere. Its basis is to be located in numerous older organizations. It is obviously inter-

<hr>

[5] See on France, J. Fauvet in *Dokumente*, January, 1956, pp. 36 ff.; recently, J.-C. Criqui in H. Hirten (ed.), Christliche Parteien, pp. 75 ff.; W. Bosworth, *Catholicism and Crisis in Modern France* (Princeton, 1962), pp. 239 ff. On Italy, see the "Report" of Lina Morino, De Gasperi's collaborator of many years, in Hirten (ed.), *Christliche Parteien*, pp. 165 ff.

[6] For a comprehensive analysis of this "infrastructure," see Fogarty, *op. cit.*, pp. 186 ff., 294 ff., and—especially on France—Bosworth, *op. cit.*, pp. 156 ff., 238 ff.

twined with the organizational forms of political and social Catholicism in the countries of the Romance languages; there, where the Christian Democratic politician has usually belonged to the upper layer of Catholic associations or to the leadership of Christian unions, there is often a close personal, non-institutional, connection between religious associations and politico-social groups or parties. In those countries Christian Democracy quickly established its political tradition. The Italian *Democrazia Cristiana* can be traced back to the *Partito Popolare Italiano*, founded by Don Luigi Sturzo; the French *Mouvement Républicain Populaire* to Marc Sagnier's *Sillon* and the *Parti Démocrate Populaire* of Champetier de Ribes.[7] Nor is the success of the German CDU imaginable without the preparatory work of the old *Zentrum* party. The part played by Protestantism in the formation of the contemporary Christian Democratic parties is more difficult to measure; although none of the parties, with the possible exception of the Dutch Roman Catholic People's Party, has a denominational coloration, only the CDU and, in a smaller way, the MRP have Protestant wings. This is a reflection of the minimal contribution of European Protestantism to the formation of Christian Democracy. The precursors of modern Christian Democracy came not from Protestant circles but from political and social Catholicism. They made their appearance when the party politics of European Protestants were moving in a completely different direction, when Protestant parties were for the most part conservative or deliberately persisted in acting out of a religio-charitable and Christian social attitude, some-

---

[7] L. Sturzo was a senator of the *Democrazia Cristiana* in the Italian senate; M. Sangnier was honorary president of the MRP. After a short period of hesitation, the *Parti Démocrate Populaire*, which had been re-established in 1944, merged with the MRP; its newspaper, *Aube*, became the official party organ of the Popular Republicans (in existence until 1951).

times in conscious opposition to political democracy.[8] Let us note here the Prussian Christian-Conservatives and the Dutch Anti-Revolutionary party and its splinter, the Christian Historical Union. More recent Protestant party formations remain conservative, at least in their concept of state. For Stoecker and Naumann the combination of a Christian social policy and the idea of a democratic and social empire are characteristic. It was only after World War I that individual Protestant parties—among them the Swiss Protestant People's party and the German Christian-Social People's Service—declared themselves for republicanism and political democracy. It is, therefore, no exaggeration to say that before 1945 the idea and the movement of Christian Democracy in Continental Europe were limited to regions of Catholic prevalence.

The situation was different in the Anglo-Saxon countries. There Christian Democracy had always been alive as an idea. That there has been no political movement or party tallying with it during the recent past can be explained by the fact that the task of such a party or movement—the reconciliation of revolution and church—had already been achieved. Since the Anglo-Saxon form of democracy presupposes both the Anglo-Saxon concept of church and Anglo-Saxon ecclesiastical history, its standards cannot easily be transferred to continental Protestantism.

[8] As late as 1928 Erik Peterson was able to write about the conditions in Germany: "From the intellectual sociological point of view the Protestant church just about corresponds to the intellectual and sociological status of the German-National People's party." (Correspondence with Adolf Harnack and an "Epiloque," *Hochland*, November, 1932, as reprinted in *Theologische Traktate* (Munich, 1951), p. 301. On the whole problem, cf. W. O. Shanahan, *German Protestants Face the Social Question* (Notre Dame, 1954); H. H. Schrey, *Die Generation der Entscheidung* (Munich, 1955), pp. 105 ff., and K. Kupisch, *Zwischen Idealismus und Massendemokratie. Eine Geschichte der Evangelischen Kirche in Deutschland 1815–1945* (2d ed.; Berlin, 1959).

Only the changes in the situation that occurred after the Second World War and the closer connections forged between denominations during the common struggle against totalitarianism created the conditions that permitted Christian Democracy to become a party of the masses beyond the confines of denomination.

The exodus of Christian Democrats from the ghetto of a denominational party has been received with mixed feelings by the public. Theological critics, especially in Protestant circles, have pointed to the dangerous secularization of the experiment.[9] Politicians, depending on their point of view, have criticized the new party as either too revolutionary or too reactionary. Emanuel Mounier, the Catholic philosopher and writer, was explicit in his critical judgment:

> Let us be frank about it. The sudden swell of Christian Democratic parties all over Europe, some of whom even are experiencing inner renewal, is only a tumor of the sick body of Christianity. There is no question of the individual value of many of the champions of Christian Democracy, their good intentions, and their usefulness. In the sociological context in which the Christian circles of Europe operate, these parties would have to be invented if they did not exist. Yet the lackadaisical unanimity with which they have taken their place left of center as if it had been their destiny from the beginning; the naïve and at the same time quite intolerant enthusiasm with which they preen themselves as an International of Wisdom, indicate that not their existence but their intentions may become one of the main dangers to Christianity in Europe. Created to liberate the Christian world from its reactionary ties, the Christian Democratic parties threaten

[9] See Karl Barth in his *Christengemeinde und Bürgergemeinde* (Munich, 1946), pp. 32 ff. Community, State and Church (Chicago, 1960), p. 29 ff.

to become their last refuge through a strange concatenation of circumstances. Risen in answer to the alliance between throne (or bank) and altar, they are limping fifty years behind history, intent on replacing the Holy Empire or the Kingship by Divine Grace by a kind of "Holy Democracy" which is no less questionable.[10]

Guy Mollet, the French socialist leader, has expressed himself in a similarly critical way, but from another point of view. He openly accused Christian Democratic politicians of treason to their national duties. His phrase "a Vatican Europe," meant as a description of an impending danger, was applauded not only in laicist France but was taken up by German liberalism (by Thomas Dehler) and by an influential group within Germany's Protestant churches (Martin Niemöller) during the struggle for the European treaties.[11]

Such negative assessments of the real or imagined intertwining of Christian Democracy and the political traditions of Catholicism have not been universal. Neutral observers have seen the value of such an alliance in the critical situation of Europe after World War II. Thus the Swiss, Herbert Lüthy, wrote:

> This irritation that so many progressives of yesteryear cannot overcome is no mere diplomatic accident: that the first concrete move in Europe was the work of a few, the work of a handful of old Catholic and conservative statesmen whose views were formed in the time of Francis Joseph and William II, the only ones who in the midst of the postwar chaos possessed a common ethos, a common tradition, and a common language.[12]

[10] *Esprit*, May 1946, p. 718.
[11] *Europe Vaticane*: see Biton, op. cit., p. 149.
[12] H. Lüthy, *Frankreich's Uhren gehen anders* (Zürich, 1954).

We can see from these few examples that apart from deeply-rooted theological considerations it was the "European" and the "Catholic" character of Christian Democracy which aroused objections. Wherever criticism assumes a special harshness, one senses the aftereffects of national and anticlerical resentment. This kind of polemics, however, seems to have decreased in the course of time. Gradually, people have begun to evaluate objectively the onset of Christian Democracy and have come to do without the questionable assistance of a terminology borrowed from the age of *Kulturkampf*.

What constitutes the unity of the European Christian Democratic movement? It is not to be found in the realm of politics (or at least not mainly there), for the Christian Democratic parties of Western Europe display such diversity in political direction that we can hardly speak of unity, certainly not to compare with the unity of liberalism or socialism. There have been and there still are conservative, liberal, and socialist Christian Democratic parties. Within the traditional parliamentary patterning of Right and Left, Christian Democracy has not yet settled on a place. Its position among the parties has been best described by the former French minister for foreign affairs, Georges Bidault:

> Gouverner au centre et faire, avec les moyens de la droite, la politique de la gauche. [To govern in the center and make the politics of the left with the means of the right.]

But this formula is too general still. The political-parliamentary place of Christian Democratic parties has changed with time and circumstance. Thus the first "Christian Democratic" party groupings, which appeared in Belgium, France, and Ireland around 1830, were liberal; their French and German successors after 1848 were conservative; those originating in France and Italy toward the end of the nineteenth century (now Christian Democratic in name) tended to accept socialist demands in their programs. And modern Christian Democratic parties differ from each other in political configuration and do not agree even about the general direction of their movement. Whereas observers are likely to observe a swing from left to right within the German CDU and the French MRP in the last few years, the very contrary swing would be noted in the Italian *Democrazia Cristiana* since the death of De Gasperi and the ascent of Fanfani and Moro to party leadership.

This is not to imply that the movement has no principles or program. There is no dearth of programs. And the constant self-criticism of political parties has been as characteristic of Christian Democratic parties as of any other. But it is likewise clear —and this is anchored in the ideological situation of these parties—that Christian Democratic political programs must be only soundings of the time and change with historical changes. There is nothing like program in the sense of the *Communist Manifesto*, based as it is entirely on belief in a foreseeable historical process (and consequently representing a kind of revolutionary realization), as Biton pointed out.[13] Christian Democracy is without such a program. Its aims are not those of preparing a revolution. For Christian politics, whatever its shadings, is never intended as a self-adulatory creation, a revolutionary "making of history"; it rather aims at the self-assertion and preservation of Christians in any of the constantly changing and therefore unforeseeable historical situations; in this sense it is more reactive than active. It is not primarily interested in the progress of history but in the way in which Christian life can be realized in each historical moment. Nor do the papal social encyclicals, though they have contributed more than any other literature to the formation of Christian Democracy, represent their political or eco-

[13] Biton, op. cit., p. 71.

nomic programs in this sense;[14] they are less representative even than the constantly changing views of the various Christian Democratic parties on political questions. The encyclicals are without any of the messianic faith in the panacea of politico-social change which pervades all revolutionary programs and also do not prescribe reliance on any particular group, class, or nation as destined to bring about change.[15] In addition they are not concrete enough in assertion to bring about political action, and this is of their very nature. Neither the Belgian nor German politician, the French industrialist nor the Italian union leader can find in them specific directions applicable to his special case, which incidentally puts a charge of onesidedness out of court. To the contrary: the foundation of its politics in natural law offers Christian Democracy precisely that broad basis which permits it to have as many variations in the structures of its everyday politics as there are national and confessional forms of Christian parties.

We should rather look for the unity of the Christian Democratic parties in their social views. It was in the social area that their characteristics first appeared. In the principles and practices

---

[14] M. Hättich, *Wirtschaftsordnung und katholische Soziallehre* (Stuttgart, 1957), p. 2: "Aus der Bestimmung dessen, was zum Heil notwendig ist, ergeben sich allerdings Massstäbe auch für zeitliche Einrichtungen . . . welche die Heilssituation stören oder den Menschen am Heilsnotwendigen hindern. Der Grund für die Äusserungen der Kirche im Hinblick auf solche Massstäbe für zeitliche Belange sind jedoch nicht die Belange selbst, sondern ist das transzendente Heil.

"Die Hinsicht unter der also sozialwissenschaftliche Aussagen gemacht werden, ist nicht der Sozialbereich an sich, sondern ist die Bedeutung dieses Bereiches für das Verhältnis des Menschen zu Gott. Es handelt sich im Grunde stets um theologische Aussagen."

[15] Technical reforms of a political and social kind are insufficient; reform of social conditions and moral improvement must go together: cf. *Quadragesimo anno* 77, 127–29; similar was *Rerum novarum* 22 (rejection of class struggle: *ibid*. 15–21).

of social policy, there is a far-reaching unity of purpose to be discerned among Christian Democrats. This can be seen in the socio-political legislation of the Western European countries which for the most part can be traced to the Christian Democratic parties. There can be no question of the importance of the Christian Democratic contributions to the security of the masses, the satisfaction of the socio-political demands of the class struggle, and the movement toward a social state. When all is said and done, it becomes clear that on those counts it made no difference whether the Christian Democratic parties supported a market economy or a planned economy and thus also proves that the socio-political thought of Christian Democracy developed independently of economic theories and ideas. The reasons for this are clear. Historically, the precursor of Christian Democracy— the Catholic and evangelical social movement—developed as a counter-current to the trend of the laissez faire economy away from concern for socio-political problems. A strong residue of emotional resistance to the market economy resulting from this anti-liberal position has remained in the make-up of the parties of Christian Democracy. This distrust has outlived both the development of modern world economics, with its responsiveness to socio-political data, and the social rise of the workers. Independent of the later development of politico-economic thinking within the parties themselves, this distrust is common to the most disparate Christian Democratic currents to this day. An outspoken anti-liberalism holds sway, a distrust in principle of any belief in social harmony as arising as an inevitable result of the individual striving for happiness. The task of making room for the individual—and not only the fittest individuals—and assuring him the necessities of life is taken more seriously and is tackled more vigorously than laissez faire politics have ever been able to do. Several motivations converge on this point: the influence of Christian social teachings; the wish of several church groups to move away from the social egotism of the proprietor classes in order to reduce the religious desertions of the working classes; and, finally, the fact that Christian Democracy—in so far as it is based on the tradition of political and social Catholicism—is the sociological politics, quite often proletarian in a purely social sense, of minorities and of separation from a "ruling class." In the political sense this is the case especially in the Irish, Belgian, and German Catholic parties of 1820 to 1850; in the cultural and church-political sense, with the later German *Zentrum* and the Catholic parties of the French Third Republic. All these parties are "proletarian" parties in the extended sense of the word developed by Toynbee—they represent groups which are not integrated in the concrete constitution of their states and stand outside of "society" as "enemies of the Reich" (Bismarck) or "ultramontanes" (Combes). In addition, the Christian Democratic parties in their social composition are founded more strongly on the lower layers of society than are their conservative Catholic or Protestant sister parties.

Hence there exists a certain anti-individualism in the theory and practice of Christian Democrats, a tendency to think in quantities, a belief in big numbers; this also explains the constantly noticeable tension between cultural and political Catholicism, manifested in France by the estrangement between the literary-artistic *renouveau catholique* and the Catholic social movement, and in Germany by the latent enmity between *Zentrum* and *Hochland* Catholicism.

The easiest way to understand Christian Democratic unity, however, is to understand it from the ideological viewpoint: as a community of people who have taken the path of politics because of certain earlier pre-political convictions. Considered from this viewpoint, many things incomprehensible at first glance explain themselves, such as the clear links between the many different Christian Democratic parties with their individual colorations; the spiritual accord that is coincident with surprisingly little political accord; the existence of a theory, but one which is not applied strictly and which leaves a great deal of room for political pragmatism. There is no doubt that in ideology is to be found the essential formative and structural principle of Christian Democracy.

Nowhere do the history of ideas and the history of a party come as close as in the case of the Christian Democratic parties.[16] We must qualify the assertion that the foundations of Christian Democracy are determined by ideology, however, by considering the relationship between religion and ideology. When a Christian is moved to act politically, ideology may be uninvolved. Actions based on biblical or natural law positions may have solely religious starting points. The true zone of ideology is entered only when religion is identified with a political system, that is, if the actor starts from a positive co-ordination of Christianity and democracy as the theological fact that determines his practical politics. In so far as such a "political theology" (which is founded neither on the Bible nor on natural law) is the foundation of Christian Democratic parties and of their political actions, we may speak of them as "ideological parties," but only in this connection.[17]

To the Continental European observer the influence of ideology, or of religion, in the Christian Democratic parties of today may no longer be discernible. He will ask himself whether politi-

[16] See H. Rothfels, "Ideengeschichte und Parteigeschichte," *Deutsche Vierteljahresschrift für Literaturwissenschaft und Geistesgeschichte* VIII (1930), 753–86, esp. 776 f.

[17] On the problem of political theology, see the thus titled work of C. Schmitt (Munich, 1922) and E. Peterson, "Der Monotheismus als politisches Problem," in *Theologische Traktate*, pp. 44–147.

cal tactics, over-flexibility, an opportunistic moving along with the tide have not blurred the outlines of the ideas with which the parties began. The Christian Democratic parties are often blamed for having drifted from their spiritual moorings, for pursuing a politics of interests, in contrast to their loudly and solemnly proclaimed principles. Even political practitioners, who do not concern themselves much with the ideological foundations of party, are inclined to admit that the growing "de-ideologization" of Continental European parties has put Christian Democracy in a difficult position: it appears to many today as an ideological party without an ideology.

This, of course, is felt differently by anyone who comes from outside of Europe, especially someone coming from Anglo-Saxon conditions: it is exactly in the Christian Democratic parties of the Continent that he feels the greatest weight of theoretical and ideological pretensions in contrast to the pragmatic concept of politics that are familiar to him. Michael Fogarty, the British Labor politician and the newest biographer of Christian Democracy, is clearly so influenced when he writes:

> Coming from the more secularised atmosphere of a country like Britain, one cannot help being struck by the way in which even the language of the Christian Democratic movements and their leaders betrays their Christian inspiration. Visit an official of one of the Dutch Protestant parties, and within five minutes one may be debating the political consequences of Karl Barth, or of the "Separation" and "Complaint" which split the Hervormde Kerk in the nineteenth century.[18] Have lunch with his Catholic opposite number,

[18] This refers to both great movements of separation from the Dutch Reformed church during the nineteenth century: the formation of the "Church in Solicitude" (1834) and of the "Church in Lament" (1886), which combined in 1891 as the "Gereformeerde Kerken in Nederland." They form the real core of Dutch Protestantism in Holland today.

and one finds the conversation channelled, often quite unconsciously, by *Quadragesimo Anno* and solidarist philosophy. The life and language of a political party like the French M.R.P., or the Italian *Democrazia Cristiana*, and of many of the social movements, is deeply coloured by the training so many of their leaders received in the Catholic youth movements. This impression is confirmed by an inspection of parties' and movements' rules and constitutions which regularly include references to revelation and the Christian tradition of the natural law.[19]

Now we must determine exactly the relation of Christian Democracy to what is called political, liberal, or social Catholicism, as well as to the corresponding phenomena on the Protestant side. Is Christian Democracy simply a form of political Catholicism (or Protestantism) as it took shape in the twentieth century? Or does it have an origin of its own, independent of these traditions? And what is its relationship to the modern social movements of the Christian denominations? It is not easy to answer these questions. They are made especially difficult by the fact that these concepts are fraught with political meanings and, in Germany particularly, are troubled by the memories of the *Kulturkampf*. Let us try first to establish some common ground through an empirical investigation.

To begin we must delimit more sharply the controversial concept of political Catholicism. If this is understood as the attempt by Catholics to obtain greater religious and political liberty within the modern constitutional state or, more generally, to achieve influence corresponding to their numbers (with such formal tools of liberalism as freedom of press, assembly, association, or religion) we may doubtless consider all political activity of Catholic circles within the framework of the nineteenth-century con-

[19] Fogarty, *op. cit.*, p. 18.

stitutional state as political Catholicism, regardless of the liberal or conservative nature of the action. Political Catholicism in this sense is nothing but a "manifestation of Catholic religiosity within politics,"[20] an attempt at religious self-assertion by political means, motivated by the weakened public position of the church that resulted from revolution and secularization and from the dissolution of the religio-church unity which had existed in absolutist principalities.[21] It reflects the inevitable change in the position of the church after the French Revolution. In a society where the liberties of the church are no longer a matter of course but depend on the activities of its members (above all, the laymen), Catholicism had to develop political forms. Hence, political Catholicism is the natural child of Catholicism per se. But again we shall be well advised to make a further distinction. Not all forms of political activity by Catholics are political Catholicism. Political Catholicism is in the main characterized by its defensiveness. Its first aim is the assurance of certain church rights and liberties; it does not concentrate primarily on the renewal of the public life in a Catholic sense. When this latter point of view becomes prevalent, when the unifying element is not of a negative but of a positive nature, then we properly speak of Catholic politics.[22] Political Catholicism and Catholic politics are not one and the same thing. The former has a defensive character, the latter an aggressive program. Most of what has been

---

[20] C. Bauer, *Politischer Katholizismus in Württemberg bis zum Jahr* 1848 (Freiburg, 1929), p. 4.

[21] Cf. H. Maier, "Kirche und Politik. Eine geschichtliche Besinnung," *Hochland* LV (1962/63), 320 ff.

[22] This distinction can be found as early as Bauer, *op. cit.*, where "political Catholicism" is defined as the attitude "regarding politics as the means to an ecclesiastical end"; Catholic politics, on the other hand, are defined "as the application of Catholic principles in politics."

said about the political character of Christian Democracy applies
to political Catholicism: it is vague in content, capable of making alliances in the prevailing political situation, and develops its
concrete shape with respect to the given historical situation.
Catholic politics, to the contrary, is convinced of the staying
quality of its ideas and rather tends to assert that certain political
forms, up to the form of the state, are Catholic forms, valid once
and forever. The concept of Catholic politics can be used in a
general sense to signify the effort to order state and society according to Catholic principles. Bauer, for example, limits himself—and this is not meant as criticism—to order political forms
of Christianity on a theological basis. We will not here discuss
the problems inherent in such an attempt. As far as an equation
of Christianity with democracy has actually had a part in the
history of Christian Democracy, objections such as those raised
by Mounier have validity. Yet we have to consider two things:
that a Catholic Democratic integralism was indispensable at
the founding of the first Christian Democratic parties in order
to supplant Catholic-monarchic integralism, and that Christian
Democrats, even if the theological foundations for their politics
were threadbare, were always convinced that they acted from
religious and ecclesiastical responsibility. In this view the choice
of the label "Catholic politics" may seem justified.

   The fact that Catholics in the nineteenth century often used
liberal means and methods in their fight for religious self-preservation—especially in the Romance language countries—has
given rise to the designation "liberal Catholicism" (*catholicisme
liberal*) for political Catholicism.[23] Doubtless, this label is much

---

[23] For a history of the meaning of this term, see Appendix. An introduction to
the history of liberal Catholicism in France is given—from antagonistic stand-
points—by G. Weill in his *Histoire du catholicisme libéral en France* (Paris,
1909), a treatise written with marked sympathy but not always up to coping with

more fitting and plastic than the rather nebulous concept of political Catholicism, chiefly because it unmistakably refers to the liberal movement characteristic of the early forms of political Catholicism. It is also more restricted, since it can be used only for those early forms.[24] O'Connell, Montalembert, Sterckx, and the young Ketteler are liberal Catholics; yet the designation does not apply to Veuillot, de Mun, and Vogelsang. And even Lamennais, the theoretician of the unity of church and democracy, though he belonged to the earlier movements, can be counted only conditionally among liberal Catholics.[25] For he especially excels as a dogmatician of great style; excursions into political ideology and theology, whether conservative or democratic, are a far cry from the realm of liberal-Catholic ideas. Therefore, the character of liberal Catholicism is most clear where the reference to the liberalism is purely formal and instrumental. This was the case, above all, with Montalembert, who developed in his Mechelner Speeches the most exhaustive Catholic political casuistry of the era of liberalism; here there can be no question of the formulation of a religio-political aim or of an identification of Christianity with certain political forms of power.[26]

Though liberal Catholicism is part of political Catholicism, this cannot now be said of the Catholic social movement (not

the theological dimension of the matter, and by E. Barbier in his *Histoire du catholicisme libéral et du catholicisme social en France* (Bordeaux, 1924), rich in material and indispensable despite its anti-liberal harshness.

[24] In the works of Weill and Barbier the notion of "catholicisme libéral" also includes the *Ralliement* Catholics of the Third Republic.

[25] In spite of the criticism expressed by K. Jürgensen (*Historische Zeitschrift* CXCIII [1961], 412), the author keeps to this opinion with regard to Lamennais' origin in traditionalism (worked out by Gurian), despite the fact that both the idea and movement of liberal Catholicism owe Lamennais their decisive push.

[26] Ch. de Montalembert, *L'Eglise libre dans l'Etat libre. Discours prononcés au Congrès Catholique de Malines* (Paris, 1863).

that there is any reason to count it among the many forms of the Catholic politics of the liberal era). While early theoreticians spoke of a *régne social du Christ* to be erected,[27] they did not mean by this a political reign. Finally, the orthodox Catholic social movement after 1870, which evolved into the social papal encyclicals, is free of ties with any particular political doctrine. Thus, as the Catholic social movement gained a form of its own it moved further and further away from political Catholicism. The latter, in its essence, is a compromise system; it labors for the assurance of liberties for the church and seeks a tolerable relation with the democratic state and aims on the whole for entente and for solutions resulting in concordat. It represents an appeal to the sovereign, "who needs to be better informed," regardless of whether he is an absolute or a constitutional monarch or a liberal majority in a parliament; its means are of a politico-diplomatic nature within the framework of institutions: interest groups, parties, parliaments. There is nothing of this kind in social Catholicism: it starts precisely at the point where the rules of concordat do not extend—in the sphere of individual and social existence. It aimed to effect matters in an individual, not an institutional, way. Its rise coincides with that time when the political dialogue between church and state had begun to suffer devaluation because of the fragility of state forms and the gradual disappearance of national sovereign states. It was a time in which the church could no longer rely on the guarantees of the state and saw itself forced to descend into the wide network of human society in order to remain present in the life of the people—by specializing its own apostolate, by forming its own social theories, and by taking missionary pains over individuals as well as groups. Thus there are two very different tasks which confront political and social Catholicism: on the one hand, the ordering of the church under the liberal constitutional state; on the other

[27] Above all, Ozanam; see pp. 225 ff.

its insertion into modern industrial society.[23] It is the intention of political Catholicism to assure for the church a right to live in the modern state, a state no longer stamped by the religio-political unity of former times and thus no longer interested in protecting the position of the church with the means of the state. In contrast to this, social Catholicism aims directly at establishing the presence of the church in society by bracketing the statal-political unity of the *cives christianus* through an invigorating embrace of the social. The unimportance of the political factor in comparison with the social becomes especially evident in Catholic social teachings. Thus, such an imposing treatise as Herder's *Sozialkatechismus*[29] gives only a quarter of its entire text to strictly political questions. In order to realize the difference, compare the fierceness of the discussions that broke out among Catholics in France after 1871 and in Germany after 1919 about the acceptability of democracy. It is significant that among the numerous encyclicals of Pope Leo XIII, mostly dealing with political matters, only the social encyclical *Rerum novarum* has gained great popularity.

What is the relationship of Christian Democracy to political and social Catholicism? Doubtless, it shares in both, since both were initially closely linked; but in essential points it transcends both. Thus it took over certain essential demands regarding church marriage and education from political (liberal) Catholicism; similarly, it possesses a concrete program of liberty based on the respective independence—not separation—of church and state.[30] What distinguishes it from liberal Catholicism, however,

[28] See traces of such an approach in J. C. Murray, "Contemporary Orientations of Catholic Thought on Church and State in the Light of History," *Theological Studies* X (1949), 177–234; and C. Bauer "Bild der Kirche—Abbild der Gesellschaft," *Hochland* XLVIII (1955/56), 519–27.

[29] Prepared by P. E. Welty (Freiburg, 1951 ff.)

[30] The French *Démocratie chrétienne* of the nineteenth century—Lacordaire, Maret, Arnaud de l'Ariège—is at last more inclined toward the idea of complete separation of church and state than (is) liberal Catholicism.

is the conviction that these programs can be realized only in a political democracy, on the grounds that Christianity and democracy have the same origins.[31] In other words: Christian Democracy believes in democracy as a fact of providential importance, whereas political Catholicism sees in it primarily a field for experimentation in practical politics. The relationship of Christian Democracy to social Catholicism is similar. Both share the wish to establish a close connection with the people and the will to renew the forms of society (into which political Catholicism demands entrance) according to a new, positive view. But Christian Democracy does not base these demands solely or primarily (as does the Catholic social movement) upon the charitable activity of man to man or upon a reform of social conditions; it hopes and expects rather that the desired society will be realized in the course of history. Thus we may say: Christian Democracy comes into being where the intent of political and social Catholicism meets with a historico-philosophical concept which recognizes in democracy, not only the providential form of the state and society of a Christian age, but also the surest guarantee of the security of the church. The natural consequence of such a way of thinking is to obligate the church theologically toward democratic solutions.

The movement of history itself shows that this is no mere conjecture or cerebration. Historically, the concept of Christian Democracy immediately had a specific meaning, sharply different from today's greatly faded version. During the Revolution of

[31] See pp. 234 ff. The thesis of an inner harmony of Christianity and democracy has been especially popular in the Anglo-Saxon world. It also appears in France, first during the great Revolution, later in romantic socialism. In our day it has been impressively revived by J. Maritain, *The Rights of Man and Natural Law* (New York, 1943), *Christianity and Democracy* (New York, 1947), *Man and the State* (Chicago, 1951). For criticism see E.-W. Bökenförde, "Das Ethos der modernen Demokratie und die Kirche," *Hochland* L (1957/58), 4 ff.

1848 in France, *Démocratie chrétienne* was the designation of that group of Catholics who supported co-operation between the church and the republican movement, in decisive contrast to de Maistre's traditionalism and the conservative glorification of the monarchy. Carried away by lofty enthusiasm, it was a movement which not infrequently literally equated Christianity and democracy.[32] When a second *Démocratie chrétienne* occurred in France, Belgium, and Italy after 1891, a similar situation arose: the label united those who saw in the social message of Leo XIII not only a program for social and ethical reform but a point of departure for the political renewal of society, hence a political program, which above all was to enable the Catholic worker to take up and win the struggle against the socialist parties.[33]

In both cases the official church kept its distance from the small avant-garde of Catholic laymen: at first in the *Syllabus* of 1864, which had been preceded by the encyclicals *Mirari vos* (1832) and *Singulari Nos* (1834), directed against liberal Catholicism; the second time, in somewhat more cautious form, in the encyclicals proclaimed by Leo XIII, *Graves de communi* (1901).[34]

The latter document is especially useful to our investigation, since in it the expression "Christian Democracy" (*Democratia Christiana*) can be found for the first time in a papal encyclical.

[32] Above all, J.-B. Duroselle has thrown light upon the history of these left-Catholic movements. Cf. his fundamental work on the early history of social Catholicism: *Les débuts du catholicisme social en France (1822–1870)* (Paris, 1951), and his two articles: "L'attitude politique et sociale des catholiques français en 1848," *Revue d'histoire de l'Eglise de France* XXXIV (1948), 44–62, and "L'esprit de 1848," in *1848, Révolution créatrice* (Paris, 1948).

[33] On the history of this second *Démocratie chrétienne*, see pp. 253 ff.

[34] See the texts in Acta Gregorii Papae XVI, 1901 ff., I, 169–74 (*Mirari vos*) and 433 f. (*Singulari nos*); the Syllabus: Acta Pii IX, Rome, 1857 ff., pars prima, III, 701–17; *Graves de communi* in Acta Sanctae Sedis XXXIII (1900/01), 385–96.

Yet the concept in this connection is circumscribed as *benifica in populum actio christiana*, that is, as having purely socio-charitable implications in clear contrast to all other special political meanings.[35] Such caution can easily be understood: under the circumstances the rather problematic equation of Christianity with a political system in an encyclical must have appeared extremely dangerous. In any case, there are pronouncements by Leo XIII which may be interpreted as signaling a cautious *rapprochement* with political democracy. It should not be condemned in and of itself, he wrote in the encyclical *Immortale Dei* (1885), that the people participate in a more or less important way in exercising the power of state; such participation under certain laws and in certain times cannot only contribute to the well being of the citizens but may even belong to their duties.[36] Here the reticence of former papal pronunciamentos has already been overcome: a door is carefully being opened. Yet decades were still necessary before the door was opened completely. It was only after 1918 that the Holy See recognized modern democracy as *fait accompli*. And it was only Pope Pius XII's Christmas Message of 1944 which, without mentioning the word, developed the positive concept of Christian Democracy, a political concept based on purely religious premises.[37]

The dialogue with modern democracy takes a less dramatic form in Protestantism.[38] Starting much later, its curve has been

[35] *Graves de communi*, p. 387.

[36] Acta Sanctae Sedis, XVIII (1885), 174. See the Latin text in the preface of this book.

[37] Acta Apostolicae Sedis XXXVII (1945) 10–23; cf. H. Maier, "Politischer Katholizismus," loc. cit., pp. 23 ff.

[38] On the whole topic of Protestantism and democracy, cf. the already mentioned article by Smend and A. Siegfried "Le Protestantisme," in *Les forces religieuses et la vie politique*, Cahier de la fondation nationale des Sciences Politiques, no. 23 (Paris 1951). Cf. also *supra*, n. 8.

more regular than in the Catholic countries of the Continent. This holds true not only for the Anglo-Saxon countries with their comparatively pale concept of church and more liberal concept of democracy, but also for Continental European Protestantism: no non-Catholic country (excepting perhaps Holland and Switzerland) experienced a crisis of religious conscience caused by the rise of modern democracy similar to those experienced by Catholic countries after 1789. The transition from the church-oriented Middle Ages to modern times was not carried out in Protestantism with the same impact and swiftness as happened during the French Revolution. The Protestant churches were spared the harsh cut of secularization, not least because a lengthy process of secularization had already achieved what Catholicism was forced to achieve in one short period. Many of the ideas which surfaced during the French and the American revolutions were already domesticated in Protestantism. Wherever the evangelical countries had contact with the ideas of democracy and liberalism, these were assimilated to their religious ethos. Only the political absolutism of the Jacobin state—which was felt to be a perverted and laicized Catholicism—was rejected by all. And only in Lutheranism was there to be found a principled and religiously-founded criticism of democracy and revolution; there, liberal ideas collided with the well-founded concept of church and the rather inflexible concept of the duties of Christians toward worldly authority. The free-church communities, originating in Calvinism, of the Anglo-Saxon world not only did not resist democracy but had already prepared the ground for it. Tocqueville's opinion that nothing in Christianity is alien to a democratic society[39] has its origin in American experiences. How

---

[39] *L'Ancien Régime et la Révolution*, chap. ii (Oeuvres complètes; Paris, 1951 ff.), II, 84, text in the preface of this book.

correct it is can be seen from the fact that the typically Continental European phenomenon of "Kulturkampf" is unknown to the Anglo-Saxon world. P. F. Drucker[40] has pointed out the religious foundation especially of American democracy.

For the Protestant consciousness it was only the religious secession of the workers about the middle of the nineteenth century that caused disharmony between the church and the modern world, although disharmony had been visible to Catholics at the time of the French Revolution and the advent of modern democracy. Whereas the liberal movement had here and there caused a conservative reaction in Protestantism without ever necessitating a thorough politico-religious reconsideration, the necessity of such reconsideration became more and more imperative with the rise of socialism and the subsequent religious rebellion of the workers. The last decades of the nineteenth century saw the birth of Protestant party movements in Europe, rising in different places under the sign of Christian socialism. The more people placed themselves outside the church, the stronger were the attempts to stem the decline of the ordinary pastoral institutions by *inner mission*. The recognition gained hold that, without new substance, even the most loving care of the traditional was condemned to sterility. "I am in politics as a pastor so that politics shall not overwhelm the church entirely," declared Stöcker, the founder of the evangelical Christian-Social Workers' party.[41] This statement reveals the central concern of the evangelical social movement of the nineteenth century.

Social Protestantism differed from its Catholic counterpart in that it was not preceded by a political Protestantism comparable to political Catholicism. The dialogue with the new forms of

---

[40] P. Drucker, "The American Genius is Political," *Perspectives U.S.A.* (vol. III, p. 118–26, 1953).

[41] Deverlein, *op. cit.*, p. 26.

the democratic age began at the lowest rung, in private and social life, but without the problems which political democracy posed for the church having first been given institutional solutions.[42] This sufficed in the Anglo-Saxon countries, for example, where the accepted concept of a free church covered the difference in style between the church and political democracy. In Germany, however, where the princely episcopate united throne and altar, the disintegration of the old state put the church itself into a revolutionary situation. The attempt at developing new forms of public weal—beyond the state concept of public weal which the church could not use after 1919 and beyond the Catholic-dogmatic church concept for which Protestant theology lacked an affinity because of inner causes—was doomed to fail. The Protestant formulation of Christian Socialism in part assumed the character of sectarianism and in part strove to maintain the authoritarian state character that clung to it even in the new and changed environment. This certainly was not a climate conducive to the growth of the thought of Christian Democracy or to the idea of combining democracy and Protestantism. As a matter of fact the old opposition of German Protestantism to democracy of a Western character remained lively until the Weimar Republic. Adaptation to a democratic environment in the end was the result of weariness, when the consequences of the social schism had disappeared and the open anticlericalism of the workers had given way to religious indifference. Yet the experiment in Christian Democracy which grew from the community of struggle of the Christian confessions in the time of the Third Reich was carried out only by a minority—a considerable one— of Evangelical Christians in Germany. It should be remembered, however, that German Protestantism was confronted with the

[42] Cf. W. O. Shanahan, *op. cit.*, pp. 37 ff., 154 ff.

problem of democracy only in 1919 and that the problem was from the beginning connected with the question of church constitution. Many uncertainties of behavior can be explained through the same kind of integralist and liberal misunderstandings as accompanied the early stages of political Catholicism. In many instances Evangelical Christianity has developed new forms of dialogue with democracy, and the old attitude of strangeness may be considered to have been generally overcome. H. Asmussen[43] has complained quite correctly "that for ten years now we have had a party in Western Germany which would like to make politics according to Christian principles, but leading ecclesiastical circles and the ministers, however, want to have nothing to do with that party"; he explains this from the fact that, although the Protestant church knows how to call upon the laity, it does not know how really to make it embrace the cause. It is doubtful, however, whether a massive commitment to an individual political party fits the structure of Protestantism at all.[44]

THE SOCIOLOGY OF PARTY FORMATION

Until 1848—and in Germany still later—parties were only formed in Western European states with ideologies to build upon.[45]

[43] Rom, Wittenberg, Moskau. Zur grossen Kirchenpolitik (Stuttgart, 1956), pp. 36 f.

[44] Cf. the remarks made by Smend (Staatsrechtliche Abhandlungen [Berlin, 1955], p. 307), as early as 1932, that the contribution of Protestantism to democracy is "not an authoritative, unanimously followed doctrine . . . , but a religious spiritual power" and that Protestantism produces this effect "not as a formally compact power, like Catholicism, but as a diffused element spread over and effective through all spiritual, political, religious circles of today's Germany."

[45] On the following, see M. Duverger, Les partis politiques (2d ed.; Paris, 1954); S. Neumann (ed.), Modern Political Parties. Approaches to Comparative Politics

"Une réunion d'hommes qui professent la même doctrine politique" ("A union of men who share allegiance to the same political doctrine") was Benjamin Constant's characterization of the parties of the liberal age.[46] His definition accorded with the political and social conditions of his times. There were none but ideological parties in the Vormärz (the period before March, 1848). It may be objected that these early parties were not exclusively shaped by ideology and that in particular conservative and liberal parties who opposed one another exhibited a healthy dose of class and interest politics. Though this cannot be denied, it does not change the fact that no party of the years 1789–1848 (with certain exceptions like the enragés of the French Revolution and the Gleichen of Babeuf) can be properly classified sociologically or linked to a particular social group.[47] The characteristics of party were not so much determined by the composition of its membership—in all there were aristocrats and bourgeois notables in varying proportions. The political doctrine, the ideology represented, was determining. Doctrine could in

---

(Chicago, 1956); above all, the following articles by Th. Schieder: "Das Verhältnis von politischer und gesellschaftlicher Verfassung und die Krise des bürgerlichen Liberalismus," *Historische Zeitschrift* CLXXVII (1954), 49–74; "Die Theorie der Partei im älteren deutschen Liberalismus," in *Aus Geschichte und Politik. Festschrift für Ludwig Bergstraesser* (Düsseldorf, 1954), pp. 183–96; "Der Liberalismus und die Strukturwandlungen der modernen Gesellschaft vom 19. bis 20. Jahrhundert," *Relazioni del X. Congresso Internazionale di Scienze Storiche*, V (Florence, 1955), 145–72. See further Th. Nipperdey, *Die Organisation der deutschen Parteien vor 1918* (Düsseldorf, 1961); E. Faul, "Verfemung, Duldung und Anerkennung des Parteiwesens in der Geschichte des politischen Denkens," *Politische Vierteljahresschrift*, V (1964), 60 ff.

[46] Duverger, *op. cit.*, p. ix.

[47] The most penetrating analysis of this kind, K. Mannheim's study on "Conservative Thinking," *Archiv für Sozialwissenschaft und Sozialpolitik*, LVII (1927), 68–142, and 470–95, clearly shows the methodological limits of the sociological decomposition of conservative ideology.

most cases be reduced to the simple, dialectic element of the party's opposition to, acceptance of, or even identification with, the French Revolution. *Conservative, radical, liberal* were not simply slogans. Political ideas are not always merely the garb of interests which can be exchanged at will: ideas may have a reality of their own which will make itself felt in changing historical situations and will resist all attempts at destruction through sociological awareness. A hasty sociological explanation of these ideological facts runs the danger of overlooking the dependence of party formation in that time on the presence of *familles spirituelles*, on the existence of ideological communities; a similar statement can be made about an attitude which does not originate in ideology but in the organization of a party. Since at this early stage the history of the party coincides with the *Geistesgeschichte* of its political doctrine, it is a work like Henri Michel's *L'idée de l'Etat*, which treats politico-philosophical trends in France since 1789,[48] that affords the deepest insights into the country's party history from the great revolution to well into the Third Republic. In other countries the situation is similar.[49] This strange condition indicates that political trends in those days were on the whole oriented toward the nation; class points of view were of minor importance as compared to interest in the theory of the state, for the formation of which each party readied its own program.

In conformity with the ideological character of the parties of the liberal age, there was widespread renunciation of technical

[48] Paris, 1895.

[49] See Th. Schieder, "Die Theorie der Partei im älteren deutschen Liberalismus," *loc. cit.*, and E. Faul, *loc. cit., passim.* Such conceptions are not limited to Germany; they also appear in France and have also in France delayed for a long time the formation of modern, non-ideologically oriented parties: replace Hegel by Rousseau!

organization. This may be explained by the fact that these parties felt themselves to be parts less of an already existing concrete state than representatives of an ideal future state; as long as their way to power led through revolution, there was no reason for or possibility of their becoming institutionally part of the body politic. On the other hand, organization in groups, cells, and sections is itself contradictory to the ideology of the liberal party, which shares with classic statism a belief in the indivisibility of the national will, in the *République une et indivisible*. It aspires to represent, not a class or a group, but the people in their entirety. Little inclined to encourage class or group representation (which would require a stable party apparatus and continuous hard work), the liberal parties stood ready to impose their will upon the state as a whole. Each of them lived in the conviction of its being "the people." Thus, in comparison with the highly prepared parties of the twentieth century, their organization was weak. There were no bureaus, no centralized superregional leadership, no program; even party names changed. Mostly there were local committees, confined to a capital, often only a loose circle grouped around a well-known personality. This does not at all mean that political life was stagnant. It could be well developed, lively, intense. Only it did not yet reach out to envelop the whole nation. It was confined to a few points of contact: the salons, the literary academies, the universities, parliament. All these places had roles in party formation. Here opinions were exchanged, mergers were made, the outlines of the fronts of enemy and allies appeared. Outside of these centers, however, the political parties and trends came to life only for the short while before elections, mostly aroused by candidates in search of a mandate who approached the voters through manifestos, visits, and letters, and without the backing of a party machinery.

In a negative sense, the loosely organized ideological party became institutionalized because the suffrage was limited by property qualifications that restricted political decision-making to a comparatively narrow group that was socially and ideologically homogeneous. It was only the February Revolution in France which breached the dam and let the flood of plebiscites reach to the core of the state. Until then, however, the political life of Western Europe had played itself out on relatively small stages, easily supervised and giving to democratic politics an elite style lacking in the traits of party government as they would later be so clearly developed under the Anglo-Saxon caucus system.[50] The broad masses were not yet politicized. Parliamentary life was far from being made up of permanent organizations. Parties formed and dissolved and no one took issue at their change or dissolution. For it was still individuals and not parties on the political stage, and while political trends fluctuated and organizations possessed little power to unify, it might happen that a book, a salon, or a particular rhetorical temperament would accidentally crystallize a political movement that could endure through some time.

Thus, political life was mainly concentrated in parliament. There the great spoken battles were fought; there crucial factors were the influence, rank, and power, which served to align the various groups in positions of conflict or alliance. The opposition strengthened itself in parliament by more or less audacious attacks on the government. Its inexperience, its failure yet to be "responsible" in the true sense of the word was the charm of such parliamentarianism. The danger which still seemed to surround parliamentary activity increased the stature of the deputy with the public, and because parliamentary resolutions were usu-

---

[50] It is no accident that the first great systems of party sociology were developed along the lines of the Anglo-Saxon model: Alexis de Tocqueville, *Democracy in America* (1835/40), and M. Ostrogorski, *Democracy and the Organization of Political Parties* (1903).

ally suggestions only without force of law, the parliamentarian's advice—given without obligation—became a more passionately enjoyable spectacle in an age that liked "to indulge in politics."[51]

Nowhere else did the character of the "fractional party based on notables" last so long as in France.[52] Here the group of ideological "friends," the ideal community, the *république des camarades*,[53] for a long time remained stronger than the power of organized associations and parties. As recently as the Third Republic and into the Fourth, loosely constituted committees of the nature of *Parti Radical* commanded the field and they have only slowly been pushed back by the modern mass- and leadership parties of socialist and Communist coloration. In spite of all surface movement, the personnel of the political scene remained uniform; even revolutions changed its traditional composition little. What always seemed to change was ideology. Thus, in 1848 nearly every deputy wanted to be known as a worker, and there was general surprise when the composition in parliament after the elections was nearly the same as it had been before: there were only a handful of true workers in a mass of lawyers and literary people.[54] Concentration of political life in the capital and in parliament continued as before. The temporary federalistic and plebiscitic mood in the era of Napoleon III was immediately followed by the anxious parliamentary regime of the Third Republic; nor could the new forces of industry and labor main-

[51] Indulging in politics: F. Schnabel, *Deutsche Geschichte im 19. Jahrhundert*, I (3d ed.; Freiburg, 1947 ff.) 309. The expression was coined by Friedrich Schlegel.

[52] Schieder ("Die Theorie der Partei," *loc. cit.*, p. 187) speaks of the "fractional party which exists virtually only in parliament and which keeps sometimes loose and irregular contact with its voters only via the circles of notables."

[53] Title of a well-known book by R. de Jouvenel (Paris, 1914).

[54] P. Bastid, *Doctrines et Institutions politiques de la Seconde République*, I (Paris, 1945), 180.

tain themselves against the overwhelming power of the party notables. What then did it mean when a Catholic party appeared in the context of early parliamentarianism, as happened in France in 1845? This was something quite unusual from the standpoint of liberal theories of party and state. Such a party stood in contradiction, not only to the ideological principles of party formation, which had obtained until then in political life, but to the apparently self-explanatory mechanism of sociological party formation. First, the *Parti catholique*, unlike other parties which claimed to mirror the whole country neutrally, could clearly be defined sociologically; it did not represent an anonymous 1 per cent of the population, but a minority of politically active Catholics. From this, however, in the liberal conception it followed that the party must have a special interest, an *intérêt particulier*, against the united interest of the nation. Taken as symbolic of the "particularistic tendency" was the appearance of Catholic priests and aristocratic lay leaders in parliament, a process which conjured again the specter of the old battle, decided in 1789, of the *trois ordres* and thus gave new fuel to the liberal nightmare of a reform of state life on the lines of guilds, aristocracy, and church. The possibility of a renewed appearance of church or guild divisions in the equalized political life of the nation formed a psychological obstacle. Even more suspect was the fact that the Catholic party seemed to have emancipated itself from the liberal conception of the state and from the practice of political action by small elite groups. By failing to confine its activities to parliamentary action and at the same time breaking through the class barrier of "bourgeois" politics by taking the side of the poor estates, it disrupted, on the one hand, the institutionalization of political life in parliament and, on the other, threatened the dam of the property qualification which protected the political privileges of citizens.

Thus the *Parti catholique*, though an ideological party in the sense of the others, was a new type among the ideological parties of the era. If its special character was not immediately noticed on its first appearance in France, it was because in the beginning the party followed a line of political conservatism and was therefore largely identified with this line. In the beginning it seemed to be no more than a new variation of the conservative and legitimistic parties, although its fight for freedom of education and association showed other, revolutionary, "democratic" traits. This view of the party as innocuous, however, changed rapidly after a section of the *Parti catholique* following the Revolution of 1848 suddenly accepted the republic. Though this orientation did not last very long—significantly, it changed as a result of universal suffrage, which created a conservative minority—it permitted a very important trait of Catholic parties to appear: these parties were able to use ideologies tactically, to use conservative or liberal programs to obtain specific religious aims. With this not only the character of the ideological party, oriented by political doctrine, but the corresponding idea of the state was brought into question.

Thus, the formation of Catholic parties ran afoul of the classic concepts of liberalism in three ways: by the obstinacy in which it brought to the fore a special interest (which, of course, had a most universal character), apparently incompatible with the unity of state and the national interest; by its application of the hierarchical principles of the church to politics (the old charge of the "*parti-prêtre*"); and by the dangerous plebiscitarian direction of its political programs. All three points culminated in the accusation that politics for the Catholic parties was subordinate to religion. This, in view of the general state of thought, was an extraordinary and most damaging accusation. For notwithstanding other differences, the liberal parties and their conservative opposition agreed on the primacy of politics; thus, a party whose real incentive came from beyond the political level naturally put itself outside the order created in 1789 to enforce the *politique d'abord* ("politics as was") in the face of all interference from the forces of the state or of religion. The Catholic party, as compared to conservatism and liberalism, seemed to be on revolutionary ground. From the point of view of classic liberalism as well as of statism and absolutism—and there is little difference between them on this point—its foundation was an offense against the dogma of national unity and a step toward the pluralistic dissolution of the state into ideological and social particularisms. We need not be surprised, therefore, to find among the critics of the Catholic parties of the nineteenth century not only liberal politicians but the standard bearers of the absolute state, including Metternich and Bismarck.[55]

The Catholic parties—and especially the Christian-Democratic parties in the narrower sense of the word—were never parties of notables in the sense of classical liberalism. They did not originate as "*réunion d'hommes qui professent la même doctrine politique*" nor as loose associations of individual personalities grouped around a political program. They were a fusion of already organized religio-political groups and associations.[56]

---

[55] See Metternich's order of December 2, 1831, to the Austrian ambassador in Rome, Count Lützow, published in L. Ahrens, *Lamennais und Deutschland* (Münster, 1930), pp. 233–36; and Bismarck, *Die gesammelten Werke* (Berlin, 1924–39), XI (1929), 238, XIII (1931), 288.

[56] See F. Schnabel, *Der Zusammenschluss des politischen Katholizismus in Deutschland 1848* (Heidelberg, 1910), and the above-mentioned book by C. Bauer. See further: K. Bachem, *Vorgeschichte, Geschichte und Politik der Deutschen Zentrumspartei 1815–1914* (9 vols.; Cologne, 1927–32); A. Dempf, *Demokratie und Partei im politischen Katholizismus* (Vienna, 1932); K. Repgen; *Märzbewegung und Maiwahlen des Revolutionsjahres 1848 im Rheinland* (Bonn, 1955), and recently K. Buchheim, *Ultramontanismus und Demokratie. Der Weg der deutschen Katholiken im 19. Jhdt.* (Munich, 1963).

Everywhere the basic elements of Christian Democracy were guilds, professional associations, and the organizations of workers, apprentices, farmers, tradesmen, and small businessmen. It was not individuals but groups who joined together. Political doctrine (which is something other than a religiously determined ideology) did not yet play any part. Of decisive importance was the appearance of Catholicism (in all its social forms) within the framework of the constitutional state with its political possibilities. In contrast to the formation of liberal parties, we do not have here a simple relationship between a political doctrine and its social correlative, in other words, the ideological party; rather between them we find the link of association, not politically, but religiously and socially, determined.

What originated in this way was a new political type, clearly distinguished from liberalism, a party of *indirect structure*.[57] This should be understood in a general sense; it does not mean that party membership was necessarily acquired by the collective affiliation of an association to which the individual belongs[58] but rather expresses the general fact that the deputies of these parties (many of which were only formed in parliament) come from "organized groups" and continued to manifest the features of the particular association or religious community. The importance of this for political action is twofold: first, Christian Democracy was no longer confined to the parliamentary state; parliamentary action was only one of its political avenues, by no means the only or most important one. Further, its elite was composed less of notables than of the functionaries and representatives of the associations, leaders of the workers' and peasants' parties, as the case might be, a structure which became continually clearer in the course of time. In any case there was a

[57] Direct and indirect party structure: M. Duverger, *op. cit.*, pp. 22 ff. See Schieder, *Der Liberalismus*, p. 145.

[58] Duverger, *op. cit.*, p. 22.

clear structural difference from the parties of liberalism and an
analogy with the structure of the future socialist parties.[59]

It is clear that such traits should not be overstressed. "Indirect
structure" is not a permanent characteristic of Christian Democracy. It characterized its beginnings and remained visible on the
order of the socialist parties only while the acceptance of Catholicism in the modern constitutional state was still incomplete.
The fully developed political party gradually leaves behind its
original structure of cells and groups. Catholicism, when it is
established in parliament, can afford to do without further group
formation within the confession. It is self-evident, then, that the
indirect structure (which was never so clearly defined in Christian Democratic parties, even those with parallel union movements, as it was in the socialist parties) in time was dissipated.
The modern Christian Democratic parties which sprang up after
the First World War were all based upon individual, not collective, membership.

Though the *subordination of the political to the social* is characteristic only of the early stages of Christian Democratic movements, the fact that these parties seemed to *repeat the revolution
of society against the state* in a new way and with important consequences has often given rise to conclusions about their ideology
and their conception of the state. Thus an attempt was made to
explain the stress on small groups and associations, on the prefer-
ence for small gatherings and the *corps intermédiaire* of Early
Christian Democratic movements—in clear contrast to classical
liberalism's concept of the state—through the peculiarities of
Catholic social teachings which were supposed to be based on
an organic concept of society and therefore opposed the claims to

[59] In this sense also Duverger, *op. cit.*, p. 23. Consider the role, for example,
which labor unions and circles like the Fabian Society played in the formation of
the British Labour party.

sovereignty of the modern state. The most remarkable and most doubtful attempt at clarification came from Joseph Hours. In a historical study which ends in political polemics, he described Christian Democracy—and above all its French species—as an antistate and antinational movement which aimed at dissolving the unity of the state into a pluralism of *pouvoirs intermédiaires*.[60] He does not see that such a reproach could be leveled against the unions, the post-liberal parties, and against any particular form of organized will outside the *volonté générale* of the Jacobin style; seen through Hours' eyes, they would all sin against the principle of national unity and, therefore, regarded from a historical perspective, would be instruments for a refeudalization of the modern state. Yet the concept of state and democracy used by Hours is an ideological construct. The "pure democracy" of Rousseau, which is his starting point, never existed.[61] We have to free ourselves of the idea that the organic concept of state and society represents a doctrine invented to refute the ideas of 1789 and which was first monopolized by Catholic traditionalism and then by Christian Democracy. It is true, however, that as far back as 1848 republican Catholics in France demanded a *démocratie des groupes*.[62] But such ideas

[60] J. Hours, "Les origines d'une tradition politique. La formation en France de la doctrine de la démocratie chrétienne et des pouvoirs intermédiaires," *Libéralisme, Traditionalisme, Décentralisation,* Cahiers de la fondation nationale des Sciences Politiques, no. 21 (Paris, 1952), pp. 79–123. For a critic see E. Borne, "La démocratie chrétienne contre l'Etat?" *Terre humaine* (July–August, 1952), pp. 76–101.

[61] For criticism of the pure or ideal democracy, cf. W. Conze in his "Epilogue" to the new edition of R. Michels, *Zur Soziologie des Parteiwesens in der modernen Demokratie* (Stuttgart, 1957), pp. 388 ff.; further W. Hennis, *Meinungsforschung und repräsentative Demokratie* (Tübingen, 1957), *passim*; E. Fraenkel, *Die repräsentative und die plebiszitäre Komponente im demokratischen Verfassungsstaat* (Tübingen, 1958), pp. 6 ff.

[62] Biton, *op. cit.*, p. 101.

were never confined to political Catholicism. Thinkers at the other end of the spectrum, like the socialist Proudhon and his disciples, criticized the individualistic democracy of 1789 and as federalists opposed the schematic reduction of the body politic to the confrontation of state and individual. No opposition against the state proper is in question here—such as is the case with anarchism—but the reaction, understandable from a historical perspective, against an absolutistic state, both in its Jacobin and its monarchist forms, which is hostile to any attempt at the social self-defense of minorities, as it only allows for an amorphous mass of individuals. In so far as Christian Democracy was one of these minorities, it also made use of the theory of *pouvoirs intermédiaires*. But in no case do such thoughts represent the decisive and organizing principle of party formation. At most it may be said that motivating the turn toward pre-statal communities is a common personalistic tradition shared both by Christian Democracy and French syndicalism. Yet it cannot be explained (as Hours thinks), just because it is common to both movements, through the old guild concept of society nor through romantic nostalgia.[63]

On the other hand and without giving attention to the constellation under which both Catholic and socialist parties fought against Jacobin democracy, there are considerable differences between the two.[64] Above all, Christian Democracy, distant as it may be from the liberal-ideological party, is not yet a class party in the true sense of the word. It appeals to all classes without distinction: workers, peasants, employees, or members of the bourgeois class. Much as the Catholic social movement of the nineteenth century took part in the formation of the Christian

[63] Hours, *loc. cit.*, p. 93.
[64] On the effect of socialism upon the formation of Christian Democracy: Dempf, *op. cit.*, pp. 21 f.

Democratic movement, especially in France,[65] the new political type which was born cannot simply be attributed to the working class, not even to the Christian working class, nor to the bourgeoisie. The distinctive characteristic of Christian Democracy can be found in the fact that it can unite within itself several classes because its structural principle lies not in the realm of the social. On the one hand this is its weakness: it has less adaptability than other parties, since different cross-currents flow through it and the interests of the individual components change. On the other hand this is its strength, once it succeeds in adjusting the disparate interests to each other. The starting point of Christian Democracy, the denomination, is much narrower than the area which is governed by liberalism and socialism, which are more extensive ideologies with fuzzier outlines. Yet within its self-determined limits, Catholicism comprehends a much greater social hinterland than the liberal and socialist parties. The hinterland corresponds to the inner spread of the social groups united within it and to the "classless" character of Catholic society.

Christian Democracy is not a liberal party in that it does not unite individuals around a political program. Nor is it a socialist party, for it is not limited to a single class. In time and type it stands between the liberal *parti-doctrine* and the socialist *parti-classe* (Duverger). In a word, it tries to reduce the concept of "class" to the common denominator of "doctrine."

Catholicism has a tendency to organize as a whole even in politics. A party formed of Catholics shows a "co-ordinating structure" of necessity.[66] Based on the social-group formation

[65] Besides the already mentioned work of Duroselle, see the book by H. Rollet, *L'action sociale des catholiques en France (1871–1914)* (Paris, 1948), which covers the later period.

[66] Co-ordinating structure: Schieder, *Der Liberalismus*, p. 166.

within the denomination, Catholicism aims to co-ordinate individual groups and goes on from there to a political form which gives to the denomination as a whole recognition within the constitutional state.

It is a matter of life to Christian Democracy how far this coordination of different groups succeeds and which formative principle wins out in the end: class or denominational. If the political forces are aligned according to the principle of denomination, they gain a coherence which is able to resist even very strong social tensions. If, on the other hand, class interests win out, the dissolution of the party is inevitable. A denominational class party is a contradiction.[67]

HISTORICAL PRESUPPOSITIONS

France was the proving ground in the nineteenth century for the first attempts to relate church and democracy—and it was there that the Christian Democratic concept first appeared—because of the aggravated public position of Catholicism in France. In no other country was the church so greatly undermined. The revolution put an end to the corporate freedom of the church and had attempted to force the clergy into the service of the state. When the attempt miscarried, the state proceeded to attack the faith by opposing the revolutionary cult of reason to church dogma. The situation approached the écraser l'infâme. The shock of it continued to be felt within French Catholicism for several decades. It is understandable that the French Catholic fight over the ideas of 1789 and the church's contest with the democratic lay state were conducted with much more asperity than in coun-

---

[67] See Rollet, op. cit., I., 339 ff., 384 ff., Dempf, op. cit., p. 27; Bauer, op. cit., p. 5; J. Becker, "Das Ende der Zentrumspartei und die Problematik des politischen Katholizismus in Deutschland," in Die Welt als Geschichte XXIII (1963), 149 ff.

tries where the break with the past occurred less dramatically. The rift between the two Frances, the traditional and the revolutionary, split French Catholicism down the middle.[68] Both partisans of Catholic traditionalism and their opponents, who sought to defend a unity of church and democracy, used logical and theological arguments to buttress their political views: at times one was ready to exorcise the Revolution, at times one was ready to Christianize it. The battle seesawed throughout the nineteenth century. Catholic opinion on the Revolution remained divided, and while conservative voices in the church were generally in the majority, there was always a minority inclined to accept republican and democratic thought.

In contrast to adulation or fear of the demoniac nature of the revolution, in time there slowly appeared a view which did not contemplate the theological significance of the events so much as their concrete historical shape. Michelet had asked: "La révolution, est-elle chrétienne, anti-chrétienne?" and added: "Cette question, historiquement, logiquement, précéde toute autre."[69] In 1848 the Christian meaning of revolution was still being fought out. Eight years later, Tocqueville cut short this quarrel by asking simply for the "how" of the past: "Quel fut le véritable sens, quel a été le véritable charactère, quels sont les effets permanents de cette révolution étrange et terrible? Qu'a-t-elle détruit précisément? Qu'a-t-elle crée?"[70] ("What is the true meaning, what was the true character, what are the permanent effects of this strange and terrible revolution? What did it destroy?

---

[68] From the abundant literature, see M. Darbon, *Le conflit entre la droite et la gauche dans le catholicisme français 1830–1953* (Paris, 1953).

[69] J. Michelet, *Histoire de la révolution française* (2d ed.; Paris, 1868), I, 17.

[70] A. de Tocqueville, *L'ancien régime et la révolution* in *Oeuvres complètes* (Paris, 1951 ff.), II, 81. English translation: *The Old Régime and the French Revolution* (New York, 1955).

What did it create?") Tocqueville found that the connection between the *ancien régime* and the revolution, even in the sphere of the church, was much closer than had been supposed under the more immediate influence of revolutionary upheavals. He attributed responsibility for the conflict between church and revolution, not to the conscious intentions of one side, but to the constraints on the church resulting from its social position in the old social order.

"It was much less in its guise as religious teaching than as a political institution that Christianity roused such passionate hatred; not because its priests wanted to regulate the things of another world, but because they were landed-estate gentry, feudal lords, masters of the tithe and administrators of this world; not that the church was not to have any place in the new society to be founded: but because it already occupied the most privileged and powerful place in the old society which one wanted to ground into the dust."[71] For the rest, in Tocqueville's opinion, there was no fundamental difference between Christianity and democracy. Rather, the Christian idea of equality of all men before God came close to democratic egalitarianism.[72]

Tocqueville wrote in the fifties of the nineteenth century. At that time Catholic traditionalism, which was born of the rebellion of Catholics against the revolution, had long lost its efficacy. It had been laid to rest with the monarchy of Charles X. But its counterpart, the early Catholic socialism of the time of Louis Phillipe, reached its crest in the 1848 revolution, but it was not generally accepted by the workers or by the bourgeoisie, which

[71] Tocqueville, *op. cit.*, p. 84. The text is found in the epigraph on p. ix.

[72] Cf. especially the "Introduction" to A. de Tocqueville, *Democracy in America* (New York, 1961), pp. 6 ff., where the development to political equality is spoken of as a "providential fact" and where it is stated: "Christianity, which has declared that all men are equal in the sight of God, will not refuse to acknowledge that all citizens are equal in the eye of the law." (P. 12.)

had forgotten the language of revolution during the Second Empire. Thus Tocqueville expressed a widely shared feeling of his time when he began the demythologization of the revolution. His findings were of the greatest importance for French Catholicism. By revealing the ideological character of revolutionary religiosity,[73] he cut the ground from under the romantic ideas of the holy character of revolutionary democracy as well as from under that of the traditionalist counter slogan of the "apostasy of the state." At the same time, he exposed the political origin of the religious crisis by closely examining the connection between *ancien régime* and revolution, confirming the views of liberal Catholics, who saw in the statehood of the church the true reason for the later dissension between church and revolution.

With these ideas Tocqueville occupied the middle ground between the two trends in French Catholicism which were ready to recognize democracy, *de facto* or *de jure*: liberal Catholicism and the minority group of the Catholic social movement which inclined toward a republican state form. Both currents, which may be designated as specifically French aspects of political Catholicism or Catholic politics, were able to rally behind them a not inconsiderable part (though not the majority) of French Catholic public opinion during the revolutions of 1830 and 1848. They gain considerably in importance as representing the beginnings of Christian Democracy in France and, therefore, in view of the theme of this book, must be considered here.

Liberal Catholicism, originating during the Revolution of 1830, avoided identification with democratic movements. However, it accelerated and eased the accommodation of Catholicism

---

[73] See the third chapter of *Democracy in America*, dealing with the question "comment la Révolution française a été une révolution politique qui a procédé à la manière des révolutions religieuses, et pourquoi." Here Tocqueville anticipates in many points the modern concept of ideology.

to democracy by snatching at the parliamentary and other public possibilities which the constitutional state offered the church. Liberal in the political sense, liberal Catholicism stressed the value of freedom over the egalitarian tendencies of the time and endeavored to erect a dam against the rising tide of state power. It recognized the dual political nature of the revolution and made a clear differentiation between the ideas of 1789 and those of 1793. Rejecting the Jacobin state, it held that the rights of the church were guaranteed in the concept of human rights. Thus, like liberalism, it opposed the individual and society to the state. With this it made it possible for the church to recover its rights within the framework of a democratic society after the church's coalition with the absolutist state had once been broken.[74]

Democratic-social Catholicism, which came upon the scene in the Revolution of 1848, distinguished itself from liberal Catholicism, on the one hand, by a sharper ideological profile, and on the other by the fact that it tried to continue the revolutionary tradition. In a way which for a long time was still opposed by Catholic dogma, it steadfastly upheld the holy character of the French Revolution, although it sharply condemned the democracy that developed within it on account of its basically individualistic attitude. It saw the religious core of the ideas of 1789, not in the concept of liberty, but in that of equality. By trying to develop the liberal revolution as a social revolution, it hoped to contribute to the spread of the Gospel and to the advent of the general fraternity among men which had been proclaimed by the church in its beginnings but which, as these partisans saw it, had never been realized.

These currents, for which the representative names are Lamennais and Buchez, often touched upon each other, and partly

---

[74] On the program of liberal Catholicism, cf. Montalembert's already mentioned (n. 26) *Discours prononcés au Congrès Catholique de Malines.*

friendly, partly hostile relationships were maintained. Both, though with different means, worked at resolving the conflicts between revolution and church. What might be termed the Christian-democratic tradition of France resulted from this mutual contact, exchange of principles and experiences, from this *rapprochement* of liberal practice and democratic ideology.

Only much later, however, and then only temporarily, did a major party on the lines of the German *Zentrum* emerge from these early Christian-democratic trends. All through the nineteenth century Christian Democracy failed to sink roots in France. There was a double reason for this: first, liberal Catholicism lacked the official approval of the church; as we have seen, it was implicitly condemned by the encyclicals *Mirari vos* and *Singulari Nos*[75] and expressly by the encyclical *Syllabus*. On the other hand the attempt at combining a Catholic social movement with political democracy met with fierce resistance from the French middle class and not only on the Catholic side: such an attitude on the part of Catholics was suspected as being an *appel peu sérieux* to democracy, as Renan says.[76] Thus Christian Democracy in France has always come between the grindstones of Catholic and bourgeois conservatism, on the one hand, and anticlerical demagogy on the other. When, finally, in the late nineties, Pope Leo XIII, breaking with the previous policy of the Holy See, attempted a *ralliement* and recommended that French Catholics accept the republic,[77] it was already too late. "Nous avons pris une trop grande avance" ("We have taken too much

[75] See above p. 23, and n. 34.

[76] E. Renan, "Etude sur Lamennais," in the new edition of Lamennais' *Livre du peuple* (Paris, 1872), p. 19. For a further reason, see A. Dempf, *op. cit.*, pp. 27 f., where the predominantly religious character of the Catholic parties is made responsible for their failure in France.

[77] Cf. *infra*, pp. 275 ff.

of a down payment"), said Clemenceau to Jacques Piou, the leader of the "rallies."[78] It was only in the twentieth century that the seed of liberal Catholicism finally bore fruit in the *Sillon*, the *Parti Démocrate Populaire*, in the Catholic Workers' movement, and finally in the MRP (*Mouvement Républicain Populaire*).

The views and attitudes of historians reflect the political disposition of groups for and against the revolution. "Right from the start the historiography of the revolution was filled with the conflicting currents of glorification of revolution and enmity."[79] Judgment of the revolution also colored opinions regarding the attempt at *rapprochement* between the church and revolutionary democracy. How this was to be judged—as possible or as utopian—depended upon whether the two powers were seen as standing in absolute or only in a relative opposition which might be resolved by history.[80]

For more than half a century opinions about the revolution were ranged within mutually exclusive categories of praise or condemnation. The revolution was regarded as a metaphysical struggle between heavenly and demonic spirits. Friends and foes

[78] D. Ferrata, *Ma nonciature en France* (Paris, 1921), p. 51.

[79] On the jumble of politics and history made by the historians of the French Revolution, cf. the strongly negative view taken by P. Geyl in his essay on Michelet (*Die Diskussion ohne Ende. Auseinandersetzungen mit Historikern* [Darmstadt, 1958], pp. 75 ff.).

[80] For a general introduction to the historical research on the revolution, see P. R. Rohden's "Preface" to the German edition of C. Brinton, *A Decade of Revolution, Europa im Zeitalter der französischen Revolution* (2d ed.; Vienna, 1951), and—with special regard to the church-state problem—K. D. Erdmann, *Volkssouveränität und Kirche* (Cologne, 1949), pp. 11 ff. The following sketch emphasizes above all the critical examination of liberal Catholicism and Christian Democracy in French historical research—"historical research" understood in that broader sense which in France up to Taine includes also philosophical-theological and literary essays.

of the revolution alike attempted to build a solid basis, theological or anti-theological, for a schema of this kind. For a long time philosophers and theologians held the upper hand vis à vis a positivist historiography which made headway very slowly, since it was greatly dependent upon its values being accepted. Such a one was de Maistre, who was the first to express the Catholic opposition to the revolution. He coined the phrase "the satanic revolution"[81] and branded as treason against the faith every kind of acceptance by Catholic thought of the ideas of 1789. Or Proudhon, the only atheist philosopher of revolution who approached de Maistre's originality and depth, who saw 1789 as the beginning of an epoch introducing the passage of justice from the hands of the church into those of men and thus an epoch decisive in the battle between human and divine law.[82] In Michelet, too, as we have seen, the question of the revolution's being Christian or anti-Christian, took precedence over all others. It was similar for Thiers, Lamartine, and Blanc. Wherever we look in France in the first half of the nineteenth century we find the debate about revolution being carried on either under the sign of theology or of metaphysics; everywhere history was in the grip of philosophy or theology of history and was occupied with tracing the hidden sense of events rather than their exact form.

Such a state of affairs confronts historical research with difficult questions. In principle, the right of theological criticism

[81] J. de Maistre, *Du pape* (9th ed.; Lyon, 1851), "Discours préliminaire" (p. 12): "La révolution ne ressemble à rien de ce qu'on a vu dans les temps passés. Elle est satanique dans son essence." Similarly *Considérations sur la France* (ed. Johannet-Vermale) (Paris, 1936), chap. v, p. 63: "Il y a dans la révolution française un charactère satanique qui la distingue de tout ce qu'on a vu et peut-être de tout ce qu'on verra."

[82] He developed this idea in *De la justice dans la Révolution et dans l'Eglise* (Oeuvres complètes de P. J. Proudhon; Paris, 1868), Vol. XXI. See especially chap. iii–v, pp. 82 ff.

with regard to such an event as the French Revolution cannot be debated. Whoever has clarified his opinion about the innermost intention of religion and revolution will have to admit that here is indeed an essential conflict.[83] The question remains, however, whether this contrast was so clearly and precisely realized in the French Revolution—or in any other—that accommodation is to be excluded once and forever. If this opinion is taken—and Catholic conservative as well as revolutionary-laicistic historiography has done so for a long time—it presupposes two rather doubtful things: First, that the revolution was a unit from beginning to end, according to Clemenceau's famous expression, *un bloc* ("of one piece"), an event which does not permit bisection into liberal and anti-liberal phases. Second, that right from the start the revolution had a definite aim, that is, the laicization of public life and the secularization of the church. Both opinions were upheld by conservative-Catholic and laicistic authors. The "bloc" thesis can be found as early as de Maistre, who stressed in the face of the opinion that the revolution underwent a decline that revolutionary history comprised several phases but on the whole represented a unity.[84] Veuillot, de Mun, and Pierre de la Gorce repeated similar opinions. Conversely, the conspiracy theory, mainly developed by Catholics, according to which the revolutionaries of 1789 intended from the start to secularize the church, was proposed also by laicist authors, whose view of the merits of the aim was different from that of the Catholic authors. At least since the times of Michelet it has not been considered

[83] Cf. C. Brinkmann, *Soziologische Theorie der Revolution* (Göttingen, 1948), p. 63.

[84] *Considérations*, chap. v, p. 66: "La révolution française a parcouru, sans doute, une période dont tous les moments ne se ressemblent pas, cependant, son caractère général n'a jamais varié, et dans son berceau même elle prouva tout ce qu'elle devait être."

objectionable to accept the program of the de-Christianization of the National Convention;[85] while laicist writers were inclined to blame the church for the breach between church and revolution, they confirm indirectly, by stressing the inevitability of the breach, that the church in the condition it found itself before the revolution could not have entered the revolutionary state—a fact which had first been expressed by Michelet when he wrote: "La Révolution n'adopta aucune église. Pourquoi? Parce qu'elle était une église elle-même."[86]

Yet it was inevitable that in time other voices should rise to contest these views and that people would begin to see the historical course of the revolution in a critical and differentiating light. This inclination grew as French Catholicism, after the extremes of the Restoration and the revolutions of 1830 and 1848 began in the Second Empire to search for a middle ground for understanding the ideas of the democratic age. From the politics of Montalembert or Falloux, who were able to maintain by their tactical maneuverability the policies of liberal Catholicism even through the era of Napolean III, clear lines lead to Tocqueville. If the *Syllabus* opposed such endeavors to adjust, it could not prevent the growing strength of liberal Catholicism in Belgium as in France during the Second Empire. Historiographically, the revolution slowly began to lose its terror for Catholics. This was the start of a period of ideological disenchantment in which revolutionary ideas seemed to dissolve and new questions, mainly of a social nature, began to agitate the mind.

Then the return to the republic, in 1871, unexpectedly renewed the old question. A new and strengthened Catholicism, with a firmer unity also apparent in inner-church affairs as a

---

[85] Cf. Erdmann, *op. cit.*, p. 16.

[86] J. Michelet, *Histoire de la Révolution française* (Paris, 1847 ff.), I, viii f.; cited in Erdmann, p. 17.

result of the declaration on infallibility, found itself opposed by
a militant laicism armed with the prestige of positivistic science
and of Comte's sociology and intent upon realizing the *République sans Dieu* in the face of "clericalism" and "ultramontanism." Again, as in the great revolution, the question of education
became the center of dispute: minds were divided over whether
the church or the state should educate French youth. When the
church-friendly regime of the *ordre moral* collapsed with the resignation of MacMahon and the era of the *république républicaine* began, the *Parti Radical* immediately attacked the church
and set about eliminating the influence of the religious orders in
education through a series of laws.[87] This led to a bitter fight between the republic and active Catholics and eventually brought
about the separation of church and state.

The first result of the laicist campaign was to reinforce the
conservative wing of Catholics. Under the pressure of the increasingly exacerbated fight, the conservative party which declared the
republic incompatible with Catholic principles gained the upper
hand and set busily at work to effect the return of the monarchy.
If the small group of republican Catholics which resisted this
powerful swing toward the right was not completely annihilated
in this situation and retained its freedom of movement and even
gained strength, it is almost exclusively due to Pope Leo XIII's
intervention. Through Cardinal Lavigerie in 1892 he made his
famous eleventh-hour attempt at preventing a breach between
the church and the Third Republic and at reconciling French
Catholics to the republican form of state.

In practical politics the *Ralliement* was unsuccessful, causing
new splits among French Catholics rather than bringing about
a unified Catholic political front. But for inner-church politics, it

[87] E. M. Accomb, *The French Laic Laws* (New York, 1941).

was an event whose importance can hardly be exaggerated. By distinguishing democracy as a political form from the democratism of revolutionary ideology, it broke through that anti-republicanism on which every attempt to open a possibility for political activity by French Catholics had foundered. Since the possibility of such a distinction had the standing of a papal pronunciamento, it became much more difficult for conservative Catholics to maintain the old charge of religious heresy against their republican adversaries. The Catholic groups alignment against Christian Democracy was thus broken at a decisive spot. The new path opened by Leo XIII with his encyclicals would now remain open for Catholics and could not be completely closed even by the curia's condemnation under Pius X of the Christian Democratic youth movement of *Sillon* (but not of the much more dangerous *Action française*).

During the years of the *Ralliement* there appeared a number of works by Catholic authors which treated the problems of modern democracy. In those writings the relationship between church and revolution was given a new and mostly optimistic meaning. During the enthusiasm of those years even the old idea of the equation of Gospel and democracy could again be taken up. Abbé Gayraud, one of the principal theoreticians of the French *démocratie chrétienne*,[88] wrote in 1899: "Le fait politique et social de la démocratie, résultat heureux pour les peuples de l'évolution progressive des sociétés, est a notre avis, l'un des fruits de l'Évangile. Voilà notre point de départ." ("The political and social fact of democracy, for the people a happy result of the progressive evolution of societies, is, in our view, one of the fruits of the Gospels. This is our point of departure.") Like Tocqueville, this movement discerned a bridge to link Christian-

---

[88] Abbé Gayraud, *Les démocrates chrétiens* (Paris, 1898), p. 3a.

ity and democracy in the concept of the equality of men before God. Gayraud noted:

> Il me semble, que l'égalité démocratique est apparue sur la terre le jour où les hommes ont appris à nommer ensemble Dieu "notre père" et à s'asseoir à la même table, sans distinction de race, ni de fortune, ni de condition pour y communier, dans la foi, l'espérance et l'amour, au même Christ, premier-né de ce Dieu Père.[89] [It seems that democratic equality first appeared in this world the day men learned together to say "Our Father" and to sit down at the same table without distinction of race, fortune, or status, in order to commune with the same Christ, first-born Son of this God Father, in faith, hope, and love.]

Thoughts of this kind permeate all the writings of Christian Democracy and the later *Sillon*; they reverberate still in the *Histoire de la démocratie catholique en France* by A. Rastoul, published just before the First World War (1913) and dedicated to the memory of Buchez. This book was the first summary by a French Catholicism friendly toward the revolution and which went beyond 1848 and 1830 to include the Great Revolution. But even where current moods did not affect historical and theological views of revolution, the general attitude toward the revolution changed. The most significant indication of this was the great work by A. Sicard, *L'ancien Clergé de France*,[90] which shed new light upon the pre-history and early history of the revolution and convincingly proved the existence of an initial unity for reform among revolutionaries and Catholics.[91]

[89] Gayraud, *op. cit.*, p. 26.
[90] Paris, 1893–1903.
[91] There are, however, also distortions and exaggerations caused by his *Ralliement* attitude; cf. Erdmann, *op. cit.*, pp. 40 ff.

Nonetheless, there was no dearth of critics who clung to the incompatibility of revolution and church; with the intensification of the differences between the church and the Third Republic, they gained the upper hand. Thus the influential anticlerical historian A. Debidour[92] in his great work, *Histoire des rapport de l'Église et de l'État en France*,[93] rejected the optimistic view of a speedy reconciliation between the church and modern democracy. He did not conceal the revolution's failure to eradicate the church among the people or the fact that the material damages which the church had sustained were more than made up by the growth of more firmly convinced Catholics. He recognized, too, that the dangers to democracy from the side of Catholicism were now much greater than before because the revolution had brought about a tightening of church organization and a spiritual unification.[94] Yet he could not say that Catholicism would triumph over revolutionary ideas: the church, he held, has lost too much ground in French society to be able to win back its former position.

Si l'ancienne noblesse et l'ancienne bourgeoisie se sont rapprochées de l'Église, depuis un siècle, il semble que dans le même temps la masse populaire s'en soit éloignée quelque peu, pour une raison facile à comprendre. . . . Le peuple sait ce qu'il doit à la Révolution, qui l'a fait libre et souverain. Il en garde pieusement au coeur le souvenir, le respect et l'amour. Les principes de 89 sont aussi devenus pour lui une religion, et toute atteinte portée à ce Credo laïque, lui paraît non seulement un attentat à ses droits, mais une sorte de sacri-

[92] He edited, together with A. Aulard, the history textbooks for the schools of the Third Republic.
[93] Paris, 1898.
[94] Débidour, *op. cit.*, pp. 643 ff.

lège.[95] [If the old nobility and the old middle class have come closer to the church, at the same time it seems that the mass of the people has distanced itself somewhat, and this for an easily understandable reason. The people know what they owe to the revolution, and that it has made them free and sovereign. They keep in their hearts a fond memory, respect, and love for it. Thus the principles of 1789 have become a religion to them, and any and every blow to this laymen's credo appears not only like an attack on their rights but as a kind of sacrilege.]

Although the implicit regard for democracy which informs these words may lack conviction, Debidour does present a true picture. He correctly points out that the return after 1849 of the middle classes and the nobility to the church could not by far make up for the defection of the workers; he correctly points out that the ideas of 1789 were stronger than the appeal of Catholic socialism because the masses sought fulfilment of their social demands, not within a corporate economy, but through a regime of political equality.

The most outspoken critic of Christian Democracy, however, was not the laicist Debidour, but a Catholic, E. Barbier. He had made his reputation on the basis of heated polemics against liberal Catholics at the end of the nineteenth century and before World War I. He published his three-volume work, *Histoire du Catholicisme libéral et du Catholicisme social en France*, in 1924. It is a gigantic indictment of liberal and social Catholicism and contains an extraordinary accumulation of material, including much information that has importance as the eyewitness of a contemporary. In those days the expression "liberal Catholicism" had a special theological meaning arising from the debate on

[95] *Op. cit.*, pp. 648 f.

Modernism. Thus, by criticizing the politics of liberal Catholicism, Barbier at the same time aimed at Loisy's theology. It is also important to note that he included the social Catholicism inspired by Pope Leo XIII in his criticism; this reflects the bourgeoisification of French Catholicism from the time of the Second Empire, a state of affairs unhampered by the separation of church and state and rather furthered by it, since the loss of state subsidies made the church completely dependent on the contributions of the *classes élevées*.

Barbier's research did not reveal much that was new about the early history of Christian Democracy. The real value of his book is to be found in the minute descriptions of the Catholic social movement of 1870–1914, its internal struggles, and its relationship to the Holy See. His judgment of *Modernisme social* is sharp and often unjust, but we must not forget that it seemed to coincide with the declaration by Pius X regarding *Sillon*. The breakdown of the policy of *Ralliement* brought about a more critical attitude of the curia vis-à-vis the French Republic. Such an intransigent policy toward the republic was difficult to reconcile with the conciliatory and reserved one of liberal and social Catholicism.

Barbier spoke in circumstances which made Pius X's rejection of liberal Catholicism appear final. Whoever surveyed the long and varied history of liberal Catholicism in France had to ask himself, however, if the attitude of rejection by the curia actually was the last word. Or was it rather aimed at the ideological pretension of *Sillon* and its dogmatic equation of Christianity and democracy as the principle of the co-operation of Catholics in a democratic constitutional state? As early as 1909, after the separation of state and church, George Weill described the three times repeated strivings of liberal Catholicism in France—1830, 1848, and 1895—for reconciliation between church and state, thrice halted by papal statements. Refusing to close the books on the question, he added: "Ce serait pourtant une grave erreur de croire que l'œuvre des catholiques libéraux a été stérile, ni même qu'elle est terminée."[96] ("It would be a serious mistake to think that the work of the liberal Catholics was sterile or that it has come to an end.") As a matter of fact after the First World War it appeared that the substance of liberal Catholicism in the Romance language countries had essentially survived: the new Christian Democratic party formations which sprang up in Italy and France would not have been viable without its prior activity.

The picture drawn by Waldemar Gurian after World War I of the development of French Catholicism since the Great Revolution is, on the whole, a confident one.[97] Gurian was the first historian to overcome the isolated treatment of liberal Catholicism. By placing Lamennais, Montalembert, and Lacordaire within the over-all development of Catholic thought since the revolution, he was able to show surprising likenesses between Catholic traditionalism and Catholic liberalism, which until then had been exclusively considered as antagonistic. Gurian showed that the dogmatization of democracy, effected by the later Lamennais, derived from a social philosophy which had its roots in the positivist attitude of de Maistre and Bonald. Along this line, which led to Comte and Maurras, he brings into relief the renewed religious Catholicity of social Catholics like Ozanam which flowered later, in the Catholic social movement. Above all, we owe to his study our detailed knowledge of the facts of 1830–48, when the political ideology of French Catholicism received its decisive remodeling, partly toward democratic-republicanism, partly toward ecclesiastical orthodoxy. Gurian

[96] G. Weill, *Histoire du Catholicisme libéral en France* (Paris, 1909).
[97] W. Gurian, *Die politischen und sozialen Ideen des französischen Katholizismus 1789–1914* (Mönchen-Gladbach, 1929).

was the first to bring into focus the inner-Catholic importance of French ideas and the connection between the political loss of power of Gallicanism and the new rise of papal power in the nineteenth century. Although Gurian could not completely free himself from the tendency to see things more harmoniously *ex eventu* than they were (thus in his view, the papacy seemed to be clearly moving toward a conciliatory church policy in the nineteenth century, a line taken only by Leo XIII) and although he judged the importance of the early Christian Democratic movements from the point of view of church orthodoxy,[98] his study as an over-all picture is superior to all previous accounts because it combines humanistic and church-historical research with sociological methodology and with an ability to perform philosophic-theological analysis.

Gurian's book starts with the *ancien Régime* and ends with a view of *renouveau catholique*, the Catholic movement after the First World War that is linked with the names of Psicharis and Péguy. It remains the only over-all presentation of the political development of French Catholicism since the revolution. In the time between the two world wars the doctrinal and theological aspect of the question has again deepened. Thus especially Jacques Maritain (after Pius XI's condemnation of *Action française*, the leading theoretician of the Catholic left in France) and the leader of the *Partito Popolare Italiano*, Don Luigi Sturzo, have investigated by their discussions of basic principles the possibilities which the democratic state offers to the political activity of Christians.[99] The merely minor successes, however, of the newly founded Christian Democratic parties in Italy and France

[98] He thus especially underestimates the importance of Buchez and the Catholic Saint-Simonists. In this respect the decisive turning point is formed by Duroselle's research, a turning point which has still to be evaluated with regard to the political importance of the early Christian-Democratic movements.

[99] For Maritain, see n. 31. L. Sturzo, *Church and State* (Notre Dame, 1961).

hardly attracted researchers into the history of liberal Catholicism. Thibaudet, who in 1928 in his book *Idées politiques de la France* described the *familles spirituelles* of modern France, counted republican Catholicism among the spiritual forces of the country without assigning much importance to its political expression, particularly *Parti Démocrate Populaire* which, in his opinion, a small crisis could sweep away.[100] This was indeed the impression which any impartial observer of liberal Catholicism in France would have carried away with him: short periods of ascent had always been followed by long stretches of fatigue.

The rise of the Christian Democratic parties after World War II, however, completely renewed and basically changed this situation.

It has also provided new conditions for research.[101] The history of liberal and social Catholicism, hovering before on the margin of historiography, has won new importance as the early history of modern Christian Democracy. This change is clearly expressed in the terminology that substitutes "Christian Democracy" for the old labels of political and liberal Catholicism, even when the political forms so described deserve the name only with many qualifications. This tendency is especially widespread in research in Latin countries. Here, under the label of *Démocratie chrétienne* (*Democrazia Cristiana*) are subsumed nearly all forms of Catholic political activity, from the liberal Catholicism of Lamennais and the Italian neo-Guelfdom of Rosmini to French and Italian social Catholicism and the Christian Democratic parties of the present oriented to the modern constitutional state. The tendency is seen in the works of Einaudi-Goguel and Tupini, as well as in those of Biton and Vaussard. Even more inclusive are

[100] Cited in J. Fauvet, *Von Thorez bis de Gaulle* (Frankfurt, 1951), p. 131.

[101] Cf. my review of Fogarty, *Christian Democracy*, in *Historische Zeitschrift* CXCIII (1961), 672 ff.

the works of Michael Fogarty and the collection, *Church and Society*, published by John Moody.[102] In these the history of Christian Democracy is seen as starting in 1820 and 1789, respectively, and the concept of Christian Democracy includes such disparate phenomena as liberal Catholicism in France, the German *Zentrum*, and the Dutch-Calvinistic *Anti-revolutionaries*. Nearly always France is at the center of these studies, corresponding to the role it played in the development of Christian Democratic theories. Thus K. Buchheim devoted a whole chapter of his book, *Geschichte der Christlichen Parteien in Deutschland* to French political Catholicism[103]; H. Guillemin, in his partisan and passionate *Histoire des catholiques français au XIXe siècle*,[104] described the battle of Lamennais and his companions as a battle of God; and R. Havard de Montagne in his pamphlet aimed in a different direction sees the line of Lamennais continuing to Georges Bidault.[105] A new comprehensive presentation of the political ideas of French Catholicism was published in 1951 by J. Roger, but it does not reach the level of Gurian, in spite of earnest attempts at objective presentation.[106]

The pressure to reorient Christian Democracy in the changed conditions of postwar Europe brought new accents to research as well and brought into question many earlier conclusions. Thus, in addition to a preoccupation with social Catholicism, whose history had been presented as essentially closed,[107] new

---

[102] Cf. *supra* n. 3.

[103] Munich, 1953; pp. 31–66.

[104] Paris, 1947.

[105] *Histoire de la Démocratie chrétienne. De Lamennais à Georges Bidault* (Paris, 1949). Only the Spanish edition (Madrid, 1950) was accessible to the author.

[106] *Ideas politicas de los Catolicos franceses* (Madrid, 1951).

[107] Besides the already mentioned works of Duroselle and Rollet, which deal with conditions in France, see on Germany E. Ritter, *Die katholisch-soziale Bewegung Deutschlands im 19. Jhdt. und der Volksverein* (Cologne, 1954).

interest has been aroused in liberal Catholicism, its predecessor, and in the early phases of Christian Democracy associated with Saint-Simon. The relative muting of the dispute between Christian Democracy and the church has made easier an objective appreciation of the heterodox precursors of the modern Christian Democratic parties,[108] and the disappearance of mistrust of political Catholicism has allowed non-Catholic circles to begin to acquire a clear insight into the necessities and problems of Catholic politics in the post-revolutionary era. The early history of Christian Democracy in Europe, which seems to be treated in existing works too much in the light of the "leonine turn" or measured against the (much later) content of Catholic social teaching, may be said to have gained not only new color but new actuality by this shift of viewpoint. One of the reasons why the existing treatises (as deserving as they are in many other respects) fail almost completely in their doctrinal analysis of Christian Democracy lies in the difficulty of reducing liberal and social Catholicism to a common denominator. Fogarty tries to avoid the problem (not without feeling the doubtfulness of his attempt) by using very broad formulations; Vaussard gives a sociological, but no doctrinal, analysis of Christian Democracy.

METHODOLOGY AND TERMINOLOGY

The first strains of Christian Democracy in France belong to the prehistory of political parties. There was no question yet of completely developed parties; there were only loose formations, groups of different structures and variable stability. There were literary and political circles grouped around a famous personality

---

[108] For a survey on the state of research today, see R. Aubert, J.-B. Duroselle, and A. Jemolo, "Le Libéralisme religieux au XIXe siècle," in *Relazioni del X Congresso Internazionale di Scienze Storiche*, Vol. V (Florence, 1955).

like Chateaubriand or Lamartine; conventual associations, like the school of Lamennais at La Chenaie; lodge-like groups like the one around Buchez, who had left the *Amis de la vérité*. Finally, there were party-like associations; like the *Cercle de la Démocratie catholique* founded by Arnaud de l'Ariège in 1849, which survived only for a short time.[109] The most important groups of democratic Catholicism had their own publications, and these are now comfortable sources for the researcher; thus the democratic spiritualism of the revolution comes to the fore in numerous reviews and pamphlets, of which those of the *Cercle social* are the most important. Liberal Catholicism appears in *Avenir*, the school of Buchez in *Européen* and *Atelier*, the Christian Democracy of 1848 in *Ère nouvelle*. Side by side with the journalistic products of the day, we find major works whose effect was felt not only in literature but in politics, as were the writings of Lamennais, Buchez, and Lacordaire. In them are mirrored all the issues which stirred Catholicism at the time of the revolution and of the restoration in France: the arguments with the Enlightenment; the battle for the Gallican tradition; the rejection of state-church infringements by the government; and the first, hesitant concern with social problems left unsolved by the revolution. Here is the place where the liveliest forces of French Catholicism meet and together search for a new politico-religious orientation.

The early history of Christian Democratic parties cannot be presented as a chapter of political sociology, nor can it be pressed into the narrow framework of party history. For it represents as well a chapter of sociology of religion and history of religion. This is borne out at every turn: the immediate reason for the formation of the Christian Democratic parties is found in the

[109] J.-B. Duroselle, "Arnaud de l'Ariège et la Démocratie chrétienne (1848–1851)" (typewritten; Paris, 1949).

changed position of the church after the French Revolution.[110] What is more, the changes in the outward situation of the church cannot be separated from the changes within: the status of the church in public life, the social constitution within which the church exists, influences theology and vice versa. It is no coincidence that Lamennais attacked both the state-church practice of the Bourbon government as well as its Gallican substructure[111] and that the emergence of laicism in the French church was preceded by the emergence of a specific lay theology, ushered in by the publication of Joseph de Maistre's book on the pope.[112]

Here we have to remind ourselves that "history of religion should not simply be studied as a branch of the humanities."[113] An organization like the church, which extends into so many phases of life, cannot be artificially reduced to the dimensions of a religious *Weltanschaung*. In our case, however, it seems proper

[110] Let us remember once more E. Mounier's already cited remark (see p. 7): "Dans la situation sociologique où se trouvent les milieux chrétiens d'Europe, si ces partis n'existaient pas, il faudrait les inventer." ("L'Agonie du Christianisme?" *Esprit*, May, 1947.) This was meant for the Christian parties coming into existence in Europe after World War II but is also valid, *mutatis mutandis*, for postrevolutionary Catholicism in its entirety. See Renan, *op. cit.*, p. 27: "Le parti catholique, d'abord repoussé par l'Eglise officielle, tend à devenir officiel à son tour."

[111] Lamennais started his career as a writer in 1808 when he and his brother edited the "*Réflexions sur l'état de l'Eglise en France pendant le dix-huitième siècle, et sur sa situation actuelle*," an historical criticism of Gallicanism prohibited by Napoleon.

[112] De Maistre still excused himself expressly in the preface "qu'un homme du monde s'attribue le droit de traiter des questions qui, jusqu'à nos jours, ont semblé exclusivement dévolues au zèle et à la science de l'ordre sacerdotal." (*Du pape*, *Oeuvres*, III, 1.) On the origin of modern lay theology, cf. the remarks made by S. Merkle in his article "Die Anfänge französischer Laientheologie im 19. Jahrhundert," in *Wiederbegegnung von Kirche und Kultur in Deutschland* (Munich, 1929).

[113] O. Brunner, "Abendländisches Geschichtsdenken," *Hamburger Universitätsreden* XVII (1954), 32.

to focus on the humanistic side of the problem and, following the usage of the nineteenth century, to speak of *Catholicism* rather than the *church*, of *Christendom* rather than *Christianity*. For we are not taking our theme into the central sphere of faith but we remain in the sphere of political theology. For the time being we shall be concerned, not with the content of the Christian message, but with the secularized form of Christendom whose origins lie in the writings of Rosseau, Chateaubriand, and Saint-Simon. But we must not forget that the marginal position held by Christian Democracy, which seemed heretical a hundred years ago, has slowly been overtaken in the course of the nineteenth and twentieth centuries by the consciousness of the church. Today's Catholic view of democracy hardly differs from the one formulated by Lamennais 130 years ago. As the church met the concepts of Christian Democrats halfway,[114] with a tendency toward church orthodoxy, facilitating the *rapprochement*, becoming evident, ideas which otherwise would have been merely of humanistic interest now became of history-forming importance and political efficacy.

What we are observing here is twofold: a process within the church and a process in the history of modern democracy. The one, *the church's adaptation to the modern democratic lay state*, has been illuminated in its religious and theological aspects in the writings of Maritain,[115] Lecler,[116] and Murray.[117] The other,

---

[114] See W. Gurian in *Perspektiven* III (1953), 69 ff.; and J. C. Murray, *Theological Studies* X (1949), 177 ff. and 409 ff.

[115] J. Maritain, *Integral Humanism* (New York, 1968), and the works cited *supra* n. 31.

[116] J. Lecler, *L'Eglise et la souveraineté d'Etat* (Paris, 1946).

[117] See Murray's above-mentioned article and by the same author: "Leo XIII on Church and State: The General Structure of the Controversy," and "Leo XIII. Separation of Church and State," *Theological Studies* XIV (1953), 1 ff. and 145 ff.

the formation of a special form of democracy out of Christian inspiration (in the dispute with the Jacobin type of state), is still awaiting a thorough summing up, despite works by Rohden,[118] Gurian, Roger, Hours, Biton, Vaussard, and Fogarty. This book does not intend to present this summary; it is restricted to the prehistory and early history of Christian Democracy in France. It is, however, meant to complement existing studies in two ways: with regard to the problem of the revolutionary origin of Christian Democracy and with regard to the connection between Catholic liberalism and Catholic traditionalism. By means of this chronological limitation the author attempts to avoid the dual extreme that is especially noticeable in French scholarship: It either traced the origin of Christian Democratic ideas to the time of the "parti dévot," the Ligue, even to the Bourgignons (Hours), or it let the history of Christian Democracy begin with the liberal Lamennais in 1830 (Borne, Vaussard), without taking note of Lamennais' origin in Catholic traditionalism. The present work seeks to prove that the history of Christian Democracy in France begins with the French Revolution.

An additional word about terminology. When we speak in the following pages of Christian Democracy, a double sense is intended. In a more restricted sense it is used whenever the French concept of *démocratic chrétienne* would justify it, that is, it marks the Christian Democratic idea and ideology proper. In a wider sense it is used to characterize, in a summary way, the differing forms of political Catholicism in the post-revolutionary era, including those which like the conservative-Catholic social movement in France are not democratic or those like liberal Catholicism which look upon democracy as an experiment only and not as an ideology. This double use of the concept was chosen in

[118] P. R. Rohden, "Zur Soziologie des politischen Katholizismus in Frankreich," *Archiv für Sozialwissenschaft und Sozialpolitik* LXII (1919), 498 ff.

order not to disrupt the historical connection between Catholic traditionalists, liberals, and democrats. If we limit the use to the more restricted sense, however, we come across a paradox described by J. Hours [119] with the words: "Les fondateurs de la > démocratie chrétienne < n'étaient pas des démocrates."

Further, we speak of a sociological church concept and of sociological Catholicism. With this we mean less the social side of the church than, to continue Waldimar Gurian's approach, a spiritual attitude which sees in the church nothing but its outward social aspect; this is a concept which negates Christianity's claim to revelation and interprets the Catholic dogma as a positive, human given.[120]

Finally, there will be frequent comment on Gallicanism and the Gallican system. We have to remember that for the time under scrutiny Gallicanism was a concept that was already being altered from a church-political system into a nationalistic ideology and retreating into literature.[121] Its social and political foundations had been eroding since the revolution. The connection between the emergence of the movements of Christian Democracy and inner changes of French Catholicism after the revolution becomes quite clear. The formation of political Catholicism runs parallel to the French church's distancing itself from the Gallican roots of its past. The church retreats from its political dominion, leaves the temporal field to the Catholic layman; it is the sign in the religious sphere that the *ancien régime* is ending and that a new era is dawning for French Catholics.

---

[119] J. Hours, *op. cit.*, p. 113.

[120] This concept found its classical expression in Voltaire, Saint-Simon, Comte, Taine, Maurras. On the problem of Catholic positivism, cf. H. Friedrich, *Das antiromantische Denken im modernen Frankreich. Sein System und seine Herkunft*, Münchner romanistische Arbeiten, no. 4 (Munich, 1935), pp. 216 ff., 297; and H. de Lubac, *Le drame de l'humanisme athée* (Paris, 1945), Part II.

[121] J. Wilhelm, *Das Fortleben des Gallikanismus in der französischen Literatur der Gegenwart*, Münchner romanistische Arbeiten, no. 2 (Munich, 1933).

2: DEMOCRACY AND CHURCH: THE REVOLUTIONARY ATTEMPT AT UNITY (1789–94)

In the history of the relations between the church and modern democracy the French Revolution is an epoch of special importance. Its consequences for the position of religion in public life all over Europe can hardly be overstated. Yet the revolution has this importance not for its religious but for its anti-religious character. This characteristic distinguishes it from all preceding European revolutions. These had left their marks on the religious consciousness of their contemporaries precisely because they were in accord with the most powerful religious movements of their times. In the French Revolution, however, all seemed from the beginning to resolve into a power struggle between religious and political authority. This conflict erupted in the first stage of the revolution and quickly escalated into a bloody struggle in which all the initially common features of the antagonists were swept away. It is not surprising that to both revolutionaries and serious Catholics the idea of reconciliation between church and revolution for a long time appeared impossible: the collision had been too powerful; on both sides too many sacrifices had been made; a return to reasonableness could appear as nothing other than a betrayal.

This course of events is the more surprising because the French Revolution, closely scrutinized, by no means lacks the

68

admixture of religious and Christian elements which can be found in all revolutions, more or less. One needs only to burrow in its documents, speeches, and declarations in order to recognize in the partly exalted, partly visionary tone the gesture of the prophet and the voice of the preacher. Not for nothing was ex-*plosion d'idéalism chrétien laïcisé* spoken of in connection with the Revolution of 1789.[1] This was true also of practical church policy, which recognized that the revolution had not begun as an anti-church movement; rather that it began under the auspices of a close alliance of clerical and political wills toward reform. This is borne out by the *Cahiers*,[2] which are full of declarations of loyalty toward the Catholic religion; it is proved by numerous declarations by clergymen on the eve of the *états généraux*[3] and by the church solemnities which accompanied the act of inauguration and later assembly meetings. The famous and often-pictured scene of the three representatives of the Estates-General walking in solemn procession, burning candles in hand, toward the Church of St. Louis in Versailles, casts a bright light upon this politico-religious unity. Like the Estates-General, the National Assembly which sprang from them retained the custom of surrounding political decisions of great consequence with religious ceremonial. Thus it lent the glamor of church pomp to its most

[1] J. Maritain, *Christianity and Democracy* (Scribner, 1947), p. 27.

[2] See A. Denys-Buirette, *Les questions religieuses dans les cahiers de 1789* (Paris, 1919); and P. de la Gorce, *Histoire religieuse de la Révolution française* (Paris, 1909; here cited after the new edition of 1948), I, 97 ff.

[3] Here especially the writings of the royal court-chaplain Claude Fauchet are to be mentioned: *Oraison funèbre de Louis, duc d' Orléans* (Paris, 1786); *De la religion nationale* (Paris, 1789). On the clergy's political attitude before the revolution, cf. A. Wahl, *Vorgeschichte der französischen Revolution* (Tübingen, 1905/07), II, 227 ff.; M. Göhring, *Geschichte der grossen Revolution*, I (Tübingen, 1950), 303, 324 ff., 327; and Gurian, *op. cit.*, pp. 15 ff. See further K. Heinrichs, *Die politische Ideologie des französischen Klerus bei Beginn der grossen Revolution* (Ph.D. diss.; Kiel, 1934).

dramatic moments, celebrated masses for the fighters of the Bastille, and climaxed the historical night session of August 4, 1789,
during which all the privileges of the old estates were swept
away, with a solemn Te Deum. Whenever the most important
spokesmen of the revolution expressed themselves on church
problems—and this they did at length and often—they stressed
their attachment to the Roman church and expressed their intention to secure it a worthy place in the new state structure. These
were not empty promises; as is now being recognized, the church
policy of the National Assembly was actually at first guided by
the wish to establish close co-operation with the Catholic church.
There was by no means a desire to separate church and state, but
a desire to unite them. Even the Civil Constitution of the clergy,
though it later became the issue of the conflict between the
church and the revolution, was originally a very clear expression
of this amalgamationist tendency, which the laicist historian
Albert Mathiez expressed in the briefest possible formula when
he spoke—not without citing respectable sources—of a mariage
d'Église et de l'État, the marriage of church and state.[4]

But is it not paradoxical from the historical point of view that
this very intention of uniting the church and the revolutionary
state, even to letting the church be completely dissolved in the
state, should have led to an acute confrontation of both powers
which after years of struggle led to the separation of church and
state? To laicist historiographers the result has always seemed incomprehensible. As a result they have constantly searched for a
guilty party, expecting to find it in the Catholic church; and they
have done so not without heated opposition from Catholic his-

---

[4] A. Mathiez, "Le mariage de l'Église et de l'État," in L'Église et la Révolution
française, Revue des Cours et Conférences, Vol. XXXIII, No. 1 (1931/32),
pp. 448–59, especially p. 459.

torians.[5] In France still any discussion of the causes of the conflict between church and revolution is likely to be confused in a
whirl of political argument.

An objective judgment will thus be possible only by a closer
look at the contestants in this uneven battle: the Catholic church
and the revolutionary state. Neither party was at all clear about
its own essence at the beginning of the revolution—and they
found out who they were and what they wanted only when they
attacked each other. This greatly contributed to the development
of that misunderstanding which culminated in the call for the
amalgamation of church and revolution and thus prejudged the
historical result considerably.

As to the Catholic church—or, rather, the Gallican church—
it was ready in 1789 for co-operation with a new kind of state,
and it thus took part in the constitutional work of the National
Assembly. But it was not political aims alone which it pursued
in the deliberations: the church was likewise intent on securing
its traditional rights by constitutional means. With regard to the
political renewal of France the church pursued a revolutionary
and a traditional aim; it was willing to reform the state but defended the positions of the church. Such a double standard,
politically bound to a moderate reformism, provoked conflict as
the revolution grew more and more radical in an opposed concept which saw the revolution as an act of political renewal and
an occasion for a deep-going politico-religious new order *par la
seule raison*. The idea of politico-religious unity, which in the
beginning had seemed to unite church and revolution, thus entered a twilight of opposing interpretations: while the church's
concept remained within the traditional scope of a "Holy Mon-

[5] Cf. the survey on the representation of the problem in the academic research
of the revolution (especially in the writings of Aulard and Mathiez) given by
Erdmann, *op. cit.*, pp. 33 ff.

archy" and aimed at the preservation of Catholicism as the religion of the state and the democratic legalization of the rights of the church in the constitution, the "philosophers," as radical interpreters of the revolutionary spirit, dreamed rather of gaining the sanction of the church for the new constitution—a thought which had been expressed by the Enlightenment, especially Rousseau, and which found expression in the deliberations of the Constituent Assembly.[6]

It is not easy to say, however, what the true aim of the revolutionary forces actually was because their intentions came to light only gradually and during the very struggle against the church. But it is certain that the defenders of revolutionary renewal—in clear contrast to the moderate reformism of the clerical *Constituents*—did not consider the church something which could be taken into the new order unchanged, and they did not intend to cease reforms at the line of the church's right of self-determination and of the old canonical forms. A close scrutiny of revolutionary church policy clearly shows the variety of the forces and ideas involved: there is only a faint dividing line between what derives in it from the *ancien régime*, in the form of the legist tradition, and what is deliberately a new formation, in the sense of the *bonne politie* of the states of antiquity and their religio-political unity. In fact, both traditions come so close that the revolutionaries in remodeling the relations of church and state could fall back not only upon the state philosophy of Rousseau but on the "good old law" of Gallican tradition. Yet there doubtless was a division between the influence of the two traditions. Nowhere is this more apparent than in the course of the revolutionary crisis itself. The cult of the Supreme Being, with which revolutionary democracy, emancipated from the church, finally ended up, was outwardly a *religion de patrie* and contin-

[6] Cf. Erdmann, *op. cit.*, pp. 99 ff.

ued patriotic traditions, but it did so quite differently from the old Catholicism of the monarchy. And in spite of its initial resistance to separation of church and state, the revolutionary state shows many more laicist tendencies and traits and conceived of its sovereignty in a much less limited manner than had been the case under the Catholic kings, in spite of all their tendencies to infringe on the legal domain of the church. The difference between church and revolution appears clearly in the changing interpretations of the relationship between state and church: while the intention of the revolutionary state culminates in a view looking to one-sided take-over, the church aims at achieving an understanding between equal partners, an idea negated by the very character of the revolutionary idea of state, whose totalistic character slowly emerged. Thus the idea of a "marriage" between church and state is a grave misconception, not only in the light of later events, but in terms of a closer examination of the original revolutionary conditions.

And yet, in the France of the waning eighteenth century, everything pointed toward such an experiment, in the church as well as in the state, in social life as well as in philosophical-religious discussion. Nowhere was the connection between state form and religion closer than in the old monarchy. It permeated private and public life in many ways and found its highest and most visible expression in the solemn anointing of the kings, which in France had the importance of an act of state. In the absence of a consciousness of unity in a state or of modern national sentiment, religion remained for a long time the strongest unifying factor in French society;[7] it also determined to a great extent the slowly increasing sphere of profane politics. Since the

---

[7] D. Gerhard, "Regionalismus und ständisches Wesen als ein Grundthema europäischer Geschichte," *Historische Zeitschrift*, CLXXIV (1952), 307–37, especially 335. Cf. also K. von Raumer, "Absoluter Staat, korporative Libertät, persönliche Freiheit," *Historische Zeitschrift* CLXXXIII (1957), 55 ff.

concept of state was slowly disengaging itself from the person of the monarch and attaching itself to the sovereign people, it was natural that the old relationship between church and state should also assume new significance: in place of a "Holy Monarchy," a "Holy Democracy"; instead of a royal church, a democratic one. In the face of this willingness to change, the freedom-loving and self-reliant element of the church, anchored in the class privileges of the clergy, carried no weight, the less so since the revolution which was transforming the public countenance of Catholicism also deprived the nobility of power and place and had installed instead a middle class affected by the idea of equal rights and hostile to the privileges of an upper strata.

Every evaluation of revolutionary church policy necessarily leads back to the history of state and church in the *ancien régime*. Here is the starting point for the later entanglements of church and revolutionary democracy; here are the strands of the knot first tied by the revolution and which it then attempted to sever with one blow. When we inquire into the relationship between church and revolution, we first must visualize, at least in outline, the church-political drama of the *ancien régime*, a drama whose protagonists are the Catholic church, the absolutist state, and the French middle class in the process of divorcing itself from the guardianship of both. Therefore, we introduce here three introductory sketches which lead us back into church history, especially of the seventeenth and eighteenth centuries. We shall consider, one after the other: the church; the church within the state; and the church in the developing bourgeois society.[8]

[8] On the following see K. Eder, *Die Kirche im Zeitalter des konfessionellen Absolutismus (1555–1648)* (Freiburg, 1949); L. A. Veit, *Die Kirche im Zeitalter des Individualismus (1648–1800)*, (Freiburg, 1931), both contained in J. P. Kirsch's *History of the Church*. On conditions in France, cf. E. Préclin and E. Jarry, *Les luttes politiques et doctrinales aux XVIIe et XVIIIe siècles* (Paris, 1955; Vol. XIX of A. Fliche and V. Martin, *Histoire de l'Église*).

PREPARATION

During the epoch which starts with the Council of Trent and ends with the French Revolution, the Catholic church underwent profound changes. As a result of the Reformation and the subsequent victory of a territorial church system, the politico-religious framework of church and laity, popes and nations, within the European world until the late Middle Ages gave way. The public position of the church changed. At the same time there appeared within the church traits different from those of earlier epochs.

The church avoided the threat of dissolution during the Reformation by drawing close to the Catholic princes. It paid for this support with the loss of its position as arbiter among the European nations. Where it had formerly been the ambition of the Holy See to "judge everybody without being subject to judgment by anybody,"[9] nothing remained of such pretensions in post-Reformation Europe. From being a universal power, the papacy shrank to being a part of the *Corpus Catholicum*, its influence more and more diminishing toward the borders of the Romance and Slavic peoples and waning slowly even in Catholic countries. Not only were Protestant states outside papal jurisdiction;[10] the Catholic states themselves sought to restrict the curia's freedom of action by closing their state churches to the outside, extending the establishment legislation, and finally by assuming

[9] Boniface VIII, "Bull Unam Sanctam" (Mirbt, *op. cit.*, p. 211); cf. also A. M. Koeniger, "Prima sedes a nemine judicatur," in *Beiträge zur Geschichte des christlichen Altertums und der byzantinischen Literatur*, Festgabe Albert Ehrhard (Bonn-Leipzig, 1922), pp. 273–300.

[10] The last judgment pronouncing the dethronement of a reigning prince was the bull of excommunication against Elizabeth I of England (1570). It had no practical effect. Cf. H. E. Feine, *Kirchliche Rechtsgeschichte*, I (Weimar, 1950), 434 f.

exclusive rights in the election of the pope.[11] The independence
of the papacy was thus more and more brought into question.
When in the late sixteenth century the papacy began to disengage itself from the exaggerations of older canonists, when in
particular St. Bellarmine reduced papal power *in temporalibus*
to *potestas indirecta*,[12] these were consequences of a loss of
power which was already quite obvious. How far it had progressed is seen in the fact that even Bellarmine's watered-down
theory could not be maintained politically.

Post-Tridentine ecclesiology's categorical affirmation of the
position of the pope as the visible head of the church is only a
seeming confutation of this view. In fact, the concept of the
hierarchy of the church which gained favor in this epoch of controversy was closely connected with the religio-political situation
of the church after Trent.[13] The stress on the visible signs of the
church and on the primacy of the pope, not only reflected the
counter-argument of Catholic theology to the *Ecclesia invisibilis*
of the reformers, but also reflected the situation of a European
Catholicism now split into isolated national churches whose
sense of unity depended on papal primacy, since it no longer
could be developed in a community of faith that transcended

---

[11] A. Eisler, *Das Veto der katholischen Staaten bei der Papstwahl seit dem
Ende des 16. Jahrhunderts* (Vienna, 1906).

[12] R. Bellarmin, *Disputationes de controversiis christianae fidei adversus huius
temporis haereticos*, t. I, Contr. III, lib. V.

[13] Hierarchical concept of church: especially since Bellarmin, *Controversiae*,
t. II, Contr. I, lib. III, c. 2. Bellarmin's catechism, the *Christianae doctrinae latior
explicatio*, shows the strongest emphasis on the visible side of the church, where
it is defined as "quaedam convocatio et congregatio hominum baptizatorum, qui
eandem fidem et legem Christi sub Romani Pontificis oboedientia profitentur."
F. X. Arnold speaks of a "cut of the pneumatic element in Bellarmin's counter-
reformatory concept of church: *Grundsätzliches und Geschichtliches zur Theologie der Seelsorge* (Freiburg, 1949), pp. 80 ff.

national borders.[14] It was for this reason that ecclesiology was increasingly concerned with the outward, vertical structure of the church and neglected its inner structure, the *Communio sanctorum*: the life of the Christian community was considered mainly from the point of view of its relation to the pope. There is no doubt that the intra-church position of the pope was thus greatly strengthened. But since the dignity of the office did not have a corresponding power, theologians could not prevent the papacy's fading into a merely juridical concept, a mere *lien d'unité*, in the consciousness of the Catholic peoples.

The externalization of the concept of the church and the dwindling of community-consciousness among the Catholic nations brought with it an increasing individualism of pastoral care during the post-Tridentine era. It would no longer try to understand man in his concrete social surroundings, in his "estate" (and was no longer able to, since the recognized orders had begun to crumble) but turned its attention more and more to the individual, the single person. It cannot be doubted that the attempts at a refined psychology, the penetration into spheres of the soul until then closed, the disengagement from the typologies of the old pastoral care brought considerable progress in many cases. But it is true as well that it was precisely this principle of individual pastoral care which in time deprived the church of the power to permeate spiritually the still existing or newly developing structures of society. Religious life was impoverished as a result, and the "collective impoverishment of the Western world progressed much faster than the pretended Chris-

[14] Cf. the statements made by F. X. Arnold, op. cit., p. 82. See also M. Ramsauer, "Die Kirche in den Katechismen," *Zeitschrift für katholische Theologie* LXXIII (1951), 129–69 and 313–46. For France, cf. Y. Congar's remarks about the catechism of Bossuet in: *Lay People and the Church*, (London, 1957) p. 361 (2d ed.; Paris, 1954), p. 465.

tianization through individual pastoral care."[15]

It was not only from the Occident that the increasing menace of social and political individualization to the traditional concepts and outward frame of Revelation was felt. Outside the borders of the old Christianity as well, the church was suddenly encountering a multitude of languages, cultures, and religions which necessitated new missionary forms. As discovery and colonization opened wide the doors of the extra-European world, missionary activity expanded: the most distant peoples began to be receptive to the proclamation of the Christian message. Hand in hand with problems of the distance between cultures went the problems of assimilation. The interrelation of the Reformation and the world mission has often been pointed out: just when Occidental Christianity was losing its religious unity, the spread of Christianity among extra-European peoples entered a new phase. But there is no evidence to show that this coincidence—or, for that matter, the opportunity that is implied here for Western Christianity—entered the consciousness of its contemporaries. Much that we learn of the mission history of the sixteenth and seventeenth centuries points to the fact that the time was not ripe for a real confrontation with the extra-Christian world: the will to conserve and to transmit religious life in forms that had developed in the West was too powerful. Where other attitudes developed, such as that of the Jesuit missionaries to China of the seventeenth century who tolerated the religious mores of the pagans, it was expressly scorned by the church. Then the later fundamental decision on the rites' question in favor of strict adherence to Western liturgical forms confirms the fact that there did not yet exist in the consciousness of the church a positive concept of historical pluralism. Hardly had the *querelle des cérémonies chinoises* split the French church into opposing camps

[15] K. Thieme, *Gott und die Geschichte* (Freiburg, 1948), p. 191.

when Bossuet gave new life to the Eusebian history of theology in his *Discours sur l'histoire universelle;* he recognized historical individuality only within the context of salvation history.[16]

The attitude of the church vis-à-vis the extra-European territories may be considered a defensive reflex, a rejection of just those particularistic and individualistic tendencies which afflicted the Catholic world of the West. As such it would be completely determined by the intra-European fate of the church after the sixteenth century. Yet this crisis in Catholicism's adaptation should not be mistaken for mere insistence on the traditional structures of the Middle Ages. Consider two other doctrinal decisions of the same time: the condemnation of Jansenism and of Quietism. In both cases there emerged countervailing movements in the church to the tendency to retain traditional structures, probably in consequence of the formal resemblance of the two movements to Protestantism. The subsequent new boundaries of dogma contained surprisingly novel, even modern traits. In Jansenism the church condemned a religious attitude which evaded the task of establishing a new relationship with the world and profane values by retreating to the religious individualism of St. Augustine.[17] And in the quarrel about Quietism the church sided with those whose aim was not the *foi nue* of religious interiority but world-storming *propaganda fides.*[18] What appears as

---

[16] On the rites' question see generally Préclin-Jarry, *op. cit.,* pp. 173 ff. and the literature cited there. On the literary consequences of the issue, see V. Klemperer, *Geschichte der französischen Literatur im 18. Jahrhundert,* I (Berlin, 1954), 97 ff.; W. Kaegi, "Voltaire und der Zerfall des christlichen Geschichtsbildes," *Corona,* Vol. VIII (1937/38).

[17] B. Groethuysen proposed to call the Jansenists Augustinians for reason of historical clarity: *Origine de l'esprit bourgeois en France* (Paris, 1927). English translation: *The Bourgeois. Catholicism vs. Capitalism in Eighteenth-Century France* (New York, 1968).

[18] See on this Préclin-Jary, *op. cit.,* pp. 165 ff. and 191 ff.

mere defensive reflex in the case of the missions, here appears in its positive significance: the will to preserve the church as an historic community and not to surrender her unprotected to the forces making for her assimilation to newly discovered realities or to the interiority of personal feelings, with its concomitant withdrawal from society.

No one can pretend that the tasks posed by the Reformation, the Tridentine renewal, and the beginning of a world mission, were solved by these temporary shifts; as a result of the weakness of the Holy See, they proved themselves very slowly. At first glance all possible gains seemed far outweighed by ensuing losses in religious seriousness and piety. Their relative value, however, can be seen in their resistance to all attempts at evasion or assimilation and to all private and inward solutions (which in the long run would have led to questioning the public mandate of the church) and in their preserving the proper place for the development of a new religious world orientation where one day it could be thoroughly worked out, that is, in the church itself. Critics of the Jesuit order (which remained victorious over Jansenism) overlook all too easily that the ethical rigorism of Port Royal had in the French society not in the least the prospects which offered themselves to Anglo-Saxon Puritanism in other circumstances. Not only political intrigues and diplomatic manipulations opposed it but life itself in a society averse to ethical extremes. On the other side it would be a misunderstanding of the essence of the church to believe that it could have accepted the road of an inner emigration by personal perfection—even if Jansenistic religiosity had more profound Christian substance than the average Christianity prevalent at that time.

Reduced nearly entirely to concerns for self-preservation and self-affirmation after the deadly threat of the Reformation, the post-Tridentine church was surprised to find itself a world church again. It was then faced with the task of becoming a world church inwardly as well. This meant that Catholicism in the following centuries faced both the positive experiences of worldliness and the dangers of secularization; it was exposed both to *laïcité* and to laicism. The exclusive predominance of the ascetic-mystical type of saint ended;[19] there was a powerful influx in the church of practical activist spirit, and the structure of the clergy changed in the long run to favor the lay element.

While in the seventeenth and eighteenth centuries laymen did not emerge in the church, it is no coincidence that the order which most decisively affected the modernity of the church, that is, the Society of Jesus, assumed even outwardly a much more layman-like aspect than had been appropriate to the older forms of Western monasticism. The Jesuit order developed a new form of monastic life, renounced the habit, the prayer in choir, and a fixed abode, and adopted a strict centralization and a far-reaching pastoral-scientific specialization. This corresponded to the situation of the church in post-medieval Europe and was an expression of a new missionary spirit. "Its shape as the church facing outward is the mark of an end to the old times with a 'Christian world' inwardly closed; it is the beginning of a new time of the 'pure world,' in which the church again is 'the mission' as it was in Christianity's antiquity."[20] As representatives of a laymen-like form of monasticism, as supporters of papal absolutism, as adversaries of princely absolutism, as modernists ready for adaptation who at the same time restored the old structures of "Christianity" in the Catholic society of the baroque period, the Jesuits represented a transition both in church matters and in politics. Their spiritual-secular world task, however, was of only short duration. With the decline of absolutism they dropped back from

[19] Jansenism may be regarded as a last reaction against this development.
[20] E. Przywara, *Ignatianisch* (Frankfurt, 1956), p. 85.

their vanguard position. Their tasks were taken up by Catholic laymen.[21]

The European "office of arbitration" of the pope[22] disappeared during the schism and the Reformation. Papal absolutism, however, continued to live on in the form of princely absolutism in the European states.[23]

In accordance with the loose constitutions of the medieval states, church and secular powers had for centuries exercised a condominium over many spheres of life in the West. Slowly, an equilibrium had evolved between the two, yet never without some trouble arising—whether it was that the church insisted on its rights in the face of the overwhelming might of the feudal powers or that the burgeoning modern state tried to take precisely those rights for itself. But in spite of a tendency, which was apparent before the struggle over investiture, toward a spirituali-

[21] In contrast to their predecessors, the nineteenth century Jesuits especially in France, are conservative also in politics. The role of the church's "left wing" is assumed by the French Dominicans. Thus, the positions of the seventeenth century are reversed in the nineteenth century.

[22] This is probably the most adequate expression to characterize the European position of the papacy since the investiture struggle. It has to be emphasized, however, that this authority was more of a moral than of a political nature. Cf. G. Tellenbach, "Die Bedeutung des Reformpapsttums für die Einigung des Abendlandes," Studi Gregoriani, II (Rome, 1947), 148. Also cautious E. Kantorowicz, "The Problem of Medieval World Unity," Annual Report of the American Historical Association for the Year 1942, III, 31–37, stressing the difference in this aspect between Western Europe and Byzantium and pointing out the non-political character of medieval world unity.

[23] Fundamental: S. Mochi Onory, Fonti canonistiche dell' idea moderna dello Stato (Milan, 1951); W. Ullmann, The Growth of Papal Government in the Middle Ages. A Study in the Ideological Relation of Clerical to Lay Power (London, 1955). For a study in the transformation of canonistic doctrines of sovereignty by the Legists (tracing an individual case), see E. Kantorowicz, "Mysteries of State. An Absolutist Concept and its late Medieval Origins," The Harvard Theological Review, January, 1955, pp. 65–91. Cf. also the collection of essays by the same author: The King's Two Bodies (Princeton University Press, 1957).

zation of secular offices and a secularization of spiritual ones,[24] neither of the two powers was able substantially to diminish the possessions of the other or to dislodge it entirely. The unity of the medieval world, at least in the West, was a unity of contrasts. It is remarkable that during the centuries-long, constantly renewed struggle between church and secular powers the attacked party always fell back on the two-power concept of Gelasius in order to defend itself against an unbridled politico-religious monism: the church so acted vis-à-vis the emperor, and kings vis-à-vis the pope.[25] Thus a middle ground was always attained between church privileges and state demands. Medieval law, innocent of the modern concept of sovereignty, was conducive to this division of rights, which was never juridically laid down but was tacitly recognized by both parties. This state of affairs was changed only when the canonists and legists renewed the Roman concept of sovereignty and thus gave form to the never quite forgotten idea of politico-religious unity and put an end to the prevailing loose overlapping of powers and forced state and church to confront each other clearly. It was only then that papal canonists advanced the exaggerated claim of direct power *in temporalibus* and, in reaction to it, were born the first radical teachings of peoples' sovereignties, proclaiming the absolute power of the state over the church.

This process determined not only the great European politics of the late Middle Ages; it also effected the internal affairs of the individual European states on their way to more and more independence. This was especially clear in France. Lavisse said that "le magistrat et le clerc portaient une robe Romaine mais qui ne

---

[24] P. E. Schramm, "Sacerdotium und Regnum im Austausch ihrer Vorrechte," *Studi Gergoriani*, II (Rome, 1947), 406–57.

[25] Schramm, *loc. cit.*, *passim*.

venait pas de la même Rome."[26] ["The officeholder and the
cleric wore Roman garb, but it came not from the same Rome."]
Spiritual and secular sovereignties clashed just where their com-
petences were closest, that is, on the question of legal jurisdiction. Here the state, through its parliaments, pushed back the
clerical privilegium fori step by step in a century-long struggle. It
used as its weapon the "appeal of abuse" (appel comme d'abus),
which permitted a defendant before a clerical tribunal to appeal
to the secular courts.[27] Such a procedure was successful chiefly
because of the social tensions which filled the French church
from the late Middle Ages on; it was to the advantage of the
state that the lower clergy, who often lived in depressed circumstances, liked the help of the secular tribunals when they wished
to assert themselves against the rich and more powerful higher
clergy. The anti-feudal modern doctrine of the state, which came
into clearer focus over the dual nature of medieval juridical life,
had great influence precisely on that part of the French clergy
which felt oppressed in the prevailing social situation. It needed
only a certain inclination of parliament toward the ideas of the
Reformation in order to bring explosively to the surface the political power of the latent Presbyterianism of the lower clergy,
which finally did shake the foundations of the Gallican church,
whose structure had newly been strengthened by the Concordat
of 1516.[28]

[26] Cited in J. Hours, op. cit., p. 83.

[27] R. Génestal, Les origines de l'appel comme d'abus (Paris, 1951).

[28] See also Préclin-Jarry, loc. cit., p. 210. G. Pagès also regards the Edict of 1695
which lessened the rights of the curés in favor of the episcopate a date decisive for
the further development of the relations between church and state. According to
him the king lost the sympathy of the lower clergy by backing the episcopate. (Revue
historique CLXVII [1931], 384.) On the connections between the Jansenist ideas
of church reform and the Staatskirchensystem of the ancien régime—as far as it
developed antifeudal tendencies—as well as the religious policy of the Constituant
Assembly, see E. Préclin, Les Jansénistes du XVIIIe siècle et la Constitution civile
du clergé (Paris, 1929).

The struggle over ecclesiastical jurisdiction originally was part of the larger argument between the popes and the Gallican church which started in the High Middle Ages and reached its first climax in the epoch of Conciliarism with the Pragmatic Sanction of Bourges (1438). Its immediate cause was the papal authorization of the mendicant orders in which the Gallican church, not without reason, saw the prolonged arm of the papacy.[29] In their resistance to the religious activating of the laity and the consequent loosening of the traditional parochial system, the French clergy at first did not look askance at the support of the crown, just as, later, king and clergy often made common cause against the papacy. But after the concordats of the fifteenth and sixteenth centuries transformed the liberties of the Gallican church into the rights of the French crown,[30] the unity of the anti-Roman front began to crumble. An ever-widening abyss opened between the "real Gallicanism" of the high prelates, who were as much concerned about independence from the state as from the curia, and the "tactical Gallicanism" of the kings,[31] who intended above all to reign with the help of the rich church prebends. It is true that the Gallican church in the declaration

---

[29] See K. Schleyer, *Anfänge des Gallikanismus im 13. Jahrhundert. Der Widerstand des französischen Klerus gegen die Privilegierung der Bettelorden* (Berlin, 1937). The French clergy's attitude toward the mendicant orders finds its eighteenth-century equivalent in the attitude of the parliaments toward the Jesuit order; cf. J. Egret, "Le procès des Jésuites devant les Parlements de France (1761–1770)," *Revue historique* 1950, CCIV, 1–27. Both attitudes show that Gallicanism was the product of national traditions and defeat the thesis that the Gallican liberties originated from the attempt to transplant the English established church to France (J. Haller, "Der Ursprung der gallikanischen Freiheiten," *Historische Zeitschrift* XCIII, [1903], 193–214).

[30] Expression in Erdmann, *op. cit.*, p. 220.

[31] On the various "gallicanisms," the best reference is P. Imbart de la Tour, *Les origines de la Réforme*, II (reprint; Melun, 1944), 88 ff. Indispensable for the understanding of political gallicanism is V. Martin, *Le Gallicanisme politique et le clergé de France* (Paris, 1929).

formulated by Bossuet of 1682 clearly backed the kingdom,[32] and in the declarations of the assemblies of the clergy until 1789 affirmations of faith in the monarchy are never absent. As the state-church concept gained and as church liberties slowly became state privileges which could easily be canceled, the position of the Gallican church between the secular and the religious central powers became more and more critical. The time was not distant when dependence on a powerful king was to be felt more sharply than dependence on a powerless pope. The Gallican liberties, as Fénelon lamented, became Gallican servitudes.[33]

What were these Gallican liberties? By denying the jurisdiction of papal legates in France, the French church assured itself the highest measure of independence from Rome. It was established that papal constitutions had to be adopted and published by the individual French bishops.[34] The Roman congregations, which since the Council of Trent were the chief factors in the formation of ecclesiastical law, were denied recognition in France as were their decrees. These were the consequences which the church drew from the Gallican liberties, but those which the king derived were much more important. Not only did he reserve to himself the right to recognize papel legates and to the regalia: he also took part in the government of the church (convoked synods and confirmed them), instructed his tribunals to decide appeals of abuse, and made papal as well as episcopal decrees dependent on his own placet. Since the king was able after the

---

[32] As Erdmann (op. cit. p. 225) deduced from the formulation of the preamble, Bossuet himself was aware, however, of the danger "that gallicanism could caricature itself into mere anti-papalism."

[33] Fénelon, Sur les libertés gallicanes (Avignon, 1790), p. lviii.

[34] On this and the following, see J. F. Schulte, "Über die sog. gallikanische Kirche," Archiv für katholisches Kirchenrecht, III (1858), 121–36; H. Hermes, Das Staatskirchentum in Frankreich von der Pragmatischen Sanktion bis zum Konkordat von Fontainebleau (Ph.D. Diss., Cologne, 1935).

Concordat of 1516 to dispose freely of the majority of French dioceses, it was the monarchy which actually profited by the Gallican liberties. Contrary to their original functions, they no longer served to insure the independence of the French church from papacy *and* kingdom but were now solely a means of royal power.

The Gallican system made sense as long as it served the interests of the national self-preservation of the French church in the face of Rome. In this respect it contributed to the comparatively long-lived respect for Catholicism in a French society that was slowly becoming secularized. Without doubt bourgeois patriotism was flattered by a national church taking its place beside a national state, a church which flaunted its independence from Rome. That this independence should be jealously defended not only outwardly but within France by the ecclesiastical aristocracy and this with all the means of feudal self-assertion was the easier to bear because the church was on the defensive in the face of a continuously growing centralization.

Indeed, Gallicanism postponed the long overdue clash of the sovereign national state and the church by an artful system of checks and balances that operated in the intrastate conflict of interests of the two powers. This system signified the existence of a very difficult and rather hazardous balance of the political claims of the national state and the privileged position of the church.

The church remains the most important unifying spiritual fact of this national state—and therefore it has to be given a special ranking in the political and social life of the state for purely political reasons; it should be done in a manner that disposes political power in such a way that no theocracy can develop. The spiritual-moral base of the *ancien régime* is determined by the church; the secular power, however, precisely because it is indissolubly tied to the church, has its special prerogatives.[35]

Thus, the Gallican system by yielding to no one's claims seemed to fulfil everybody's wishes. Its only weakness appeared in the need, if it was to function satisfactorily, for there to be approximately equal power between the two partners. At the slightest shift in weights, it lost its equilibrium. Although the authoritarian attitude of the kings vis-à-vis the church was offset by the inclination toward feudalism among the high clergy, the church was far less well defended against the unashamed state-church practice of a bourgeois-ruled parliament. The problem that all church liberties were based on the class privileges of the episcopate was clearly revealed. Although the bourgeoisie welcomed the verbal Gallicanism of the church (mainly expressed against a powerless pope), the real Gallicanism of the bishops, expressed in the privileges of the high clergy, in the residue of clerical jurisdiction, and in the moral influence of the church upon public life encountered a far more serious opposition from parliament than from the monarchy.

The decline of royal power in the eighteenth century, however, seemed to offer the aristocratic church another chance. This can best be seen in the social change that took place in the episcopate itself. While commoners advanced to high positions in the French church under Louis XIV, in the subsequent period the episcopate again became the exclusive preserve of aristocracy. At the assemblies of the clergy the Gallican church, despite outward loyalty, expressed itself in very arrogant language concerning the monarchy. There is no doubt that at least a part of the high clergy thought the time had come to recapture the political position which they had not held since the time of Richelieu.

[35] Gurian, Ideen., pp. 8 f.

This is the only explanation of the formation, at the very moment that royal power was beginning to gain strength as a consequence of the reform ministers' policies, of the contradictory coalition of clergy and parliament, which forced the resignation of the last reform minister and therefore made inevitable the summoning of the Estates General. The particular motive for this coalition was Brienne's attempt to enforce a tax reform against the will of the parliaments and the clergy. This unexpected *rapprochement* of old enemies has been regarded as the most important political event on the eve of the Revolution.[36]

Whereas the Gallican system brought about the outward exclusion of the French church from the general and universal church communion—as borne out by the fact that the Tridentine reforms were never accepted as a whole in France and were activated only in individual cases by the king[37]—it had a conservative effect internally on the social composition of the French church. Although advancing centralization and increasing concentration of state power in the hands of the king had overwhelmed the aristocratic church long before, the church still held to its old social make-up. As a result, the abyss between the "poor church" of the curés and *desservants* and the "rich church" of the aristocracy became so wide that not even the power of church discipline was enough to bridge it finally. In this, too, the revolution effected the climactic break; during it the lower clergy made themselves independent and went their own political ways.

These ways paralleled those of the bourgeoisie. The idea of a

[36] See, e.g., K. Heinrichs, op. cit., pp. 53 ff.; Erdmann, op. cit., pp. 72 ff. On the sociology of the eighteenth-century nobility in general, cf. also F. L. Ford, *Robe and Sword. The Regrouping of the French Aristocracy after Louis XIV* (Harvard University Press, 1953).

[37] Schulte, loc. cit., pp. 126 ff.; Hermes, op. cit., pp. 41 ff.

single middle class, *cette idée qui aurait plu à Richelieu*, as Mirabeau remarked to Louis XVI, not only strongly attracted the bourgeois deputies of the Estates General and caused the transformation of the revolt of the estates into a movement for political equality; it similarly and as strongly impressed the clerical members or followers of the third estate. This shows up during the assemblies of the estates in the new political self-assertion of the *démocratie cléricale*, which expressed itself effectively despite episcopal exhortations to obedience which were considered manifestations of aristocratic presumption. Pastor Jallet, representing his clergy, who had joined the third estate, told his episcopal superiors:

> Nous osons dire, que nous sommes vos égaux: nous sommes des citoyens comme vous; nous sommes députés de la nation comme vous. Vos droits ne sont pas plus étendus que les nôtres, et avoir un avis opposé au vôtre, ce n'est pas lever l'étendard de la rébellion.[38] [We dare say that we are your equals; we are citizens like you; we are deputies of the nation like you. Your rights are not more extensive than ours, and to hold an opposing opinion from yours is not to lift the standard of rebellion.]

Here the tie between the upper and the lower classes of the clerical hierarchy is already seen to be broken. The alliance of the lower clergy with the middle classes, which was to have such important consequences, had already begun.

As a *class* the middle class grew up outside the church.[39] This

---

[38] Cited in J. Leflon, *La crise révolutionnaire*, Vol. XX, Fliche-Martin, *Histoire de l'Église* (Paris, 1949), p. 44.

[39] See B. Groethuysen, *op. cit.* The formulation used above is not (as in the opinion of W. Lipgens, *Neue Politische Literatur*, [1960], 661) an exaggeration of the results of Groethuysen's research, but, as any closer study will show, its exact résumé; cf. also the passages quoted *infra* p. 92. See also Elinor G. Barber, *The Bourgeoisie in 18th Century France* (Princeton University Press, 1955).

is not to say that the *individual* bourgeois was a roistering free-thinker rather than, as he was, honest, strictly moral thinking, and even an outright pious and believing man. But on the whole the bourgeois world and its class ethics were foreign to the church; it was no longer reached by traditional proclamation. The fact that theologians retired to the individualistic teaching of virtues signified the church's capitulation in the face of the social phenomenon as such. In fact, clergy and bourgeoisie spoke a different language, as Groethuysen has shown in his analysis of the sermon literature in the seventeenth and eighteenth centuries: a static, class-conscious life teaching strung between the unchangeable poles of poor and rich, of high and low, remained perforce unintelligible to the bourgeoisie, whose dynamics were acquisition, ascension, and change. We must remember that even to charge interest was vigorously contested in the moral theology of the eighteenth century! On the other hand the bourgeois found nothing in the formularies and typologies of the church that corresponded to his specific life situation. There was no archetype of bourgeois or, in a wider sense, of lay sanctity.[40] Furthermore, the theological scheme of a "Christian middle class,"[41] which conceded the bourgeois a place halfway between king and beggar, could be valid only as long as the bourgeois was willing to remain in this position.

The difficulty for the church in finding access to the bourgeois concept of life is apparent in the writings of the theologians who tried to lead the bourgeoisie to a religious attitude corresponding to its nature. Such attempts were made, above all, by the Jesuits and the Jansenists. Both started from opposite ends: the Jesuits from a society ordered by classes, in which the religious duties of

[40] Cf. on this problem as reflected in more recent Catholic theology: H. Urs v. Balthasar, *Der Laie und der Ordensstand* (Einsiedeln, 1948); Y. Congar, *op. cit.*, 380 ff.

[41] Groethuysen, *op. cit.*, 39.

the individual were delimited by his position in the social structure; the Jansenists from the religious personality which seizes
and masters its task in the world from a center of the individual's
relation to God.[42] Both methods failed because neither made
concessions to bourgeois characteristics. One failed because it
presupposed an unaffected social order; in reality it no longer
existed. The other failed because it overlooked the constantly
growing class consciousness of the bourgeoisie. Thus the bourgeoisie slipped from the church. It constructed its own world
outside the church.

> The individual bourgeois might remain a Catholic; the
> bourgeoisie, the bourgeois State, did not. The bourgeois, see-
> ing himself abandoned by the God of the Christians who
> appeared never to approve of him save to the extent that he
> stayed prudently within the narrow confines of his sphere,
> went on to the conquest of power without the cooperation
> of the Church and, without asking the advice of the God of
> the Christians, he asserted what he called his rights and
> established a new order.[43]

To be sure, the separation of morality and religion and the
construction of an autonomous class morality was not solely the
work of the middle classes. Since the Renaissance, the Western
church has been faced with a rapidly growing number of spheres
of life striving for independence and threatening to throw off
church influence. Evolution did not stop at the doors of the
church. Individualization was the fate of Christianity, too. Post-
Tridentine Catholicism, in ever-increasing measure, turned to the
individual and the positive-historical; the appearance of empiricism in Jesuit philosophy, heretofore free of systems, is but one

---

[42] Cf. Groethuysen, op. cit., p. 46, 83, ff.
[43] Groethuysen, op. cit., p. 233.

example among many.[44] We have already seen that the difficulty of finding a positive relationship to modern values had evoked in Catholicism the dual extremes of tactical adaptation to the world and rigorous denial of the world; in condemning Jansenism and Quietism, the church made a first, but only a temporary, decision.

Individualistic tendencies, however, were not dangerous to the church, even if they involved deviations from traditional religious foundations, as long as they concerned only individuals and were without consequence in the collective mentality of a people or in the social order of classes. This style of affairs explains the astonishing social ineffectiveness of the merely unecclesiastical tendencies of Renaissance humanism and also the fact, so confusing to the modern observer, that skepticism and even irreligious attitudes often went hand in hand with formal faithfulness in many of the personalities of the sixteenth and seventeenth centuries. In France Rabelais and Montaigne are the most famous examples.[45] Under close scrutiny this attitude is less astonishing. It is not to be confounded with modern "double-think" but is only proof of the existence of certain psychic and social circumstances which hampered thought and imposed a certain direction upon it. The tendency to individualism increased with time and, slowly, espe-

[44] See G. Gundlach, Zur Soziologie der katholischen Ideenwelt und des Jesuitenordens (Freiburg, 1927), pp. 60 ff.

[45] On Rabelais, cf. the very stimulating book by L. Febvre, Le problème de l'incroyance au XVIe siècle. La religion de Rabelais (2d ed.; Paris, 1947). H. Friedrich says about Montaigne's relation with the church: "Montaigne is faithful to the church. But he does not deduce his conservatism from approval of the objective truth of Catholic teaching. For him the church is something existing from ancient times and squaring things up; born in its sphere of influence one ought to yield to it. The approbation of its institutional might is no more . . . than an act of useful behavior undisturbed by the critical results of theoretical considerations." (Montaigne [Bern, 1949], p. 142.)

cially during the Enlightenment, took the direction away from the church. There can be no doubt that, as sovereign reason possessed itself of the recognized and discovered realities, the old Catholic harmony of reason and revelation broke down and a kind of optimistic rationalism began to take its place. The actual disintegration of religious life, however, only started when this individual process became general and forms of life were developed which permitted the individual to turn his back on Christianity without expressly denying it. The ideational understanding of existence had to be systematized, and the church had to be confronted with an "autonomous, collectively determined consciousness."[46] This was precisely the role of the middle classes.

It is only in the eighteenth century, therefore, that "modern unbelief" can be spoken of. The unbelief of the sixteenth century remained a passing and singular reflex movement which never attained historic importance; it could fall back neither upon collective conviction nor upon the prestige of a science which might act as a bulwark against criticism.[47] The seventeenth century in France passes for the *siècle croyant*.[48] It is only in the eighteenth century that unbelief loses its doubting, and skepticism its questioning, character. Criticism of religion changes into a "dogmatism of rational reason which goes by evidence apparent to all and which rejects everything that it cannot reason out."[49] As a fact belonging to an order of the supernatural, the church finds no acceptance in the eyes of reason; it may justify itself in the

[46] Groethuysen, *op. cit.*, p. 235.

[47] Febvre, *op. cit.*, pp. 492 ff.

[48] Cf. especially H. Bremond, *La vie chrétienne sous l'Ancien Régime, Histoire du sentiment religieux en France*, Vol. IX (Paris, 1932). For a different opinion on the seventeenth century, see J. Maritain, *Antimoderne* (Paris, 1932). For a commentary on this opinion, see E. R. Curtius, *Französicher Geist im zwanzigsten Jahrhundert* (Bern, 1952), pp. 429 ff.

[49] Friedrich, *op. cit.*, p. 169.

here and now by reasons of social usefulness, by pointing to the
service it does for society when it calms the poor and admonishes
the rich to a modest use of their means. In this respect the following confession by Necker is quite characteristic: "The more
the people has to live in sorrow and misery as a consequence of
the high taxes the stronger is the necessity to grant it a religious
education."[50] But it is precisely through this socialization and secularization that the credibility of its heavenly mission is dimin-
ished and it loses its most meaningful attribute—the ability to
transcend social conditions.

That such a process of dechristianization could develop silently
behind an undamaged facade depended also in part on the inner
constitution of the church after the Council of Trent. The more
the institutional character of the church gained the upper hand
over its community character, the more faith itself threatened
to become only an outward form, lacking all qualities of personal decision. As *fides implicita* it finally faded into a mere
reflection of sociological status. Because post-Tridentine Catholicism showed the observer above all the visible face of the church
and because the church in contemporary consciousness lived
principally as a social entity, changes in the structure of society
became vastly more dangerous to Catholicism than purely philosophical criticism of dogmas. Thus the self-confident existence
of a separate middle-class world of values and a way of life was
a challenge of a new and special kind for Catholicism and confronted revelation with unusual tasks. Pushed back to a kind of
cultural apologetics that actually contradicted her essence, the
church became involved in a fruitless and theologically ambigu-
ous battle for its middle-class reputation. It tried to prove that
the "secular values," which the middle class had discovered, were

[50] Cited in Groethuysen, *op. cit.*, p. 237.

present in it to the same extent or even more abundantly.[51] More insistently than ever before, the church was swept from its leading position to the sphere where its usefulness could least be contested: to the sphere of social life and moral rules.

Both the philosophy of Enlightenment and the middle class were ready to give it asylum in this sphere, not because they were convinced of the truth of the church's teaching but because they valued the social benefit of its moral teachings. Voltaire was not alone in his slogan *"Il faut un Dieu pour le peuple"* ("The people need a God"). Montesquieu, Helvetius, Holbach, and Rousseau also combined rejection of dogma with recognition of the social utility of the church.[52] The utilitarian socialization of the church concept thus reduced Catholicism to a mere social religion long before Rousseau drew the theoretical consequences of this fact in his *religion civile*. For social reasons people retained what rationalist criticism rejected.

On the other hand, it was quite clear that a social utilitarian foundation of the mission of the church was an impossible theological undertaking. If church apologetics were adapted to the

[51] There is almost no research at all on the deep penetration of utilitarian thought in the theology of the late eighteenth century. Groethuysen, in accordance with the subject of his work, scarcely considers this side; he describes above all the struggle of the church against the rising bourgeois spirit. For a few remarks, see Erdmann, *op. cit.*, pp. 184 ff.

[52] For a survey, see the second part of the series of lectures: *L'Église et la Révolution française*, delivered by A. Mathiez. *Revue des Cours et Conférences*, Vol. XXXIII, no. 1 (1931/32), pp. 327–38. According to him, the whole philosophy of the Enlightenment adheres to the notion of the politico-religious unity of society. This is also valid for the revolutionaries of 1789. On Voltaire's practice in religious matters, cf. two typical passages from his letters: "Je ne suis pas obligé d'aller à la messe dans les terres d'autrui, mais je suis obligé d'y aller dans les miennes" (Voltaire to Fiérot, January 31, 1761; cited in F. Boulard, *Premiers Itinéraires en Sociologie religieuse* [Paris, 1954], p. 43). And: ". . . je vais à la messe de ma paroisse, j'édifie mon peuple, je bâtis une église, j'y communie . . ." (Voltaire to d'Argental, January 14, 1761).

thought of the Enlightenment, they were bound to be caught up in contradictions which in the end might endanger the religious independence of the church. For the revolution was not slow in advancing demands for changes in the structure of the church with the same arguments that the conservatism of the church used against religious revolution. The decision had to be made whether the church was to be an instrument for middle-class life insurance here and now or would seek a renewed consciousness of religious mission in confrontation with the middle-class world, a consciousness strong enough to break outmoded historic forms and to redeem Christian life from an institutional numbness.

RUMBLINGS

We can draw two conclusions from the situation of the French church on the eve of the revolution: the church was in need of reform; it was unable to reform itself. It stood in need of reform because of the ever-sharpening contradiction of its privileged position in the context of the times;[53] its social constitution caused grave damage to the peace of the church and to religious life. Many bishops having commitments at court neglected their duty of residence and had thus become estranged from the people and the diocesan clergy. The situation of the lower clergy, above all of the country parsons, worsened through the increasing depreciation of currency. The tendency of the beneficiaries to look for substitutes who were only paid a minimum wage, the *portion congrue*, led to the existence of a clerical proletariat which was,

[53] This is especially true of the ecclesiastical tax privilege: Erdmann, *op. cit.*, pp. 63 ff. The church used to pay a voluntary *Don gratuit* every five years which, however, did not exceed 3 per cent of the direct inland revenue. Considering its income from the estates and the tithe, the charitable and educational duties fulfilled by it did not matter much. According to Leflon, *op. cit.*, p. 22, the church owned 10–16 per cent of the French soil.

of course, open to revolutionary emotions. Before the revolution
there had thus been in several dioceses organizations of the lower
clergy, similar to modern trade unions, which had tried to enforce its representation in the diocesan bureaus.[54]

But the church was unable to reform because the very diminu-
tion of imperial power was compensated for by increased pressure from the estates, and this put further and further off any
voluntary resignation of inherited privileges or any redistribution
of the burden of the lower and the higher clergy.

All this changed with the revolution. The revolutionary state
itself took a hand in church reform. It transformed the church
according to its own ideas, making it an *église salariée,* and tried
to incorporate it in the new political system by means of a civil
constitution.

The revolution could claim to continue a tradition deeply
rooted in French history. As a matter of fact, the most pious
Christian kings had always interfered widely in the internal affairs of the church; since the Concordat of 1516 the Gallican
church had increasingly become an instrument in their hands.
The Constituent Assembly, in prescribing the legal form of the
church, only seemed to be drawing the logical consequences of
an enterprise begun by the kings and their councillors.

And the *bon curés,* as well, who opted for the civil constitution could believe that they were following an old tradition: a
presbyterian concept of the church, given form in France by
Edmond Richer and which had survived among the lower clergy
in the Gallican church during the years of autocratic class
reign.[55] Thus it was possible to give the impression of a far-

---

[54] See Préclin, *Les Jansénistes du XVIIIe siècle,* pp. 389 ff. It goes without say-
ing that a clergy strained by economic worries to such a high extent could fulfill
its ecclesiastical duties only in a very inadequate way.

[55] E. Richer, *De ecclesiastica et politica potestate liber unus* (Paris, 1611). On
Richerism and its consequences, cf. Préclin's already mentioned book.

reaching accord in goals between the two groups; political and ecclesiastical constitutionalism seemed to converge in revolutionary church politics.

It was on this basis that during 1789–93 there occurred the first attempts at alliance between church and revolution. Our task will be to examine its political presuppositions and its individual forms.

As early as the *Cahiers* of the third estate the question of church reform was prominent, corresponding to the position of the church in French public opinion. The church constitution, the character of benefices, and the relationship of church to king and pope attracted the greatest attention.[56] Reduced to its simplest formula, the question was: which privileges would the church retain, which ones would it relinquish or modify? The object was the separation of the religious prerogatives of the church from the liberties enjoyed by the clergy as a class.

[56] The Cahiers, according to A. Brette, "l'ensemble des voeux émis . . . par une assemblée de membres de l'un de trois ordres, réunis en exécution de lettres royales de convocation, pour rédiger leurs doléances, voeux, plaintes, remontrances, petitions, etc." (*Recueil de documents relatifs à la convocation des États généraux de 1789*, I [Paris, 1894], lxx) are only partly published, a.o. in the *Archives parlementaires de 1787 à 1860*, première série, Vols. I–IV).

For a supplement and continuation of A. Brette's *Recueil*, cf. now *Recueil de Documents relatifs aux séances des États Généraux, mai–juin 1789*, préparé sous la direction de Georges Lefebvre et d'Anne Terroine, t. I: *Les Préliminaires, la Séance du 5 mai* (Paris, 1953). The existing repertoires are fragmentary; the most comprehensive of them—although to be used with care—is the one by B. F. Hyslop (cf. the criticism by G. Lefebvre, *Revue historique* CLXXVI [1935], 63–66).

In contrast to other problems of the history of revolution, there is scant literature on the religious questions dealt with in the Cahiers; for a survey see A. Denys-Buirette, *Les questions religieuses dans les cahiers de 1789* (Paris, 1919), and—especially on the Cahiers of the clergy—C. L. Chassin, *Les Cahiers des Curés* (Paris, 1882). For a critical examination of the value as source material of the *cahiers de paroisse*, cf. H. Sée, "La rédaction et la valeur des cahiers de paroisse," *Revue historique*, CIII (1910), 292–306.

On the religious privileges of the church, the recommenda-
tions of the voters' assemblies aimed at leaving untouched the
status of Catholicism as a national religion. Only occasionally
were there voices for equality of the different sects or which were
indifferent toward religious questions.[57] Nor were the clergy
opposed on the administrative and charitable work which they
did for the common good, for this specific activity passed as the
result of that practical love of neighbor which made Christianity
acceptable even to the most ardent opponents of the church.
There was also hope that the influence of the clergy over the
people might be harnessed for political reform. That the educa-
tive functions of the clergy were hardly ever attacked (with the
sole exception, as always, of the order clergy in the *Cahiers*) was
the more notable, since it was precisely the school which later
became the issue between church and revolution. The relative
absence of aggressive laicism in the *Cahiers* bears out our con-
tention that at stake in the church politics of the Constituent
Assembly was less the process of separation than that assimilation. All in all, it may be said that the scope of the church's
religious liberty was remarkably broad and undoctrinaire in the
Cahiers of the third estate, and these can by no stretch of the
imagination be considered antireligious.[58]

This is not equally true of the proposals which concerned
economic redirection of the church. That these questions were
extraordinarily delicate and cut deeply into the constitution of
the church seemed not always to have been clear to the reform-
bent authors of the *Cahiers*. Many proposals, therefore, come

---

[57] Leflon, *op. cit.*, p. 42; Denys-Buirette, *op. cit.*, pp. 394 ff.

[58] The opinion of Robinet (*Le mouvement religieux pendant la Révolution
1789–1801* (Paris, 1896), pp. 110 ff., according to which the Cahiers contained
a complete plan for church reform, is untenable in view of the sources.

very close to the church-state line of the later Constituent Assembly. It should be pointed out, however, that nationalization of church properties was demanded only occasionally and that the opinion of the third estate was not at all unanimous on the question of abolishing the tithe: there were those who voted for retaining it.[59] Prior to the convocation of the Estates General, no one had ever thought of an *église salariée* in the form in which it later was created by the civil constitution. This is not to say, however, that sympathy for the lower clergy and antipathy to the higher, as is so clearly expressed in the *Cahiers*,[60] did not by itself lead to a loosening of the hierarchical structure of the church, independent of the nature of individual reform proposals. The tendency of the *Cahiers* is crystal clear. Although there were the efforts, on the one hand, to curtail the power of the bishops by giving greater rights to the chapters and to make the nobility and their prebends more a part of the state by taxing their incomes, the greatest concern of the third estate was for the *pauvres curés*. Not only was it intended that they be paid better (which they urgently needed) but, what is more, they were supposed to be given greater rights vis-à-vis their religious superiors. Some of the *Cahiers* went so far as to allow the lower clergy the right to vote in the election of bishops.[61] It may be mentioned in passing that there was as much antagonism to the bishops as to the pope in the third estate. The demand for the abolition of the concordat, which appears in many of the *Cahiers*,[62] may have had

---

[59] Denys-Buirette, *op. cit.*, pp. 155 and 252 ff.

[60] "Toutes ses faveurs vont à la paroisse et aux pauvres curés auxquels on souhaite plus d'indépendance, et un sort matériel moins précaire." (Leflon, *op. cit.*, p. 42.)

[61] Denys-Buirette, *op. cit.*, p. 308.

[62] Denys-Buirette, *op. cit.*, pp. 441 ff. The royal court-chaplain Fauchet in his *De la religion nationale* (1789) also called the concordat a "conception infernale," demanded its abolition and a return to the Pragmatic Sanction.

its roots more in this than in the wish to curtail royal privileges.

Did the claims of the third estate form a basis for co-operation with the clergy? If the *Cahiers* of the clergy are compared with those of the third estate, the answer is affirmative. There are at least three points on which the two estates agreed: in the fundamental conviction that church reform was necessary; in a determination to preserve the public position of Catholicism; and in the Gallican reaction against the power of the pope. It is true that the *Cahiers* of the clergy differed from those of the third estate on the questions of the abolition of tithes and of the concordat (and the clergy were by nature more cautious in the formulation of reform proposals). Considering, however, that the texts were as a rule the result of compromise between the bishop and his diocesan clergy (and the bishops, because of their authority, usually still had the upper hand)[63] the differences are far less than may appear at first glance. In any case the reform proposals of the third estate tended to divide the lower clergy from the episcopate and to win them to collaborate with the communes; it was at this point that the class structure of the old society seemed most vulnerable. Before long the coalition of higher clergy and the parliamentarian *noblesse de robe*, which had been introduced by the revolution, was joined by a coalition of the democratic wing of the communes and the lower clergy, a process which greatly assisted in divesting the revolution of the character of a class revolt and made the drive for political equalization immediately apparent through the acceptance of the *vote par tête*.

Necker's voting law, which gave the third estate the same number of representatives as the other two estates combined, strengthened the political position of the *démocratie laïque*, the

[63] Leflon, *op. cit.*, p. 41.

third estate: it also helped the lower clergy, the *démocratie cléri-cale*, to obtain a majority among the clergy, a development which was to have important consequences, since the majority threw its full weight on the side of the revolution while the epis-copate remained with the minority during the elections.[64] When the third estate declared itself to be the National Assembly on June 17, 1789, the coalition party in the chambers of the clergy won against the wishes of the bishops. Pierre de la Gorce called it *la fusion de la démocratie et de l'Église.*[65] It meant, however, that the decision by the communes, until then without legal foundation, had the sanction of constitutional law through the attitude of the clergy. A decision by two of the three estates was legally binding on the king, according to the rules of the Estates General; the nobility had no alternative but to acquiesce.[66]

The beginning of the revolution thus confirmed the political accord of the two estates. Although a specific political program was not initiated under this accord—it was at this point that the process of differentiation began which ultimately led to the for-mation of the different clubs and parties—the accord neverthe-less formed the right mood and background for the work of the Constituent Assembly during the first months of the revolution, when it was not yet torn by divergent opinions. Nothing is more expressive of this unity of the wills for church and polit-ical reform than the fact that the high clergy, which at first fol-lowed the democratic turn of the revolution hesitantly, was swept along on the wave of patriotic feelings. During the famous

[64] Of 296 deputies of the clergy 47 were bishops, 23 abbots, 6 chapter vicars, 12 canons and 208 members of the lower clergy.

[65] P. de la Gorce, *op. cit.*, p. 117.

[66] The mood of the nobility is characterized by the winged words of D'Antrai-gues: "Ce sont ces . . . curés qui ont fait la Révolution" (cited in A. Latreille, *L'Église catholique et la Révolution française*, I [Paris, 1946], 72).

night session of August 4 the high clergy solemnly and voluntarily renounced their feudal privileges and did not resist when
the National Assembly later abolished the tithe without com-
pensation. They even voted for the sale of church silver to allevi-
ate the most urgent financial needs of the state.[67]

It is quite clear that the alliance between the two "democra-
cies," the bourgeois and the clerical, was based on revolutionary
enthusiasm and on sober political considerations. Without the
help of the countless curés in city and country, political renewal
in France was impossible in view of the still very loose structure
of the administrative organization. It was the curés task to read
the royal decrees (and later the decisions of parliament) from
the pulpit and it was they who by dint of this semi-official
position formed the natural link between the people and the
National Assembly. This alone would have made impossible an
offhand treatment of the Church. Beyond this, everybody—
including the circles of the enlightened philosophes—was convinced of the usefulness, even the necessity, of having the
new state constitution sanctioned by religion. On this, too, the
co-operation of the clergy was essential. Finally, the Catholic
religion was so valuable a symbol of national unity that the
National Assembly could only with difficulty do without it,
despite the assembly's inclination toward religious tolerance.
Whatever administrative, ideological, or political reasons lay in
the background, in any case the picture of the simple, upright, and
unselfish country curé—since Rousseau a figure of romantic literary attraction—was a natural mediator. The bourgeois législateur
needed the clerical ministre de bonté, just as the developing nation needed the religion nationale. The alliance between church
and revolution was forged in the name of France as it was in the
uninterrupted tradition of Gallicanism.

[67] Erdmann, op. cit., pp. 129 ff.; Latreille, op. cit., pp. 73 ff.

The revolution needed the church. But the church needed the revolution as well. The lower clergy, in alliance with the bourgeoisie, was not always on the giving side; it received much from the state. Compared to the past, its position under the civil constitution considerably improved. Moreover, the renewed concentration of state power which evolved during the revolution would likewise profit the power of the church in public life, if the alliance of the political and ecclesiastical reform movements endured. Doubtless, many clergymen had this in mind when they joined the ranks of the revolution, remembering especially that one of the main reproaches leveled by the church against the *ancien régime* had been for moral laxity.

Shortly before the revolution, Abbé Fauchet, who later was to be one of the main advocates of the democratic tendencies in French Catholicism,[68] developed the task of a *gouvernement sur la base de l'Évangile* in his book *De la Religion nationale*. The main points of his program were legal property restrictions on the basis of a fixed maximum of capital, state encouragement of marriages between classes in order to dissolve social differences, and the regulation of inheritance laws to render the amassing of great fortunes impossible. A democratic kingdom was to reform the state and manifest Christian principles in public life. Prostitution was to be suppressed, the theater was to serve moral purposes only, and freedom of press was to be kept within the strictest limits of religion and ethics.

> Ainsi la législation sera conforme à l'esprit de l'Évangile, à la morale essentielle de la fraternité, qui est la base et le couronnement du bien public dans une Nation sagement ordonnée pour le bonheur de tous les Citoyens.[69] [Thus will

---

[68] On Fauchet: H. Cros, *Claude Fauchet* (1744–1793). *Les idées politiques, économiques et sociales* (Paris, 1912).

[69] Fauchet, *De la religion nationale* (Paris, 1789), p. 248. (Cf. also n. 51.)

the legislature conform to the spirit of the Gospels, to the
inherent morality of brotherly love, which is the basis and the
crowning glory of the public weal in a nation which is wisely
governed for the happiness of all its citizens.]

Fauchet prefigures the ideals of the *Démocratie chrétienne* of
the nineteenth century and, above all, of the generation of 1848,
ideals directed against middle-class liberalism and for a social
order emanating from the idea of "evangelical equality." The
Revolution of 1789, though, did not fulfil the expectations of
Fauchet, the passionate and romantic reformer. With the development of a new aristocracy of property, the old social class
structure according to social groups, apparently canceled by the
abolition of estates, returned under a different form. The cry of
the "Unfinished Revolution" retained its inspiring force for a
long while. It was later taken up anew in the social Catholicism
of Buchez and Ozanam. Thus Fauchet's *démocratie fraternelle*[70]
and Ozanam's *démocratie chrétienne*[71] are revealed as a mixture
of Christian romanticism with prophetic hints of socialism.

At this point we must recall the various ways in which the
democratic-religious spiritualism of revolutionary times was expressed. One can hardly speak of a broad, politically unified
movement. We are confronted, rather, with the sect-like activities
of small circles whose ideas were spread by a great number of
periodicals. Most accessible proved to be the long-known *Cercle
social*, which was founded in the flaming months following the
storming of the Bastille.[72] It may best be characterized as stand-

[70] Fauchet, *Sermon sur l'accord de la Religion et de la liberté prononcé le 4
février 1791*, p. 6.
[71] Ozanam, *Oeuvres complètes* (Paris, 1872), VII, 174 ff.
[72] On the *Cercle social*, see L. Blanc, *Histoire de la Révolution française* (Paris,
1847 ff.), III, 24 ff.; H. Cros, op. cit., pp. 26 ff. J. B. Duroselle (*Catholicisme
social*, p. 11) sees in Fauchet an "*ancêtre du catholicisme social*."

ing between a revolutionary club and a political academy.[73] It differs from comparable groupings in that its publications have a distinctly religious tone.[74] Its aim was to blend revolutionary ideas and Christian tradition. A social backing for this plan was to be obtained through the reconciliation of Catholics and Freemasons. This intention of the *Cercle social* was carried out with zeal and much publicity: it can be partially explicated through the characteristics of Bonneville and Fauchet, its founders.

Of the two, the Marquis Nicolas de Bonneville was the more important, though Fauchet's fame at times outshone his.[75] Nodier, leader of older French Romanticism, described him as

le coeur le plus simple et le plus exalté que j'aie connu de ma vie, avec son imagination de thaumaturge et sa crédulité de femme, son éducation d'homme du monde et ses moeurs d'homme du peuple.[76] [The simplest and most exalted man I ever met, with the imagination of a miracle worker, the credulity of a woman, the education of a man of the world and the manners of a man of the people.]

During the revolution Bonneville, a young man from Evreux, made a name for himself as a translator of German literature. In the years 1782–85 he published *Théatre allemand*, with translations from Lessing, Goethe, and Schiller.[77] A Freemason, he belonged to the order of the Illuminates founded by Weishaupt

---

[73] The most accurate analysis is given in A. Mathiez, *Le Club des Cordeliers pendant la crise de Varennes et le massacre du Champ de Mars* (Paris, 1910), p. 5 f.

[74] *Bulletin de la Bouche de Fer* (1790); *La Bouche de Fer* (1791/92); *Cercle social* (1791/92).

[75] On Nicolas de Bonneville, see Ph. le Harivel, *Nicolas de Bonneville, préromantique et révolutionnaire (1760–1828)* (Strasbourg, 1923).

[76] Ch. Nodier, *Souvenirs et portraits*, Oeuvres, Vol. VIII (Paris, 1828), p. 333 f.

[77] *Nouveau Théâtre allemand de Friedel et Bonneville* (12 vols.; [Paris, 1782–1785]).

in Bavaria in 1780.[78] The revolution seems to have extraordinarily
stimulated both his weaknesses and talents. While it carried his
fantasy to the realm of dreams, it increased the wilful doctrinaire's yearning to achieve something. During the preliminaries
of the great dispute between church and revolution, Bonneville
appeared as a creator of systems of a peculiar kind. But after his
scurrilous and confused writings of the revolutionary epoch, his
philosophy of religion crystallized.[79] It culminated in the concept
of a political theocracy. This turn to theological problems is the
more astonishing when it is remembered that the pre-revolutionary Bonneville had all the characteristics of the typical, rather
than the unusual, young liberal nobleman; he was a representative of that early Romantic and Germanophile generation that
was dominant in French aristocratic circles before the revolution.
It is most likely that his friend Fauchet exerted great influence
on this theological turn. The persuasive Abbé, who even before
the revolution had the title *prédicateur ordinaire du Roi* and
who seemed to become more and more a clerical people's trib-
une after the storming of the Bastille, is known chiefly from his
book *De la Religion nationale*. He was at the height of his fame
when he met Bonneville and founded the *Cercle social* with
him. He had taken part in the storming of the Bastille and delivered grandiloquent funeral orations over the fallen heroes: he
implored the judgment of heaven against the kings and the aristocracy who had "crucified the Son of God."[80] He was the first
to receive a citizen's crown from the people. His sermons quite
movingly celebrated the unity of church and revolution:

[78] On the revolutionary Illuminates, cf. A. Barruel, *Mémoires pour servir à
l'histoire du jacobinisme* (Hamburg, 1800), Vol. V.; A. Viatte, *Les sources occultes du romantisme* (Paris, 1927), I, 262 ff.

[79] N. de Bonneville, *De l'esprit des religions* (Paris, 1791).

[80] *Premier Discours sur la liberté française prononcé le 5 août 1789*, pp. 7 f.

Dieu, est l'humanité. Jésus Christ n'est que la Divinité Concitoyenne du Genre-Humain. La Catholicité n'est que l'Assemblée, la Communauté, l'Unité des frères, fidèles à la Patrie de la Terre, pour s'élever ensemble à la Patrie des cieux.[81]

And in a frenzy of religious nationalism, there is the passage in the third *Discours sur la liberté française*:

Dieu de Genre-Humain! Avec quelle unanime ardeur nous vous adorons comme le Dieu des Français![82] [God is humanity. Jesus Christ is only the co-citizen divinity of the human race. Catholicity is nothing but the Assembly, the Community, brothers united and faithful to the Fatherland of the Earth, to rise together to the Fatherland of Heaven.] [God of the Human Race! See the unanimous ardor with which we worship you as the God of the French!]

According to its founders, the *Cercle social* was to be a club neither of the Jacobin nor any other revolutionary kind. Its aim was the union of the international lodges of Freemasons into a universal *Confédération des Amis de la Vérité*. In the midst of a dissolving social order, according to Bonneville's and Fauchet's arguments, only the lodges kept intact the ideas of liberty, equality, and unity. They were, therefore, destined to act as the proclaimers of that gospel of brotherly and universal love which the revolution had given new life. France and the world were to be renewed through the spirit of early Christianity which lived on in the secret societies. A new code of laws rising from the fundamental belief that man is *un être aimant*, an altruistic being, was destined to refashion the old political forms that had been born of a pessimistic philosophy, and to replace them by newer and

---

[81] *Second discours sur la liberté française prononcé le 31 août 1789*, p. 21.
[82] *Troisième discours sur la liberté française prononcé le 27 septembre 1789*, p. 7.

better ones. The model of such a new legislation was the *Contrat social*: Rousseau and the Gospels were to be the pillars of the new social order.[83]

The gatherings of the *Cercle social*, held in the Royal Gardens, attracted great numbers. Four thousand were present at the opening session, when Fauchet spoke on the *Contrat social*. Among the visitors were Madame Roland, Abbé Sieyès, Condorcet, and Camille Desmoulins. The Club of the Jacobins, concerned by the activities of the *Cercle social* in which it suspected a rival, let no occasion pass for accusing Fauchet of demagogy and causing social unrest. On the other hand, the *Cercle social* wooed the Jacobins, but without success.[84]

Although Fauchet was not a member of the National Assembly, he agreed with its policies. Despite reservations concerning the Declaration of Human Rights and a desire to see it rounded out with his own catalogue of civic duties,[85] Fauchet was in basic agreement with the work of the Constituent Assembly, especially with its religious policies. Fauchet was among the defenders of the civil constitution, one of the first priests to swear allegiance to the constitution. Later, he was elected constitutional bishop of Calvados. In his pastoral letters he referred to himself as "Bishop by the grace of God and the will of the people."[86] As a member of the legislature Fauchet vigorously fought those who refused to take the oath: whoever would not swear the oath, *le plus*

---

[83] *La Bouche de Fer*, January 10, 1791.

[84] *La Bouche de Fer*, July 7, 1791.

[85] *La Bouche de Fer* of June 17, 1791, cites affirmatively a speech by Mandard, in which the Declaration of Human Rights is criticized for social reasons: "Les représentants de la nation ont prêté l'oreille à cette assertion mal conçue que ce sont les propriétaires qui composent l'état. . . . Les droits de l'homme et du citoyen s'y opposent."

[86] The full title was: "Claude Fauchet, par la grâce de Dieu et la volonté du Peuple, dans la communion du Saint Siège apostolique et dans la charité du Genre-Humain, Evêque de Calvados."

catholique qui fût jamais, was a godless man opposed to the commands of the Gospels.[87] One has to consider the meaning that the word *catholique* carried for Fauchet: for him Catholic meant unity above all, the means to keep religion and society together.

The fact that Fauchet's political activity in the *Cercle social* had as its chief goal the unrealistic plan to reconcile Catholics and Freemasons considerably curtailed his effectiveness. Both serious Catholics and such spokesmen for the philosophy of Enlightenment as la Harpe[88] criticized his nebulous political enthusiasm and his gushing style. Indeed, the alliance of Bonneville and Fauchet very soon broke apart and with it the *Cercle social*. The *Société des Amis de la Vérité* was dissolved in April, 1791, and the review, *La Bouche de Fer*, published by Bonneville and Fauchet, also died. Later, however, Fauchet founded another review, *Journal des Amis de la Vérité*, to fight those who refused the oath and also—in ever-increasing political isolation—to fight against the religious radicalism of the left and against the idea of separation of church and state.

In his battle for the civil constitution, Fauchet saw eye to eye with the other spokesmen of democratic-radical Catholicism, such as the Abbé Grégoire of Lorraine who later became a bishop of the Constitutional church.[89] Grégoire, too, believed in a "holy alliance of Christianity and Freedom";[90] he too equated the duties of a Christian with those of the citizen. In one of his

[87] *Sermon sur l'accord de la Religion et de la liberté*, p. 31.
[88] Cf. Cros, *op. cit.*, p. 38.
[89] On Abbé Grégoire, see A. Pouget, *Les idées religieuses et réformatrices de l'évêque constitutionnel Grégoire* (Paris, 1905).
[90] *Essai historique sur les libertés de l'église Gallicane* (Paris, 1818), as cited in Pouget, *op. cit.*, p. 442. Grégoire urged his own diocesans to see to it "que par nos soins l'alliance si naturelle du christianisme et de la démocratie devienne indissoluble." (Lettre pastorale of March 12, 1795, as printed in A. Gazier, *Etudes sur l'histoire religieuse de la Révolution française* [Paris, 1887]. pp. 370 ff.)

pastoral letters we read: *"Qui n'aime pas la République est un mauvais citoyen et conséquement un mauvais chrétien."*[91] ["He who does not love the Republic is a bad citizen and therefore also a bad Christian."] Grégoire's republican attitude was older and better founded than that of Fauchet, whom it had been possible to think of as a follower of the monarchy until the very eve of the revolution.[92] As a representative of the presbyterian wing of the French church, Grégoire was a democrat out of religious conviction. His political ideas, thus, are an exact mirror image of his concepts of the inner structure of the church. A democratic church, for him, was not a demand arising only from national tradition—he, like Fauchet, demanded the re-establishment of the Pragmatic Sanction[93]—but in his view corresponded to the laws of early Christianity, to the spirit of brotherly love that had been resurrected by the revolution.

When the civil constitution of the clergy permitted the amalgamation of clerical and political voting bodies and gave presbyterian tendencies, under strict state control, the sanction of the constitution of the church, it acted consistently with the ideas of Grégoire, who expected a democratic church to exercise a stronger public influence through Christian morals.

How large a following did Bonneville, Fauchet, and Grégoire have? It is impossible to gather exact data. In the fast-moving epoch of the revolution, when new ideas appeared and disappeared from the surface of things in never-ending sequence, even a foundation like the *Cercle social* kept its attractiveness only for a short time. The idea, however, of a *religion nationale* continued to live and survived in the ranks of the constitutional church that had separated from Rome. If it is remembered that a sig-

[91] Gazier, *op. cit.*, p. 390.
[92] Cros, *op. cit.*, p. 103.
[93] *Essai*, chap. x and xi.

nificant number of priests swore the oath[94] and that the constitutional church maintained itself until the time of the Napoleonic concordat, it may be seen that the presbyterian and democratic tendencies of the French church at the time of the revolution represented a considerable power.[95]

It is in the constitutional church that the concept of "Christian Democracy" has its origin. On November 21, 1791, during the legislative assembly's deliberations over religious disorders in France, Lamourette, the constitutional bishop of Lyons, declared in an opinion about the draft of a law before the respective committee:

> Séparez donc, Messieurs, je le veux et je le désire autant que vous; séparez la constitution de la théologie qui date de Constantin, c'est-à-dire, de l'époque ou Rome vaincue, par l'impossibilité d'étouffer les principes lumineux de la démocratie chrétienne, a fait sa paix avec l'évangile, afin de l'aristocratiser, et de travestir le Sage de Nazareth, cet ami vrai du peuple, en une divinité protectrice des ravisseurs du monde, et ouvrit d'éternels abymes sous les pas de quiconque songerait à briser les fers de la servitude.[96] [Separate, gentlemen:

[94] The statistical inquiries in hand do not allow a final conclusion; cf. Leflon, *op. cit.*, p. 71. Latreille, p. 95, estimates that the number of those who swore the oath comprised half of the parochial and one-third of the entire clergy.

[95] That the possibility of a presbyterian development in the French church really existed can be deduced from a comment made by Talleyrand (cited in Leflon, *op. cit.*, p. 75) who justified his willingness to ordain bishops with the necessity "d'éviter le presbytérianisme et de sauver la constitution hiérarchique de l'Église." (*Mémoires*, I, 135 f.)

On the presbyterian tendencies in the French church, cf. also H. Leclercq, *L'Église constitutionelle* (Paris, 1934), especially chap. vi ("Le retour à l'Église primitive"). One has to take these trends very seriously and must not play them down *ex eventu*.

[96] Observations contre l'article XV du projet de Decret du comité de législation, sur les troubles religieux, prononcées le 21 novembre 1791, par M. Lamourette, Evêque du Département de Rhône et Loire, p. 5.

I wish it and desire it as much as you do; separate the constitution from the theology which goes back to Constantine,
that is to the times when Rome, vanquished by the impossi-
bility of suppressing the luminous principles of Christian Democracy, made its peace with the Gospels in order to make a
travesty of the Wise Man of Nazareth, the true friend of the
people, and to make him into an aristocrat, and a deity which
protects the rapist of the world, and opened the eternal abyss
under the steps of whoever would think of breaking the
chains of servitude.]

The theological motivations which are the basis of these statements deserve special attention. Their meaning becomes clear
when considered together with similar expressions of Fauchet
and Grégoire. An analysis of these theological-political thoughts
will illuminate the bases of the democratic-religious movement
of the revolution.

It has already been said that Grégoire's democratic impulse
originated in his concept of church. For him the church is not
a series of hierarchies, but the *communio sanctorum: une assemblée des fidèles.* The *Journal chrétien,* the organ of the constitutional church, attacked the hierarchical concept of church by
referring to Cyprian.[97] As expressed in a letter to the publisher:
"It [the constitutional church] has as its aim to restore religion
to its original beauty, to free her from superstitious rites which
an unenlightened piety put in the place of religious duties."[98]
Grégoire's democratic passion had as its goal an early Christian
kind of restoration. His work on the liberties of the Gallican
church—which is the testament of the bishops of the constitutional church to posterity—ends with a quotation from St. Ber-

---

[97] *Journal chrétien,* August 28, 1791, "L'esprit du christianisme."
[98] *Journal chrétien,* November 5, 1791, "A l'auteur du Journal chrétien."

nard: "*Quis mihi det, antequam moriar, videre ecclesiam Dei,
sicut in diebus antiquis?*" ["Who will grant me to see the
Church of God before dying, as in the old days?"]

The restoration movement is also to be seen in certain his-
torico-theological turns of phrase in Fauchet. The *Sermon sur
l'accord de la Religion et de la liberté* reports that God the
Father himself originally gave the Jews, His chosen people, a
democratic constitution and that the Son of God had written
into the hearts of those redeemed by Him the laws of fraternity,
of brotherly love, that is, the content of true democracy.

> La divinité, dans ces deux interventions solennelles, s'est
> montrée populaire;[99] elle a dicté des lois de la démocratie na-
> tionale au peuple juif,[100] et ensuite des lois de la démocratie
> fraternelle au genre humain. La loi de Sinaï et la loi de
> l'Évangile écartent toute puissance arbitraire de dessus des
> hommes, ne leur imposant de règle que la raison suprême, et
> les mettant sous le régime de la liberté. [The deity, in its two
> solemn interventions, dictated the law of brotherly love to all
> mankind. The law of Sinai and the law of the Gospels do
> away with any arbitrary power above the level of men by not
> imposing any rules except those of supreme reason, putting
> them under the reign of liberty.]

Fauchet endeavored to make this intervention of the deity
appear, not as forced upon man, but as a free offer. For the dec-
alogue, the basis of the biblical "nation," had been accepted
voluntarily by the Jewish people:

> La loi rédigée, inscrite et proclamée, devait être librement
> acceptée par tout le peuple assemblé en familles, en canton-

---

[99] Cf. the passage mentioned *supra*, p. 109, speaking of a "Divinité Concitoyenne
du Genre-Humain."

[100] Cf. W. Schöllgen, *Die soziologischen Grundlagen der katholischen Sittenlehre* (Düsseldorf, 1953), p.225.

nements et en tribus. Ce ne fut qu'après cette acceptation libre que la volonté générale ayant consommé son acte, l'alliance fut jurée et le pacte national déclaré inviolable. Non seulement le code des lois fut définitivement sanctionné par l'exercice complet de la liberté générale, mais le gouvernement lui-même, proposé par la divinité et voulu par le peuple, fut démocratique: Le partage du territoire fut égal et librement convenu; les juges furent à la nomination du public et les chefs du pouvoir exécutif, au choix de la nation. [The law, tendered, inscribed, and proclaimed, had to be freely accepted by all the people assembled in families, tribes, or in billets. Only after this voluntary acceptance, which completed the act, was the alliance sworn and the national pact declared inviolable. Not only was the legislative code definitely sanctioned by the complete exercise of general freedom: but the government itself, proposed by the deity and desired by the people, was democratic; the division of land was voluntarily agreed upon, the judges were nominated by the people and the heads of the executive power were the people's choice.]

Democracy—Fauchet describes it, anticipating Lincoln's formula, *tout pour le peuple, tout par le peuple, tout au peuple*— therefore is the form of government sanctioned by God: "*La législation et le gouvernement de Dieu.*"

The recognition of human reason and divine will, however, is not of long duration. The original democratic revelation is immediately followed by the revolt of the Jews against the divine law. By installing kings above them, the Jews betrayed the social contract. The immediate consequence was the loss of their national existence.

Les rois que la nation voulut se donner malgré les avis réitérés du père de la nature,[101] quoiqu'ils n'eussent aucune

---

[101] Cf. Grégoire's remark: "Le célèbre discours de Samuel aux Hébreux, qui voulaient changer la forme de leur gouvernement, n'a jamais été cité par les

autorité législative, furent la plupart des despotes que firent leurs propres malheurs en faisant le malheur public. Tant il est difficile à la souveraineté du peuple de contenir le sceptre qu'elle confie au mandataire de sa puissance. [The kings, which the nation wished to give itself despite the opinion of the Father of Nature, and although they had no legislative power, were for the most part despots who caused their own misfortune by making public misfortune. This shows how difficult it is for the people's sovereignty to retain the sceptor once it has passed it on to mandatories of its power.]

Thus it is only Christ, who came to the earth in the time of Augustus, the *lâche tyran*, who re-established God's alliance with man:

> Il veut vivre toujours l'égal, l'ami, l'homme du peuple, mais il ne ménage jamais les riches, les grands, les puissants ennemis du peuple: ses anathèmes ne tombent que sur les têtes insolentes qui dominent arbitrairement le peuple; il réunit, contre lui-seul, toutes les aristocraties qui avilissent ou écrasent le peuple, et il meurt pour la démocratie de l'univers.[102] [He always wants to live as an equal, the friend, the man of the people, but he never spares the rich, the great, the mighty enemies of the people: his anathemas fall only upon the heads of the insolent, who arbitrarily dominate the people; he unites against himself all the aristocracies which degrade or crush the people, and he dies for the democracy of the universe.]

It was my intention here to give Fauchet's thoughts in detail, for they illuminate the ground in which the democratic spiritualism of the clerical constitutionalists was rooted. Since the church

prédicateurs de cour. Supposons que le prophète eût parlé dans un sens absolument inverse, Dieu sait quels beaux commentaires nous eût valu ce texte." (A. Pouget, *op. cit.*, p. 441.) Grégoire probably hinted at the *Politique tirée de l'Ecriture Sainte* by Bossuet.

[102] *Sermon sur l'accord de la Religion et de la liberté*, pp. 6 ff.

follows the same course of ascent and descent as does the history of the people of God, it is necessary within it, too, to free the "pure spirit," the "original beauty," of Christianity from the defacings of human customs. The *Journal chrétien* in its issue of August 28, 1791, treats the question comment *l'esprit du Christianism s'est altéré* in the same tone.[103] The expressions *Christianism pure, religion pure,* are continually repeated in Fauchet, Bonneville, and Grégoire.

There is no mistaking the spiritual and terminological relationship of Fauchet's thoughts to the teachings of Rousseau's *Contrat social*. It is no coincidence. Fauchet looked upon himself as a disciple of Rousseau.[104] There is no need to seek express mentions of the *volonté générale* or of the highly significant turn against representative democracy to recognize this dependence: Rousseau's sequence of natural innocence and cultural degeneration shows up in Fauchet, where it is applied to the history of the church. The return to nature is given a Christian orientation, and it is now seen as a return to the early church. By changing the democratic legislator who in Rousseau appears as the steward of autonomous reason, to the Christian God, he simultaneously re-christianizes the *Contrat social*; the secular law of reason becomes Christian natural law which originates in God, the *père de la nature.*

But is such a metamorphosis possible? One thing is sure: it can be achieved only at the price of a spiritualist dissolution of the church which would seem to be incompatible with Catholic thought. And is it possible at all to speak of Fauchet's and Grégoire's ideas of church reform? The idea of the "church," as used by the faithful, seems in them to come critically close to

[103] See n. 97, *supra*.
[104] See *infra*, pp. 126 ff.

meaning those human and historical accessories which deface pure religion. It may be that to the defenders of *religion pure* true Christianity had ceased to exist with the coming of royal absolutism or with the abolition of the Pragmatic Sanction, perhaps even with Constantine. To maintain the connection with the democratic early church, Fauchet was forced to construct a curious chain of tradition, leading from Origen through Hieronymus, Erasmus, Morus, Bacon, Montaigne, Charron, and Richer, right up to the lodges of the Freemasons.[105] Clearly, when church history is given over to such arbitrariness, it loses all connectedness and appears as an unstructured sequence of spiritual eruptions. From this it is no great distance to Bonneville's a-Christian metaphysics of religion, in which all the fixed boundaries of religion are dissolved in a pantheistic *tout est dans tout*.[106]

In Fauchet the church completely loses its institutional outlines. What remains is a democratically conceived "People of God."

The *Contrat social*, conceived as God's covenant with man, shapes the people into a nation in such a way that political cannot be separated from religious existence. The two tracks of state and church merge in the unity of a *religion nationale*. Democratic government becomes a means to theocracy. These ideas are close to those that will be proclaimed by Lamennais and his school in the nineteenth century.[107]

Did Fauchet's ideas make possible any kind of collaboration between church and revolution? At least until the outbreak of the religious crisis following the proclamation of the civil constitution, the answer is affirmative. At least one point of contact

---

[105] *La Bouche de Fer*, January 10, 1791.
[106] N. de Bonneville, *De l'esprit des religions* (Paris, 1791), Vol. II, § 157.
[107] Cf. F. de Lamennais, *Essai sur l'indifférence*, Vol. II (Paris, 1820), Preface.

between revolutionary and "Christian" democracy is quite apparent: both conceive of Catholicism mainly as a religion of unity,
a connecting link in the national community. Hence formal
structure is more important than dogmatic content: the latter
may even recede into the background in favor of the formally
creative, unifying element of church order. In *De la religion nationale* Fauchet explains that a state organism cannot live without the *croyances pareilles*, without obligating convictions that
are common to all its members; hence the necessity that Catholicism be the religion of the state.[108]

It can be seen that Fauchet's arguments here are quite in
keeping with the spirit of the times and with it with the majority of the bourgeoisie. The church policy of the National Assembly confirms this. When Mathiez pointed out that the members
of the Constituent Assembly, carried away by a passion for unity,
"a Roman and Catholic passion," did not try to separate church
and state but on the contrary tried to combine them, he was
absolutely right.[109] Yet the desire would signify little as long as
state and church had no clear notion of their own essences, their
mutual interdependence, and their common limitations.

Was such a formalized notion of Catholicism as Fauchet employed really apt to shed a useful light upon the question of the
mutual relations between church and democracy? It is doubtful.
It is more likely that it misled, because it pretended to discern a
unity that did not exist. Theoretically, the passion for unity could
materialize in one of two ways: as democratic theocracy or as
democratic caesarism and caesaro-papism. As things were, however, there was little chance for the first. When Deputy Camus
defended the civil constitution in the National Assembly on the
grounds that religion was in the state but the state not in reli-

[108] Pp. 45 ff.
[109] A. Mathiez, *Rome et le clergé sous la Constituante* (Paris, 1911), p. 78.

gion,[110] it was clear that the premises of Fauchet's political theology no longer existed. Camus' next sentence, *"Nous sommes une convention nationale, nous avons assurément le pouvoir de changer la religion"* ["We are a National Convention; we surely have the power to change religion"], made quite apparent the change in the political and religious balance of power, without, however, yet drawing the consequences of such a sovereignty. The church's will to survive was crushed *a priori;* only as an instrument of official policy could it hope to continue a frugal existence in the shadows of an omnipotent state. As a matter of fact, the "secular religion"[111] which was finally admitted to the structure of the revolutionary state could not have been Catholic. It was but a creation to serve the aims of political common sense.

FAILURE

On April 13, 1790, the National Assembly rejected the proposal by the Carthusian monk Dom Gerle, a member of the Jacobin Club, to make Catholicism the state religion.[112] Three years later, on the 20th of Prairial (June 8), 1793, in the midst of the Terror, Robespierre, in a celebration in the gardens of the Tuileries, proclaimed the new religion of the Supreme Being.[113]

These two events, the dethroning of the old and the elevation of the new state religion, comprehend in time the outline of the revolution. Between them there is the fall of the monarchy, the

---

[110] *Moniteur*, IV, 515.

[111] Term used by J. L. Talmon, *The origins of totalitarian democracy* (London, 1952), pp. 21 ff.

[112] *Moniteur*, IV, 103 ff. Cf. Erdmann, *op. cit.*, pp. 180 ff. and Leflon, *op. cit.*, p. 54. Latreille, *op. cit.*, p. 83, makes the remark: "On peut dire qu'à cette date apparaît et s'élargit la fissure entre les patriotes et les représentants de l'Église gallicane."

[113] Latreille, *op. cit.*, p. 168; Leflon, *op. cit.*, p. 126.

beginning of war at home and abroad, and the transition from liberal constitutionalism to totalitarian democracy.[114] In terms of religio-political developments, this epoch is distinguished by the fact that the Catholic idea of unity definitely was transferred from the side of the church to the side of the state. While the revolutionary followers of religious democracy lost more and more ground politically, the democratic lay state began to form its own religious sect. The victory of the Jacobins was the victory, too, of the principle of religious absolutism, with the power of the state being extended over conscience.

At the beginning of the revolution the bishops had tried to save the clergy as a class by voluntary financial concessions. The bourgeoisie, however, tried to break the special political position of the clergy by rescinding the economic privileges of the church. Its aim was a nation of no classes, only individuals. The discussions of the National Assembly on the subject of church and state reflected this conflict. The dispute over the privileges of the clergy soon led to a battle of principles, in which the claims of state and church were sharply opposed. After the sequestration of ecclesiastical properties, a reordering of the legal and social position of the clergy became imperative. It was supposedly to be achieved by a thorough-going *Constitution civile du Clergé*. But the civil constitution of the clergy was not a solution of the conflict: in the attempt to destroy the class-consciousness of the clergy, the foundations of Gallicanism, along with the structure of the old church, buckled.

We need not discuss the question, so often raised since Taine,[115] whether the church policy of the National Assembly was dictated by political or economic motives, that is, whether

---

[114] Talmon, *op. cit.*, pp. 69 ff. The sociological changes of the years 1792/93 are described in an article by A. Rüstow: "Der Umbruch von 1792/93," *Die neue Rundschau* LXIII (1952), 331–70, which complements Talmon's study.

[115] H. Taine, *Les origines de la France contemporaine* (Paris, 1876), III, 265.

the precarious situation of the state forced it to expropriate church property or whether the revolution acted out of political principle. We need mention only the result: during the revolution the Gallican church ceased to exist as an autonomous institution. In the course of events its autonomy was lost, piece by little piece: politically, through the association of the *bons curés* with the bourgeoisie; socially, through the abolition of feudal privileges; economically, by the nationalization of church property; and, religiously, through the Civil Constitution of the clergy.[116]

The Civil Constitution, which hastened the final breach of church and revolution, was unacceptable to the Gallican position.[117] This is apparent in the behavior of the majority of ecclesiastical deputies in the National Assembly. As speaker for the clergy in the National Assembly, Archbishop Boisgelin stated that the National Assembly had overstepped its authority in acting without regard to the canonical principle; to become legally binding, its decisions needed the assent of the church.[118] As a Gallican, Boisgelin was not thinking here of the pope so much as of a French National Council. But precisely this was rejected by the radical majority in the assembly, who feared the resurrection of the clergy as a class with the creation of an aristocratic assembly of bishops. It was its express wish to regulate the new structure of the church.

With this the way to unity was blocked. The *Exposition des*

[116] Leflon, *op. cit.*, p. 56.

[117] Erdmann has rocked the foundation of the concept of the Gallican character of the civil constitution by his detailed comparison of the Civil Constitution and the texts of the Gallican traditions. See his results, *op. cit.*, pp. 227 f. His opinion has not yet been fully accepted. The older French treatises and most recently Leflon, *op. cit.*, p. 58, regard the Civil Constitution as a "synthèse des doctrines gallicanes."

[118] Boisgelin, "Discours sur le rapport du comité ecclésiastique, concernant la constitution du clergé prononcé le 29 mai 1790."

principes, a pamphlet in which the episcopal deputies defended themselves,[119] showed clearly the straits into which the Gallican church had foundered in its attempt to anchor democratic rights in the constitution, just as ecclesiastical liberties had until then been secured in the class order. Since the majority of the French church—and now, more and more, the lower clergy also—refused to swear allegiance to the Civil Constitution, the church policies of the National Assembly terminated in failure. Instead of the desired religious-political unity, there was a split between church and nation. The Catholic and the constitutional church opposed each other as bitter adversaries: the one persecuted by the state, the other favored by the state, both wrestling for the faith of their believers and for official recognition. As a consequence and by a concatenation of diverse circumstances, the attack on the old church became a general wave of de-christianization that adversely affected the *église constitutionelle* also. The legal basis for the constitutional church was void when the constitution of 1791 was repealed. There were, therefore, two rival churches in France without clearly-defined status under public law. The advocates of the "république une et indivisible" could not grant tolerance to both of them in accordance with the principle of human rights. The logical result was that every institutional form of religion was banished from the state and that the republic tried to achieve social unity of itself in the shape of a "religion civile" based upon remnants of the Catholic cult.[120]

[119] Complete title: *Exposition des principes sur la constitution du clergé, par les évêques députés à l'Assemblée nationale* (end of October, 1790). See Erdmann, *op. cit.*, pp. 238 ff.; Latreille, *op. cit.*, pp. 91 ff.

[120] Latreille, *op. cit.*, pp. 169 f. Both of them revoked their teachings and made their peace with the Catholic church. On the revolutionary cults, cf. A. Aulard, *Le Culte de la Raison et de l'Être suprême* (Paris, 1904); A. Mathiez, *L'origine des cultes révolutionnaires* (Paris, 1909); J. Tiersot, *Les fêtes et les chants de la Révolution française* (Paris, 1908). In general, A. Aulard, *Le christianisme et la Révolution française* (1925).

Not only Roman Catholics abjured the oath; many priests of the constitutional church mounted the scaffold as well; among them were Fauchet, who had proclaimed the unity of church and state in his sermons, and Lamourette, who had been the first to speak of Christian Democracy in a French parliament.

It was only after the complete failure of the constitutional experiment in state and church relations that the radical movement for the complete separation of the revolutionary state from Christian tradition gained momentum. Only then did the movement for philosophical-political reconstruction, which at first had been noted for its reformist traits, assume its true shape. The cult of reason, the calendar based on decades, the new measures of time, were all expressions of a deliberate breaking with the past and at the same time were signs of the religious messianism which saw in the revolution the beginning of the new time and of the redemption of the human race. For intellectual history it is worthy to note that, just as the enlightened ideal of *bonne politie* was oriented to the model of the Roman republic,[121] the cult of state which was supposed to take the place of Christianity showed clear Roman traits. The painter David portrayed the revolutionary festivals in the character of Roman *dies fasti*. Roman fasces and tablets were used in public. The orators of the revolution adopted the vocabulary of the Roman republic and identified themselves with Roman heroes like Brutus, Cassius, and Gracchus.[122] As little successful as the revolutionary cults were in

[121] A. Schinz, *La pensée de Jean-Jacques Rousseau* (Paris, 1929), pp. 417 f.

[122] Thus Madame Roland concluded a letter to Brissot with the words: "Adieu tout court. La femme de Caton ne s'amuse point à faire des compliments à Brutus." Cited in Brinton, *Europa im Zeitalter der Französischen Revolution* (2d ed.; Vienna, 1948), p. 259. For an interpretation of this, cf. the remarks made by Hannah Arendt, "Was ist Autorität," in *Fragwürdige Traditionsbestände im politischen Denken der Gegenwart* (Frankfurt, 1957), pp. 166 f., which are based on the Marxian opinion that the French Revolution appeared on the stage of history in a Roman costume.

doing away with Christian spiritualism, it was clear that their aim was to renew the civic virtues of antiquity and its unity of religion and politics, and form a new spirit that could survive without Christianity.

The persecution of the old church did not end with the fall of Robespierre. The Directory disavowed the religion of the Supreme Being that had been introduced by the fallen dictator and resumed propagandizing for atheism. Rapidly dwindling in power, however, it was no longer able to give political meaning to the antireligious messianism of the revolution. By the end of the century, the revolutionary attempt at forcibly blending religion and church can be considered to have failed in its caesaro-papistic shape. In the Concordat of Paris (1802) Napoleon restored the old church to its traditional rights. This, after all that had happened, was an act dictated by reasons of state.

The group of revolutionary romantics around Fauchet and Bonneville had attempted to blend Christian and revolutionary theories of natural law. In detail, their program was based on a mixture of Rousseauian and biblical principles. This is true especially for the Cercle social, the meeting place where revolutionary Catholics and atheists analyzed the Contrat social together. Those of Fauchet's lectures to the Cercle social which have been preserved permit us to follow this process in detail.[123]

In the third of these lectures we find:

> Nous allons nous servir, pour poser les principes de la législation qui convient à tous les hommes des idées d'un grand homme.[124] [To pose principles of legislation which apply to all men, we are going to use the ideas of a great man.]

For Fauchet, Rousseau was the true legislator, and his work la

---

[123] They are published in the periodical La Bouche de Fer.
[124] La Bouche de Fer, October, 1790.

plus complete démocratie de l'amour et de la vertu.[125] The basic
principle of *amour universel*, laid down in the Bible in a general
way, is to be found here translated into clear legal and political
concepts. In Fauchet, Rousseau and the Bible are the indispensable foundations of the system.

At the same time, Fauchet did not read the *Contrat social*
uncritically. He disputed Rousseau on many points, simplified
him, and sharpened his expressions or turned them around.[126]
Rousseau's anthropology, based upon passion, is pessimistic;[127]
Fauchet put forward one in which man is seen as an *être aimant*
(loving being). Rousseau saw primitive man as changing from
the state of nature to the social state through an act of will: in
Fauchet the state of nature and the social state blend. Rousseau
was a historical relativist, though far less than Montesquieu:
in contrast, Fauchet believed in a "true legislature," common to
all peoples and all countries. These shifts of values, which are
reminiscent of Taine's *esprit classique* in its naïve form, are characteristic of Fauchet. In him, Rousseau's severity of thought
became a romantic and fanatic doctrinarism that tried to solve
every political question by a universal recipe and without close
analysis.

Nevertheless, we may say that Fauchet only radicalized and
popularized the ideas of his master, and his interpretation corresponds, if not to the letter, then to the spirit of Rousseau, except
for the section of the *Contrat social* on the relationship of state
and religion,[128] precisely that one which seriously questions the
possibility of a Christian form of Rousseau's ideas.

[125] *La Bouche de Fer*, January 17, 1791.
[126] Cf. H. Cros, *op. cit.*, pp. 53 ff.
[127] At least in the *Contrat social* and in the *Lettres de la Montagne*. On the
conflict between Rousseau *romantique* and Rousseau *romain* in the anthropology
of *Emile*, cf. Schinz, *op. cit.*, pp. 421 ff.
[128] *Contrat social* IV, 8 (Oeuvres complètes de Jean-Jacques Rousseau [Paris,
1832], V, 146 ff.).

Fauchet analyzed only a part of the *Contrat social*. He fails
to mention the chapter on religion. In any case, his attempt to
change Rousseau's *législateur* into the theistic God of the Covenant is manifest. This, of course, is a hopeless attempt. For Rousseau's remark, *"il faudrait des dieux pour donner des lois aux
hommes"*[129] ["It would take gods to give laws to men"], cannot
be understood as an allusion to a divine creator. The meaning of
législateur is qualified by references to Plato, Lycurgus, and Calvin. Quite plainly, it is declared: *"Le législateur est à tous égards
un homme extra ordinaire dans l'État."*[130] There is nowhere a
question of a divine legislator in the sense of Fauchet. Calvin,
too, is only mentioned in passing; Rousseau admires him more
as the founder of states and the helmsman of the state than as a
theologian.[131]

Nor does the attempt to regard Rousseau's project of a *religion
civile*[132] as a kind of democratic legitimation of Catholicism fare
better. Here too the wording of the *Contrat social* opposes all
attempts at Christian assimilation. For Rousseau expressly excludes Catholicism from the types of religion which may be considered for a state constituted according to the *volonté générale*:
he calls it *religion du prêtre*, arguing that since it imposes on
man two different "homelands" (state and church), it would
destroy the unity of society, the true *raison d'être* of religion,
according to the *Contrat social*:

[129] *Contrat social* II, 7, *loc. cit.* p. 59.
[130] *Ibid.*, p. 60.
[131] *Ibid.*, pp. 60 f.
[132] *Contrat social* IV, 8, and *Lettres de la Montagne*, I, 1. See K. D. Erdmann,
*Das Verhältnis von Staat und Religion nach der Sozialphilosophie Rousseaus
(Der Begriff der "religion civile")* (Berlin, 1935). See also P.-M. Masson, *La
religion de Jean-Jacques Rousseau* (Paris, 1916), pp. 178 ff.; and Schinz, *op. cit.*,
pp. 364 ff.

Tout ce qui rompt l'unité sociale ne vaut rien; toutes les institutions qui mettent l'homme en contradiction avec lui-même ne valent rien.[133] [Anything that disrupts social unity is of no value; institutions which put man in discord with himself have no value.]

There is no bridge here which could lead to Fauchet's concept of Catholicism as the "religion of unity."

It might be objected that Rousseau meant the Catholic church and that, on the other hand, Fauchet started from an uneccle-siastical and undogmatic formalized concept of Catholicism. Although true, this does not alter the case. For Rousseau's judgment of the *pure et simple religion de l'Évangile*, that is, of the primitive Christianity which Fauchet and Grégoire had in mind, was by no means more favorable than his view of Roman Catholicism. In the same place we read:

Cette religion, n'ayant nulle relation particulière avec le corps politique, laisse aux lois la seule force qu'elles tirent d'elle-mêmes sans leur en ajouter aucune autre et par la, un des grands liens de la société particulière reste sans effet. Bien plus, loin d'attacher les coeurs des citoyens à l'État, elle les en détache comme de toutes les choses de la terre. Je ne connais rien de plus contraire à l'esprit social. [This religion, which has no particular relation to politics, leaves to the law the only force which it takes from itself without adding any other, and thus one of the great means of the special society remains without effect. And what is more, far from bringing the hearts of the citizens close to the state, it detaches them from it as it does from all the things on earth.]

Rousseau's remarks conclude: "*Une société de vrais chrétiens ne*

---

[133] *Contrat social*, IV, 8, *loc. cit.*, p. 161.

serait plus une société d'hommes."[134] ["A society of true Christians will no longer be a society of men."] And later on: "*Je me trompe en disant une république chrétienne; chacun de ces deux mots exclut l'autre.*"[135] ["I am in error to say 'Christian republic': These words are mutually exclusive."]

It cannot be assumed that Fauchet was ignorant of these passages. If he had overlooked them in the flush of his apologetic enthusiasm, his friends in the *Cercle social* certainly would have pointed out to him the contradictions in his interpretation of Rousseau. For we have proof that the question of the possibility of Catholicism existing in the framework of the revolutionary state had the attention of the *Cercle social* and that Rousseau's rejections caused heated discussions there.

In his book *De l'esprit des religions*, published in 1791, Bonneville remarked in the chapter entitled *Unité sociale*:

Dire brusquement que "la Religion chrétienne est si mauvaise que c'est perdre le temps de s'amuser à le démontrer" (*Contrat social*, Book 4. Chapter 8) c'est de la rudesse à pure perte; c'est manquer le but qu'un vrai philosophe doit se proposer; c'est avoir dit la vérite, bien plutôt pour l'honneur de l'avoir dite, que par un désir sincère de la faire aimer.[136]

J. J. Rousseau trouve que la liberté et l'humanité sont incompatibles;[137] je ne le pense pas, après avoir longtemps réfléchi. Peut-etre que, privés de nos secours et de la facilité que nous avons de nous communiquer nos lumières, les plus sages d'entre les Druides ne purent jamais venir à bout de réunir

---

[134] *Ibid.*, p. 152.
[135] *Ibid.*, p. 154.
[136] Vol. II, ¶ 10.
[137] This is an allusion to Rousseau, *Lettres de la Montagne*, I, 1: "Le patriotisme et l'humanité sont . . . deux vertus incompatibles dans leur énergie, et surtout chez un peuple entier." (*Oeuvres*, Vol. VIII, p. 40, n. 1.)

l'une et l'autre.[138] . . . L'auteur du *Contrat social* a prétendu que le christianisme romain était plus nuisible qu'utile à la forte constitution d'un état libre.[139] Warburton soutenait que nulle religion n'était utile au corps politique. C'était anéantir tous les systèmes religieux; le philosophe Anglais est, ce me semble, allé trop loin. Une religion qui ferait de la patrie et des lois l'objet de l'adoration de tous les citoyens, serait aux yeux du sage une religion excellente. Le suprême pontife serait le roi, le régisseur suprême. Mourir pour son pays, serait aller à la gloire éternelle, au bonheur éternel. Celui qui aurait violé les lois de son pays, serait un impie; et le premier magistrat de la nation, pontife et roi, aurait le droit de la dévouer à l'exécration publique, au nom de la société qu'il aurait offensée, et au nom du Dieu suprême qui nous a tous également soumis à des lois impartiales.[140] [To say curtly that "the Christian Religion" is so bad that it is a waste of time to amuse oneself at proving this (*Social Contract*, Book 4, Chapter 8) is the purest rudeness. This would mean missing the goal of what true philosophy should have as a purpose; it means having said the truth for the honor of having done so rather than from a sincere desire to make it loved.

J. J. Rousseau finds that liberty and humanity are incompatible; after long reflection, I do not think so. It may be that the wisest among the Druids, who did not have the help and the facilities which we have to communicate our findings to each other, never were able to unite the two. . . . The author of the *Social Contract* has stated that Roman Christianity harmed more than helped the strong constitution of a free

---

[138] Cf. Rousseau, *loc. cit.*: "Le législateur qui les voudra toutes deux n'obtiendra ni l'une ni l'autre: cet accord ne s'est jamais vu; il ne se verra jamais, parce qu'il est contraire à la nature, et qu'on ne peut donner deux objets à la même passion."

[139] Rousseau, *Contrat social*, IV, 8, *loc. cit.*, p. 161.

[140] This is a paraphrase of Rousseau's statements under the catchword *religion civile (loc. cit.)*.

state. Warburton remarked that no religion was useful to the body politic. This view nullifies all religious systems. I think the English philosopher went too far. A religion which would make the fatherland and its laws the object of its citizens' adoration would be an excellent one in the eyes of the sage. The Supreme Pontiff would be the king and the first director. To die for the fatherland would mean to attain eternal glory, eternal happiness. Whoever violated the laws of his country would be impious, and the first official of the nation, pontiff or king, would have the right to disavow religion, in the name of the society which it offended and in the name of the supreme God who subjected all of us to impartial laws.]

But where is the religion to be found that will be compatible with a good constitution? Bonneville thinks he has found it: "*la religion de nos pères.*" This, as we know, is Fauchet's view, too. But it is not Rousseau's. The *religion civile*, as outlined in the chapter on religion of the *Contrat social*, is composed of remnants of the Catholic cult, but it is expressly separated from the *christianisme romain*, that is, from the church itself. Fauchet's and Bonneville's desire to find in Catholicism—or at least in its Gallican species—Rousseau's *religion civile*, is wishful thinking; it is not founded on Rousseau's texts.

In a nearly imploring tone, *La Bouche de Fer* turns to the Freemasons of the *Cercle social*, conjuring with Rousseau's authority:

> Amis de la Vérité, ne perdez jamais de vue ce que Hobbes et Jean Jacques ont écrit pour vous engager à réunir les deux têtes de l'aigle, et pour tout ramener naturellément et religieusement à l'UNITÉ politique, sans laquelle jamais État ni Gouvernement . . . ne sera bien constitué.[141] [Amis de la

---

[141] No. 9, October, 1790.

Verité, never forget what Hobbes and Jean Jacques have written in order to unite the two heads of the eagle and to lead
everything together religiously and naturally, towards a political unity without which neither state nor government would
exist.]

Fauchet here alludes to a statement in the chapter on religion
of the *Contrat social*. Because of its importance, it is given here
in full:

> De tous les auteurs chrétiens, le philosophe Hobbes est le
> seul qui ait bien vu le mal et la remède, qui ait osé proposer
> de réunir les deux têtes de l'aigle, et de tout ramener à l'unité
> politique, sans laquelle jamais État ni gouvernement ne sera
> bien constitué. Mais il a dû voir que l'esprit dominateur du
> christianisme était incompatible avec son système et que l'in-
> térêt du prêtre serait toujours plus fort que celui de l'État.
> Ce n'est pas tant ce qu'il y a d'horrible et de faux dans sa
> politique, que ce qu'il y a de juste et de vrai, qui l'a rendue
> odieuse.[142] [Among all Christians only the philosopher Hobbes
> has seen the evil and its remedy, has dared propose to unite
> the two heads of the eagle and to bring everything together
> religiously and naturally towards political unity without which
> neither state nor government could be constituted. But he
> had to admit that the dominating spirit of Christianity was
> incompatible with his system and that the interest of the
> priest would always be stronger than that of the state. It is

[142] *Loc. cit.*, p. 150. The last sentence is especially conclusive. Rousseau explains
it in the *Lettres de la Montagne* I, 1 (*loc. cit.*, p. 39) with the following words:
"Telle est . . . la plus forte conséquence qu'on puisse tirer de ce chapitre (sc. du
Contrat social), où, bien loin de taxer le pur Evangile d'être pernicieux à la
société, je le trouve, en quelque sorte, trop sociable, embrassante trop tout le genre
humain, pour une législation qui doit être exclusive; inspirant l'humanité plutôt
que le patriotisme, et tendant à former des hommes plutôt que des citoyens."

not what is so horrible and false in this policy but what there is true and just which has made it hateful.]

If we compare this to the similar remarks in *De la Religion nationale*, it is clear that Fauchet's arguments, seen in the light of their original, terminate in a conclusion that is exactly opposite to it. Where Fauchet is searching in Catholicism for the principle of the *unité sociale* that is lacking in Rousseau's contractual state, the author of the *Contrat social* argues against the national political usefulness of Christianity exactly on the grounds of its binding power in the nation. For Christianity is a humanitarian and supranational principle: *trop sociable—inspirant l'humanité plutôt que le patriotisme*; it is in conflict with the need to concentrate national sovereignty and national power.[143] The highest interest of the national state is the *législation exclusive*, an anticipation of the concept of national sovereignty used by Camus and Neufchateau against the church during the revolution. Its exercise, however, is not possible as long as the political power is opposed by an *intérêt particulier* in the shape of the church. Reasons of state, therefore, demand that the church be sheared of its status as a sovereign body. Thus the matter is turned upside down, so to speak: what is to be attained in Fauchet with the help of Catholicism—the reunion of political and religious power, the renewed blending of the "two heads of the eagle"—is in Rousseau supposed to heal a malady caused by Christianity.[144] The reunion of religion and politics can occur only when the social body of the church is destroyed. There is no room for Catholicism in a sovereign state formed on the basis

[143] The *Contrat social* here only continues the trend of the occidental doctrine of sovereignty. The old problem of the canonists and Legists is treated by Rousseau from the point of view of the nation-state.

[144] Cf. especially the historical introduction to the chapter on religion of the *Contrat social*, loc. cit., pp. 146 ff.

of the *volonté générale*. In such a state nothing is left of Christianity but a dogmatic spirituality, devoid of all firm institutional characteristics, that is, a Christianity without the church.

But a Christianity without the church cannot be a Catholic Christianity. For spirituality and ecclesiastical form, the content of faith and its social application in the community of worship, form an indissoluble whole in Catholicism. If the state reduces church dogma to a deistic credo, if it prescribes the form of worship in the church, if it alters the church constitution and attacks the church's autonomy, there can no longer be serious talk of a Catholic Christianity.

Those who argue from the *Contrat social* can do so only from the utilitarian point of view. They can point out the church's social usefulness and recommend certain of her tenets as moral rules for public life. They can define the Catholic priesthood as an institution of public servants and clerical guardians of the law.[145] But then the church ceases to exist.

The step toward a utilitarian formulation of the concept of the church was taken by Fauchet when he deduced the necessity of Catholicism on purely social grounds quite independent of the question of truth. "*La meilleure religion sera donc celle qui fortifierait, d'un lien plus indissoluble, toutes les parties de la Législation.*"[146] This was Rousseau's procedure exactly when in the *Contrat social* he sifted the remaining stock of religions to discover their social advantages and disadvantages.[147] Had Fau-

---

[145] "Le sacerdoce, dans le gouvernement, lorsque le peuple élit ses officiers, évêques ou surveillants, ou gardiens de la loi, c'est le souverain toujours assemblé pour créer, connaître et cultiver la loi." (N. de Bonneville, *De l'esprit des religions*, Vol. I, ¶ 29.)

[146] *De la Religion nationale*, p. 45.

[147] *Contrat social*, IV, 8, loc. cit., pp. 146 ff. In this context Rousseau's strong sympathies for Islamism are remarkable.

chet followed Rousseau one step further, he would have had to recognize that even the "divine legislator" of the *Contrat social*, upon which his theory is based, is only a postulate of political reasoning, the necessity for which had been determined by Rousseau on a basis of purely practical considerations.[148] The consequence of his failure to take this last step was that he—and with him the Christian Democracy of the revolution—remained helplessly suspended between the teachings of revolutionary and Christian natural law.

Rousseau was the first of the philosophers of the Enlightenment who systematically thought through the relationship of state and religion. He had seen the difficulties in a state founded on a blending of autonomous reason and the church and saw the difficulties incomparably more clearly than Voltaire or Montesquieu, both of whom inclined to rather practical, traditional, solutions in political as well as religious spheres. The theoreticians of popular sovereignty were also theoreticians of *religion civile*. Whoever went along with the revolution, as it gradually became more radical on the path from monarchy to Jacobinism, and simultaneously clung to Catholicism or attempted to strengthen the influence of the church through its alliance with "the people," sooner or later was forced to come to terms with Rousseau's philosophy of state.

The *Cercle social* tried in vain to break or to weaken the antinomy boldly set forth by Rousseau of the church and popular sovereignty. This resulted only in its powerless protest against the view in the *Contrat social* that the Catholic religion and the revolutionary state were incompatible. The real significance of the *Cercle social*, however, does not lie in its attempts at mediation or criticism. It is to be found in the fact that its own history mirrors the systematic contradiction which Rousseau revealed. At

[148] *Contrat social*, II, 6, loc. cit., p. 58.

the very moment that the church policy of the revolution took a trend inimical to Catholicism and the *religion civile* was put to its test, the alliance of Catholics and revolutionaries began to dissolve. With it ended, even before it began, the possibility of a history of a revolutionary Christian Democracy.

At the beginning we asked why the experiment of amalgamation of church and democracy during the revolution was doomed to fail. Now we can complete our earlier statements: the revolution wanted not orderly co-operation but the subordination and incorporation of the church; the democratic-presbyterian base in the French church was too narrow to support a serious alternative solution; thus, the amalgamation of church and state could be realized only in the form of revolutionary caesarism. The church's structure and the political aims of the revolution were in conflict. Catholic France was not Cromwell's England. Once more we quote Michelet: *"La Révolution n'adopta aucune église. Pourquoi? C'est parce qu'elle était une église elle-même."*[149]

There has always been a strong temptation to see Rousseau, the proud son of the Calvinist state of Geneva, as the herald of a democracy founded on religion.[150] There are, indeed, many

---

[149] See *supra*, p. 51, n. 86.

[150] This thesis has again been put forward by F. Glum, *Rousseau* (Stuttgart, 1956). However, his book is too little qualified in its subject to be taken seriously; cf. the criticism by I. Fetscher, *Politische Vierteljahresschrift* III, (1962), 93 ff. But Fetscher's excellent book on Rousseau (*Rousseaus politische Philosophie* [Neuwied-Berlin, 1960]) also harmonizes things too much in this point; I cannot endorse his interpretation of the chapter on religion especially in view of the revolutionary *experimentum crucis* described supra. This is still much more the case with the interpretation by O. Vossler (*Rousseaus Freiheitslehre* [Göttingen, 1963], p. 352) where the scandals of capital punishment and intolerance, although noticed, are regarded as harmless rhetoric or are argued away with a view to Rousseau's idea of freedom. Unfortunately, none of the interpretations (with the exception of the book by Erdmann, *supra* n. 132) draws upon Rousseau's own commentary on the *religion civile*, the "Lettres de la Montagne."

passages in the *Contrat social* in which the conception of the religio-political unity of the state—not quite clearly developed—oscillates between theocracy and caesaro-papism. What had been possible on the foundations of a secularized Calvinism—the combination of the theory of state of the *Contrat social* with the credo of the *savoyard vicar* was impossible in French Catholicism. Rousseau himself left no doubt on this,[151] and the course of the revolution bore him out. The application to Catholicism of the church-political ideas of the *Contrat social*, which presupposed the separation of Christianity and the church, resulted in the dialectic turn of religious democracy toward an excessive "Staatskirchentum" ("establishment" churchdom).[152] The revolution, therefore, could establish the unity of political power as Rousseau demanded only at the price of terror and the destruction of the old Gallican church.

Undoubtedly, the problems of church and state, as they came to light during the revolution, were prefigured in the *ancien régime*. It was because the liberties of the church were class privileges that religion became politically vulnerable. It was because the spheres of church and state were intermingled in the old monarchy that the totalitarian monism of Jacobinism developed in the course of the secularization which filled the eighteenth century. Much responsibility (not yet established by intensive research but obviously important) for the fate of the French church during the revolution belongs to the restrictive and ob-

[151] Cf. again the chapter on religion in the *Contrat social* and the *Lettres de la Montagne*, I, 1, *loc. cit.*, p. 37.

[152] In the field of politics the transfer of direct democracy of the Swiss pattern to a centralized area state like France (suggested, but not articulated by Rousseau himself) similarly led to immediate *démocratie directe* of the revolutionary clubs and to Jacobin control. Cf. G. Ritter, "Wesen und Wandlungen der Freiheitsidee im politischen Denken der Neuzeit," in *Vom sittlichen Problem der Macht* (Bern, 1948), pp. 116 ff.

stinate Catholic concept of church that developed during the Counter-Reformation, and Jacques Maritain is right to speak of a *hypocrisie majestueuse* in reference to the Catholic absolutism of the seventeenth century.[153]

This, however, does not alter the fact that Catholic absolutism, even when it misused the church as *instrumentum regni*, kept its church-political practice within strict limits; the monarchy did not deny that the church was a sovereign society (*societas perfecta*). This is indeed the difference that separates even a Louis XIV from the legislators of the *Constituante*. It was only the Revolution which opposed the church's claim to social unity and sovereignty before the law. Something altogether new had begun; it can only be characterized partially by the concepts of *Staatskirchentum* or Gallicanism.

Since Talmon, this "something new" has been called *totalitarian democracy*.[154] It is a concept of democracy which is inspired by the idea of the religio-political unity of the state, a concept far from the liberal idea of the separation of religion and politics, of civic duties and human rights.[155] In Rousseau's early works the vision of the original state had already acquired the characteristics of the polis of antiquity; antiquity's unity of religion and politics was opposed to the Christian dualism of state and church.[156] The

[153] J. Maritain, *Integral Humanism* (Scribners, 1968, p. 179). New translation by J. W. Evans.

[154] J. P. Talmon, *op. cit.* (cf. n. 111). Cf. also to the following, J. C. Murray's article, "The Church and Totalitarian Democracy, *Theological Studies* XIII (1952), 525 ff., which is built upon Talmon.

[155] Talmon, *op. cit.*, p. 10.

[156] See K. D. Erdmann, *op. cit.*, pp. 35 ff., and K. Löwith, *Von Hegel zu Nietzsche* (Stuttgart, 1953), pp. 256 ff. On the interpretation of this phenomenon in the history of the revolution, cf. Talmon, *op. cit.*, p. 246, who sees in Buonarotti's comment on revolutionary religious policy, "Le culte doit se confondre avec les lois," the revival of antiquity's ideal of the polis.

revolution, although it certainly cannot be derived from Rousseau,[157] followed him in the effort to meld law and worship, state and religion, in political symbiosis. This, incidentally, was the aim of the idealistic revolutionary Christian Democratic groups; they envisioned an order which "combined the Gospel with legislation, church with the state, morals with laws, God himself and men completely."[158]

Such an order, however, is incompatible with the spirit of Christianity. For the Christian idea of separation of powers[159] excludes the notion of a sovereignty which includes both the political world and the church. The borderline between religious and political power, as history shows, cannot be crossed with impunity, even when the direction taken is toward theocracy. The attempt to deify the state is absolutely incompatible with Christianity.

As long as the revolution remained a "church," appeasement of Catholicism was out of the question. This could take place only when Jacobin political monism was transformed into the liberal dualism of separate spheres, one governed by state authority and one, a sphere of conscience, free from state intervention. Just as civil[160] rights, first conceived as intrastate affairs, were transformed into human rights that preceded the state, the Catholic and democratic concepts of society drew closer to each other. This statement may provoke opposition, considering the Syllabus and similar papal declarations. We have to bear in mind, however, that the revolutionary state's claim to totality was much

---

[157] According to the ingenious paradox of A. Schinz, op. cit., p. 519, Rousseau is the "père illégitime de la Révolution." Cf. also Erdmann, op. cit., p. 12.

[158] Fauchet, De la Religion nationale, cited in Erdmann, Volkssouveränität und Kirche, pp. 78 f.

[159] Matth. 21, 22; Jo 18, 36.

[160] As late as at the time of Mirabean cf. Erdmann, op. cit., p. 102.

more dangerous for the church than the liberal tradition of human rights, whose origin in Christianity and natural law is not concealed by the fact that the church was not able to adopt the individualistic formulation given to them in the eighteenth and nineteenth centuries.[161] Based upon the principle of freedom of conscience, liberal Catholicism could bring the church back to democracy (and democracy back to the church) by opposing the interference of the state in religion and by postulating the freedoms of both the *civis christianus* and the *civis politicus*.

The settlement of these fundamentals in the relations of church and democracy took place in the nineteenth century, but it developed only slowly and step by step and was continually interrupted by setbacks and hesitancy. Catholics only reluctantly agreed to democratic principles. In France, especially, democracy and the church remained for long at odds; it was in France that traditionalism first spawned a political ideology that indiscriminately rejected the principles of the revolution and aimed at renewing the old monarchic order.

[161] Cf. H. Maier, "Kirche und Demokratie," *Zeitschrift für Politik*, X (1963), 320–37.

3: THE TRADITIONALIST
CONTRADICTION (1795–1829)

Traditionalist is the name given a group of French Catholic writers who first distinguished themselves at the time of the Directory and later under Napoleon and the Restoration. Most of these men belonged to the French nobility; often they had spent years in exile; and in their writings they sharply opposed the revolution. The best known of them are Lamennais,[1] de Maistre, and de Bonald. In their works they treat various matters pertaining to state theory and state-church relations. The underlying theme

---

[1] For a general introduction, see M. Ferraz, *Histoire de la philosophie au XIXe siècle*, Vol. III: *Traditionalisme et ultramontanisme* (Paris, 1880). For information on the theory of state, see H. Michel, *L'ideé de l'État. Essai critique sur l'histoire des theóries sociales et politiques en France depuis la Révolution* (Paris, 1895), pp. 108 ff.; D. Bagge, *Les idées politiques en France sous la Restauration* (Paris, 1952), pp. 187 ff., who—unlike Michel—vividly advocates Traditionalism. (For criticism, cf. the review by Bertier de Sauvigny, *Revue d'histoire de l'Église de France* XXXIX [1953], 93–96). J. Bellamy's book, *La théologie catholique au XIXe siècle* (Paris, 1904), pp. 7 ff., deals with religious Traditionalism. For German literature, see the already-mentioned books by H. Friedrich (*supra* p. 67, n. 120) and W. Gurian (*supra* p. 58, n. 97), and P. R. Rohden, *Joseph de Maistre als politischer Theoretiker. Ein Beitrag zur Geschichte des konservativen Staatsgedankens in Frankreich* (Munich, 1929). R. Spaemann, *Der Ursprung der Soziologie aus dem Geist der Restauration. Studien über L.G.A. de Bonald* (Munich, 1959).

which binds their works as a group is criticism of the revolution,
a stress on historical development and on providence over mechanism in human autonomy, and finally in the demand for the
re-establishment of the old monarchical order in France. Because
of this inherent direction of their thought (but chiefly because
of their historical effects) their writings may be spoken of as
the traditionalist school.[2] Although the influence of the school
was not very widespread, it had considerable influence on the
political thought of the Catholic elite of France, Belgium, and
Germany for over a quarter of a century, that is, from the end
of the Great Revolution to the beginning of the Revolution of
1830.[3] It plays a role that cannot be emphasized too strongly in
the formation of political Catholicism in those countries. The
year 1795–96, with the appearance of de Maistre's *Considérations sur la France* and de Bonald's *Théorie du pouvoir politique*, may be regarded as the beginning of the publicistic influence of the traditionalists.[4] Its terminus may be designated by
the appearance of Lamennais's *Des progrès de la Révolution*, in
which he concluded his own passage from traditionalism to liberalism a year before the outbreak of the July Revolution. Between
these dates the traditionalists produced a mass of literature, including two masterpieces: de Maistre's *Du Pape* (1819) and
Lamennais's *Essai sur l'indifférence* (1817–23).

[2] French scholars usually refer to the Traditionalists as "royalistes", "réaction-
naires," or "ultramontains." Even more accurately Bagge, op. cit., speaks of an
"école théocratique."
[3] Cf. L. Ahrens, *Lamennais und Deutschland. Studien zur Geschichte der
französischen Revolution* (Münster, 1930), pp. 43 ff., and H. Haag, *Les origines
du catholicisme libéral en Belgique (1789–1839)* (Louvain, 1950), pp. 43 ff. and
recently the comprehensive description by K. Jürgensen, *Lamennais und die Gestaltung des belgischen Staates* (Wiesbaden, 1963).
[4] The complete title reads: *Théorie du pouvoir politique et religieux dans la
société civile démontrée par le raisonnement et par l'histoire.*

As a political movement, traditionalism directed itself mainly against the revolution and the Enlightenment. A product of the catastrophes which had befallen France since the time of the Jacobin dictatorship, it gave expression to the longing for the well-ordered and sturdy social order of the *ancien régime* which had become increasingly popular after the twin failures of the Jacobin and Napoleonic adventures. There was a general longing for peace, order, and harmony, not only in the remnants of the old aristocracy but among much of the middle classes; it seemed that it could be assuaged only by the old triad: *une foi, une loi, un roi.* Thus, traditionalism put its faith in the living features of the past rather than in the progressive ideals of the revolution; in a retreat back to national tradition with its particular benefits (church, monarchy, a stable society) rather than in possible future achievements. De Maistre defined the political program of traditionalism as "the contrary of revolution."[5] In effect, the traditionalist movement drew its life chiefly from the contrast of its ideas to those of 1789. It is possible, as Jean Lacroix demonstrated, to understand their thought as a system deriving logically from opposition to the revolution.[6] The revolutionary images of order convert into their opposites: *expérience* v. *raison, société* v. *individu, ordre* v. *progrès.*

Yet to proceed in this manner is to reach only a partial understanding of the traditionalist movement. The achievements of the traditionalists are by no means limited to vociferous denigration of the revolutionary ideal or to aristocratic revolt against democracy. Their contributions to a new theory of state and society, based on religion, must not be overlooked simply because

---

[5] *Considerations sur la France, Oeuvres* (4 vols.; Paris, 1851/52), I, 186. Hereafter de Maistre's works are quoted according to this edition and not according to the complete edition of 1884–86, which is not easily accessible.

[6] J. Lacroix, *Vocation personnelle et tradition nationale* (Paris, 1942).

counter-revolutionary criticism forms the best known (but by no means the most important) part of their writings. It should be noted, too, that their *critical* achievement was not so much their polemic against democracy—a form of state which they had known only in a distortion; it lay rather in their giving the clearest and most precise expression of the doubt in the viability of political orders and of the skepticism about political activism which had taken hold of French society after the revolution and under Napoleon. Yet the traditionalists no more gave themselves over to the reserved skepticism of conservatives who made premature peace with the revolution in the monarchy of the charter than they had to the Jacobin reign or to Bonaparte. Daringly, they propounded a theocratic order against the revolutionary reign of reason. By linking theocratic order to national tradition through the monarchy, the traditionalists exerted considerable influence upon the Catholicism of the Restoration. But they were never merely defenders of the status quo, and their thoughts often had effects in spheres which seemed far removed from their origins.

In connection with the theme of this study traditionalism has a twofold interest: *politically*, as the form of the Catholic dispute with the revolution; *religiously*, as a form of Catholic lay theology and lay apologetics.[7] These aspects intersect, for as everywhere the profane and the intra-ecclesiastical sides of political Catholicism are almost indistinguishable. This difficulty appears in the most varied forms: in de Bonald and Lamennais the question of Catholic political attitudes in post-revolutionary society touches closely upon the question of the traditional status of the church; dogmatic and constitutional points of view intermingle

---

[7] On that S. Merkle, "Die Anfänge französischer Laientheologie im 19. Jahrhundert," in *Wiederbegegnung von Kirche und Kultur in Deutschland* (Munich, 1929), pp. 325–57.

in the traditionalists' metaphysics of society; everywhere *political theology* appears to be the single unifying factor in traditionalism.[8] Criticism of revolutionary state theory and social theory is only a point of departure. It furnishes the basis for social renewal. But this renewal is itself to be reached with the help of religion. Thus, traditionalism translates into political terms certain models of ecclesiastic-hierarchical order: it intends to reconstitute society on the basis of religion: *Reconstituer la société politique à l'aide de la société religieuse*[9]—this formula of Lamennais is the key to understanding the traditionalist theory of society.

Traditionalism can here be considered only in its most important forms. We, therefore, restrict ourselves to the authors who most clearly show both its religious and political content: de Maistre, de Bonald, and Lamennais. For Ballanche, we can only mention the work of Frainnet;[10] for Chateaubriand and Balzac, who were close to traditionalism in their political views, the works of Andre Vincent[11] and Guyon.[12]

De MAISTRE

Considérations sur la France, published by the nobleman from Savoy, de Maistre, in Switzerland in 1794, itself contains the sum of the traditionalist criticism of the revolution. In it we find the very harshest condemnation of the revolution, in a time rich in passionate attacks and in equally passionate apologias. The critical asperity of the work derives not, as might be expected, from the class consciousness of the aristocratic author, although there are ample expressions of contempt for the plebeian revolu-

---

[8] C. Schmitt, *Politische Theologie* (Munich, 1922).

[9] *Infra* p. 244.

[10] G. Frainnet, *Essai sur la philosophie de P. S. Ballanche* (Lyon, 1904).

[11] Ph. André-Vincent, *Les idées politiques de Chateaubriand* (Paris, 1936).

[12] B. Guyon, *La pensée politique et sociale de Balzac* (Paris, 1947).

tionaries; reasons other than class are decisive in de Maistre's rejection of the revolution. Most important is a reason that is theological in nature. In de Maistre's view, the revolution is "satanic." Chapter iv of the *Considérations* begins: *Il y a dans la revolution française "un caractère satanique qui la distingue de tout ce qu'on a vu et peut-être de tout ce qu'on verra."*[13] ["There is a satanic character of the revolution which distinguishes it from all that we have seen or, perhaps, will see."] This judgment is repeated in de Maistre's book on the pope. *"La révolution française ne resemble à rien de ce qu'on a vu dans les temps passés. Elle est satanique dans son essence."*[14] ["The French Revolution resembles nothing ever seen. It is satanic in essence."]

The very de Maistre who rejects the revolution as a satanic revolt discovers traces of divine providence in it. He justifies it as the providential judgment of God called down upon the French nation:

> Il fallait que la grande épuration s'accomplît, et que les yeux fussent frappés; il fallait que le métal français, dégagé de ses scories aigres et impures, parvînt plus net et plus malléable entre les mains du roi futur. Sans doute, la Providence n'a pas besoin de punir dans le temps pour justifier ses voies; mais, à cette époque, elle se met à notre portée et punit comme un tribunal humain.[15] [It was necessary that the great purge fulfil itself, and that our eyes be beaten; it was necessary that the French metal, freed from its sharp and impure defects, come out cleaner and more malleable in the hands of a future king. Doubtless, providence has no need to inflict punishment here on earth in order to justify its ways; but in

---

[13] *Considérations, loc. cit.*, p. 66.
[14] *Du Pape, Oeuvres*, III, 12.
[15] *Considérations*, pp. 17–18.

that particular span of time it put itself within our reach and meted out punishment in the manner of a human tribunal.]

The revolution, though satanic, is at the same time a messianic event which introduces a new time, a new religious epoch.

How can we explain the strange ambiguity in these statements? The ambiguity is resolved when we consider that de Maistre is concerned, first, with man and then with history. As a work of men, the revolution appears satanic, a revolt against God. As divine punishment, a *révolution décretée*, however, it appears as a well-earned punishment that leads to rectification and renewal. In this sense, pessimistic condemnation and eudemonic justification are, for de Maistre, not opposed. They are sides of the same coin. The uninitiated eye will see the revolution only as an accumulation of senseless horrors. The wise man, however, perceives the secret order which reigns in the disorder.

How human liberty and divine providence coexist in history is metaphorically expressed by de Maistre in the *Considérations*. A flexible chain holds men to the throne of the Supreme Being; *librement esclaves*, (voluntary slaves), men are tools in the hands of the eternal geometer, *"qui sait étendre, restreindre, arrêter ou diriger, la volonté sans altérer sa nature."*[16] ["Who knows how to stretch, restrain, stop, or direct the will without altering its nature."] When man seeks to disengage himself from his state of dependence, God shortens the chain and thus humiliates him with blind submission. This happens especially in times of revolution: *"dans les temps de révolutions, la chaîne qui lie l'homme se raccourcit brusquement, son action diminue, et les moyens trempent."*[17] ["During revolutionary times the chain which connects with man is suddenly shortened, his actions diminish and

[16] *Considérations*, p. 1.
[17] *Considérations*, p. 3.

the means deceive."] Man, who passes himself off as a creator, thus becomes a puppet in the hands of providence. The more self-assured he is, the more he proves his historic impotence.

On a remarqué, avec grande raison, que la révolution française mène les hommes plus que les hommes ne la mènent. Cette observation est de la plus grande justesse; et quoiqu'on puissé l'appliquer plus ou moins à toutes les grandes révolutions, cependant elle n'a jamais été plus frappante qu'à cette époque.[18] [It has been said and rightly so that the revolution guided men, and not men the revolution. This remark is indeed right, and even though one might apply it more or less to all the great revolutions, it was never more clearly true than at that epoch.]

With these words de Maistre disassociates himself from all revolutionary expectations, from all reliance upon man's arbitrary power of decision. To enlightened deism he opposed a concept of history that stresses man's impotence and God's omnipotence. His anthropology is pessimistic. Man is nothing; he is unable to create anything that endures; his will is weak, his reason a pale light which leads him astray. What delusion, then, to believe that men could give themselves a constitution! Nothing is more erroneous, but—as de Maistre states regretfully—it has not disappeared, the catastrophe of the revolution notwithstanding.

L'homme ne peut faire une constitution, et nulle constitution légitime ne saurait être écrite. . . . Seulement, lorsque la société se trouve déjà constituée, sans qu'on puisse dire comment, il est possible de faire déclarer ou expliquer par écrit certains articles particuliers; mais presque toujours ces déclarations sont l'effet ou la cause de très grands maux, et toujours

---

[18] *Considérations*, p. 5.

elles coûtent aux peuples plus qu'elles ne valent.[19] [Man cannot make a constitution, and no legitimate constitution will
ever be written. . . . Only when society finds itself constituted,
without anyone being able to say how, is it possible to make
explicit or to explain certain articles in writing—but nearly
always they are the effects or the cause of evil and the people
more than they are worth.]

That the revolution dared to re-establish the political world
par la seule raison was its real crime for de Maistre. At the same
time he sees in this its metaphysical blindness, the failure to
realize that man is not a creator.

The revolution is satanic, because it expresses the human
passion to revolt. It is divine, because it is the judgment of
providence.

> La première condition d'une révolution décrétée, c'est que
> tout ce qui pourrait la prévenir n'existe pas et que rien
> ne réussisse à ceux qui veulent l'empêcher.[20] [The first con-
> dition for a sanctioned revolution is that everything to prevent
> it is absent and that nothing works out for those who want
> to avoid it.]

This provides a proof that the revolution did not proceed from
human arbitrariness but was an act of divine retaliation. Another
proof is to be found in the consequences of the revolution. Conditions in France show that, far from having destroyed it, the
revolution prepared for the kingdom's return and its coming
triumph.

> La France et la monarchie ne pouvaient pas être sauvées que
> par le jacobinisme.[21] . . . Tous les monstres que la révolution a

---

[19] "Essai sur le principe générateur des constitutions politiques," *Oeuvres*, I. 39.
[20] *Considérations*, p. 4.
[21] *Considérations*, p. 20.

enfantés, n'ont travaillé, suivant les apparences, que pour la royauté.[22] [France and monarchism were saved only by Jacobinism. All the monsters which the revolution spawned have, apparently, only contributed toward the kingdom.]

The church, too, was renewed in the course of the revolution.

Le premier coup porté à l'Église fut l'envahissement de ses propriétés; le second fut le serment constitutionnel: et ces deux opérations tyranniques commencèrent le régéneration.[23] [The first blow which the church sustained was the invasion of her properties, the second the constitutional oath: these two tyrannical actions were the start of her regeneration.]

Thus, the effects of the revolution turned out to be blessings.

En vérité, on serait tenté de croire que la révolution politique n'est qu'un objet secondaire du grand plan qui se déroule devant nous avec une majesté terrible.[24] [Actually, it is tempting to believe that political revolution is only a secondary part of the Great Plan taking place before our eyes in all its terrible majesty.]

De Maistre was not the only person seeking a theological interpretation of the revolution in those years. At the same time, Louis-Claude de Saint Martin, then an unknown philosopher, was uttering similar thoughts.[25] Nothing could be more enlightening about the first hesitant attempts of historical thinking to come to terms with the unknown quantity "revolution" than a comparison of these two thinkers, who were in many ways akin to each other although they lived through the revolution in dif-

[22] *Considérations*, p. 22.
[23] *Considérations*, p. 26.
[24] *Considérations*, pp. 28–29.
[25] L.-Cl. de Saint-Martin, *Lettre à un ami ou considérations politiques, philosophiques et religieuses sur la révolution française* (Paris, 1795).

ferent ways and different places.²⁶ Like de Maistre, Saint-Martin saw in the revolution *"l'exécution d'un decret formel de la Providence"*²⁷ ["the execution of a formal decree of providence"], and the events through which France had passed in 1789 seemed to him an *"image du judgement dernier"*²⁸ ["a vision of the Last Judgment"]. Like de Maistre, he concluded his apocalyptic reflections with an optimistic image of the future. In his eyes the revolution was the beginning of a political and religious upheaval which would transform the faith and its institutions, replacing the letter by the spirit and leading the kingdom of man into the kingdom of God. A prince of peace, *vrai commissionaire de Dieu*,²⁹ would govern the peoples and the blood-soaked reign of the French Revolution would be transformed into the kingdom of truth and justice.

De Maistre takes up this same thought but does so in a way that moderates Saint-Martin's optimism. He will not explain the future. His are only conjectures about the future, conjectures which may hit upon the truth or miss it completely. Where the concept of providence, in Saint-Martin, is completely absorbed by the historic event, there is for de Maistre an area between divine will and its human embodiment which liberty may use for submissive obedience or satanic revolt. De Maistre thus escapes having to interpret and justify history in every detail. He avoids the sort of panlogism which questions the ethical ordering of historical events and man's historical responsibility. As a work of man, the revolution remains indictable; that providence uses

---

²⁶ On the relationship between Saint-Martin and de Maistre, cf. Sainte-Beuve, *Portraits littéraires*, II (Paris, 1836), 422 ff.; A. Franck, in *Journal des Savants* (Paris, 1880), pp. 246–56, 269–76, and 329–45; A. Viatte, *Les sources occultes du Romantisme* (Paris, 1928), I, 279.

²⁷ *Lettre à un ami*, pp. 73–74.
²⁸ *Lettre à un ami*, p. 12.
²⁹ *Lettre à un ami*, p. 60.

it for its proper aims does not cancel its *caractère satanique*.

De Maistre was no blind reactionary, belittling the disagreeable present in favor of an idealized past. He is outspoken in his feeling for the spiritual decay of France in the eighteenth century, for the dissolution of law and morality which had started as early as the regency. Saint-Martin's interpretation of the revolution is welcome to him because it permits him to see a divine judgment in the events of 1789. "*Si la Providence efface, sans doute c'est pour écrire.*"[30] ["When Providence wipes the slate clean, it is certainly done so she can write again."]

Criticism of the past is above all criticism of Gallicanism. "*Pourquoi dit-on l'Église gallicane, comme on dit l'Église anglicane?*" ["Why do we speak of the Gallican church as one does about the Anglican church?"] We find in a pamphlet by de Maistre which appeared in 1817 under the title, *De l'Église gallicane dans son rapport avec le Saint-Siège* ("On the Gallican Church and Its Rapports with the Holy See"):

> Quelquefois on serait tenté de croire qu'il y avait dans cette Église quelque chose de particulier qui lui donnait je ne sais quelle saillie hors de la grande superficie catholique, et que ce quelque chose devait être nommé comme tout ce qui existe.[31] [Sometimes it is tempting to believe that there was something special within that church which gave it some sort of eminence above the great surface of Catholicism and that this thing should have a name like everything else that exists.]

The Gallican church had forgotten that it was only a province of the *empire catholique* and that there are no special credos in this regime. What do expressions like "we believe" or "we do not believe," which are common in the French church, mean?

---

[30] *Considérations*, p. 28.
[31] *De l'Église gallicane*, Oeuvres IV, 1.

"Comme si le reste de l'Église était tenu de se tenir à ce qu'on tenait en France!" ["As if the rest of the church were beholden to observe what one observed in France!"] The word "we" in the Catholic community makes no sense except if it applies to everybody. Gallican separatism is therefore religious heresy. The glory of the French church lies in its professing a universal truth, and not in persevering in a *"caractère particulier. C'est là notre gloire, c'est là notre caractère distinctif, et c'est manifestement celui de la vérité."*[32] ["Here is our glory, here is our special character and this is evidently the one of truth."]

Where does the *esprit de schisme*, the spirit of schism, which had spread through the French church come from? De Maistre unhesitatingly answers: it derives from the Reformation. Calvinism had caused the parliaments of France to refuse the Tridentine reforms. Jansenism filled the French church with a spirit of revolt against Rome.

> Protestant dans le XVIe siècle, frondeur et janséniste dans le XVIIe, philosophe enfin, et républicain dans les dernières années de sa vie, trop souvent le parlement s'est montré en contradiction avec les véritables maximes fondamentales de l'État.[33] [Protestant during the sixteenth century, rebel and Jansenist in the seventeenth, finally philosopher and republican in the last years of its life, parliament found itself too often in conflict with the true and basic guidelines of the state.]

According to de Maistre, it was the parliaments and the School of Port-Royal, the Calvanistic laity and the Jansenist clergy, who were the real carriers of the spirit of reform in France.

> Le parlement devint en totalité un corps véritablement

[32] De l'Église gallicane, loc. cit., p. 3.
[33] De l'Église gallicane, p. 7.

anti-catholique, et tel que, sans l'instinct royal de la maison de Bourbon et sans l'influence aristocratique du clergé . . . la France eût été conduite infailliblement à un schism absolu.[34] [Parliament as a whole became so truly an anti-Catholic body that without the royal instinct of the House of Bourbon and without the influence of the aristocratic clergy France would surely have been led to total schism.]

The dawn of reform thinking in French society had consequences not exclusively religious. It had brought changes in the complete politico-religious structure of the *ancien régime*. For Calvinism was essentially democratic and, therefore, incompatible with the monarchic state. There was a direct link between the ecclesiastical presbyterianism of the lower clergy and political democracy. Thus, France's catastrophe was simultaneously political and religious: together with the absolutistic state the revolution destroyed the Gallican church.

But since Gallicanism and Protestantism were intertwined, de Maistre's program of reform could not call for a return to Gallicanism. It had to call for a return to the universal church and to its visible head, the pope. This thought is carried to its utmost logical consequences in de Maistre's main work, *Du Pape*. Not only is the concept of papal infallibility defined in a way that anticipates the declarations of Vatican I: the papacy is granted jurisdiction over secular sovereignties exceeding what sixteenth century doctrine had granted the Holy See.[35] De Maistre sketches

[34] *De l'Église gallicane*, p. 15.
[35] *Du Pape*, Oeuvres, III, p. 17 ff. and 223 ff. As for De Maistre, however, infallibility is not vested in the transcendental realm; it is just another term for sovereignty which *ex definitione* is component to any political power. "L'infailli-bilité dans l'ordre spirituel, et la souveraineté dans l'ordre temporel, sont deux mots parfaitement synonymes. L'un et l'autre expriment . . . cette haute puissance qui les domine toutes, dont toutes les autres dérivent, qui gouverne et n'est pas gouvernée, qui juge et n'est pas jugée" (*loc. cit.*, p. 18).

a Christian League of Nations under the spiritual leadership of the pope.[36]

L'hypothèse de toutes les souverainetés chrétiennes réunies par la fraternité religieuse en une sorte de republique universelle, sous la suprématie mesurée du pouvoir spirituel suprême; cette hypothèse, dis-je, n'avait rien de choquant, et pouvait même se présenter à la raison, comme supérieure à l'institution des Amphictyons. Je ne vois pas que les temps modernes aient imaginé rien de meilleur, ni même d'aussi bon. Qui sait ce que serait arrivé si la théocratie, la politique et la science avaient pu se mettre tranquillement en équilibre, comme il arrive toujours lorsque les éléments sont abandonnés à eux-mêmes, et qu'on fait faire le temps.[37] [If it is hypothesized that all Christian sovereignties are united through religious brotherly love into a kind of universal republic under the measured supremacy of a spiritual power, such a hypothesis, as I said, has nothing shocking about it and could even be presented to reason as superior to the institution of Amphitryon. I cannot see that modern times have envisioned anything better or as good. Who knows what would have happened if theology, politics, and science had had a chance to find their equilibrium, as always happens when the elements are left to themselves and time is left to work.]

There is no doubt that de Maistre's use of the spiritual principle of organization, the *pouvoir spirituel*, was the result of his experiences with the revolution. When de Maistre's book on the pope appeared, the revolutionary period and Napoleon's reign over Europe were only a few years past. The failures of the tyrant, first to re-order Europe and then his catastrophe in Russia, his defeat at Waterloo, and the Congress of Vienna, were still fresh in everyone's memory. The plans for unions and leagues of

[36] Du Pape, p. 233.
[37] Du Pape, p. 247.

nations, fashionable after 1815 and finally having taken shape—
in a form far from de Maistre's theocratic concepts—in the Holy
Alliance of Tsar Alexander I, gave his book its historical background and political resonance. They originated from the same
mood which pervades his book on the pope: as a result of the
malaise of destructive forces released by the centrifugal powers
of the revolution, all of Europe clamored for spiritual, religious,
and political unity.

Therefore, the political motives behind de Maistre's theological construction cannot be overlooked. His concern was not really
the defense or restoration of papal rights, but the delimiting of
absolute political power. Sovereignty needs a counterweight in
order to prevent its deterioration into limitless despotism: *"c'est
une loi, c'est une coutume, c'est la conscience, c'est une tiare,
c'est un poignard; mais c'est toujours quelque chose."* ["It may
be a law, a custom, the conscience, a tiare, a dagger, but it is
always something."] Why not the pope? Was not the pope's
authority erected in the Middle Ages *"pour faire équilibre à la
souveraineté temporelle, et la rendre supportable aux hommes"*[38]
["to create a balance to temporal sovereignty and to make it supportable to men"]? De Maistre based his claim for a *potestas
indirecta in temporalibus* on political arguments, just as he sup-
ports his claims concerning papal infallibility on questions of
faith not by theological, but by political-philosophical, reasoning.
The limitation of powers and the control of sovereignty are the
main motives behind his political theology. Apart from its primarily political argumentation, the importance of de Maistre's
work is to be found in his forceful rejection of a state power comprising at the same time both politics and religion. It is here that
the figure of the Savoyard noblemen, often scorned as a reactionary, takes on astonishingly modern, even liberal traits. By pitting

---

[38] *Du Pape*, p. 230.

the spiritual power of the church against the political absolutism of the revolutionary state, he returns to the classical theory of double powers, a concept opposed by the revolution which harkened to the *bonne politie* of the states of antiquity.

De Maistre entered history as the founder of "ultramontanism." His proposals for political reform have been given much less attention. In spite of his emphatic proclamations of loyalty to the king, his monarchism always seems to have a kind of declamatory character. De Maistre could not overlook the fact of the monarchy's great guilt in the degeneration of the *ancien régime's* relations with the church (in which he himself sees the cancer of the pre-revolutionary form of state and the main cause of the revolution); he bitterly reproached Louis XIV in the dispute over the regalia.[39] And the Bourbons who continued the state-church usages of pre-revolutionary times and took over the Napoleonic concordat together with all the organic articles, found no favor in his eyes. Thus, he does not give an absolute justification to monarchy: the legitimacy of the forms of state is made entirely dependent upon the proof of time.[40] It was only de Bonald who tried to furnish monarchy with a background of divine law through theological-political analogies.

De BONALD

De Bonald is the systematizer among traditionalists.[41] Though more sober and plain than de Maistre with his paradoxes, de

[39] *De l'Église gallicane*, p. 117 ff.
[40] "Quant à la légitimité . . . Dieu s'explique par son premier ministre au département de ce monde, le temps" (*Essai sur le principe générateur, loc. cit.*, p. 38).
[41] De Bonald's works are quoted according to the edition of Migne, *Oeuvres complètes de M. de Bonald* (3 vols.; Paris, 1859). On de Bonald we have only a small literature; for an introduction, see H. Moulinier, *De Bonald* (Paris, 1916). The best monograph (the first complete description of de Bonald's philosophy) is by R. Spaemann (see *supra*, n. 1).

Bonald possesses qualities which the other lacks: accuracy, tough-
ness of mind and power to convince philosophically. If de Maistre is anti-Voltairian in style and substance, de Bonald is similarly
anti-Rousseau: he develops the social theory of the traditionalists.[42]

In de Bonald's criticism of the revolution the arguments are
the same as those already encountered in de Maistre. The revolution reveals the impotence of the individual and the impotence
of reason; it demonstrates that its preconditions—individualism
and rationalism—are brittle. History has put the theories of Enlightenment to the test and found them lacking. The social contract of Rousseau cannot serve as the foundation of states. De
Bonald draws the philosophical conclusions of 1789 by affirming
the primacy of society over the individual and the subordination
of individual reason to collective reason. In both regards he goes
far beyond de Maistre.[43]

Man does not form society; society forms man. "*L'homme
n'existe que pour la société, la société ne le forme que pour elle-
même,*" this is the opening volley of his book, *Théorie du pouvoir politique et religieux.*[44] In the introduction he writes: the
origin of society does not lie in an act of human will, nor is
its concrete historical form determined by human reason. Society
does not need a constitution; it is already constituted according
to its innate law.

> L'homme ne peut pas plus donner une constitution à la
> société politique qu'il ne peut donner la pesanteur aux corps,
> ou l'étendue à la matière; bien loin de pouvoir constituer la
> société, l'homme, par son intervention, ne peut empêcher que
> la société ne se constitue, ou, pour parler plus exactement, ne

[42] P. R. Rohden, *op. cit.*, pp. 13 ff.
[43] Michel, *op. cit.*, pp. 113 ff., and Bellamy, *op. cit.*, pp. 13 ff.
[44] *Théorie du pouvoir*, Oeuvres, I, 123.

peut que retarder le succès des efforts qu'elle fait pour par-
venir à sa constitution naturelle.[45] [It is as possible for man
to give political society a constitution as it is for him to determine how heavy his body will be or to stretch matter; far
from constituting society, man's intervention cannot prevent
society from constituting itself, or, to put it more precisely,
he cannot prevent the success of the efforts society makes to
achieve its natural constitution.]

With this the ground is cut out from under Rousseau's idea of
social contract. For if society finds its own best form by its very
nature, there is no need for man's active intervention; it follows
that it is no longer necessary (and, incidentally, no longer possible) to re-establish state power on the grounds of social agree-
ments or to correct existing constitutions to the standard of
natural law. The relationship of nature-culture, individual-society
also shifts quantitatively: the natural, in de Bonald, is no longer
the norm; rather, it is a undeveloped stage which must be left
behind if culture is to originate at all. Thus, it is no surprise that
the author of the *Pouvoir politique* also attacks the anthropologi-
cal tenets of the *Contrat social*. He does it with the kind of anti-
thetical logic characteristic of him: "*Nous sommes mauvais par
nature, bons par la société,*"[46] we read in the *Pensées* (first published in 1815). This is the antithesis of Rousseau's statement of
a natural human innocence spoiled by the effects of culture.

Not only the individual, but reason, too, for de Bonald is *fille
de la Cité.*[47] Left to itself, without the corrective influence of
society, individual thought goes astray; only the *quod ubique,
quod omnibus,* is assurance that reason will not stray from the
path of truth. De Maistre had written: "*On ne raisonne que trop*

[45] *Loc. cit.,* p. 122.
[46] *Pensées, Oeuvres choisies,* ed. by de Montesquieu (Paris, 1908), p. 293.
[47] J. Lacroix, *op. cit.,* p. 30.

en France, et le raisonnement en bannit la raison."[48] ["We reason too much in France and the arguments ban reason."] De
Bonald, who similarly distinguished between argumentation and
reasoning, makes individual reason dependent upon a *raison générale*, which assumes the character of infallibility. He ties truth
to the norms of society, just as de Maistre tied it to the testimony
of time. This, however, by no means signifies that truth for him
is one with the social-historical movement; society, as a form en-
compassing individuals, has a better chance to preserve undimin-
ished the deposit of truth for mankind and to transmit it to
future generations. Unable to reach truth on their own, men
derive truth from tradition, the mediators of which are family,
community, people, and church. This tradition, however, is immediately connected with God through a *révélation primitive*. It
is based upon language, which man has received, not invented.[49]
Together with language, he receives at birth the religious and
ethical truths which he needs for coexistence with other men:
the existence of God, the immortality of the soul, the rules of
social behavior, and the laws of politics.

The world order—both divine and natural—does not develop
from the individual will or sovereign reason. It originates in the
rhythm of the Trinity that is imprinted on the structure of the
world.

> Ainsi, tout ce qu'il y a de plus général au monde et dans
> nos idées est soumis à une combinaison ternaire: trois caté-
> gories d'êtres dans l'univers: cause, moyen, effet; trois per-
> sonnes dans la société: pouvoir, ministre, sujet; trois temps
> dans la durée: passé, présent, futur; trois dimensions dans

---

[48] *Considérations, loc. cit.*, p. 131.
[49] This idea, which prevails throughout de Bonald's entire work, is developed
in the second chapter of the *Recherches philosophiques* (Oeuvres, III, 61 ff.).

l'espace: longueur, largeur, profondeur.[50] [Thus, everything which is most common in the world and in our ideas is subject to a trinitarian combination: three categories of beings in the universe; cause, means, and effect; three persons in society: power, ministry, subject; three times: past, present, future; three dimensions in space: length, breadth, depth.]

This trinitarian organization pervades the whole of political and social life. It is the inherent law of states. In de Bonald's political thinking the attachment to the trinitarian scheme has two consequences: first, since trinity in its essence is unity, it brings the concept of *unité des pouvoirs* into the focus of his social theory, with the consequence that the separation of powers in the political sphere is rejected just as is the variety and the variability of extra-Catholic denominations. On the other hand, the trinitarian concept of society prevents the transformation of political unity, so necessary for the existence of the state, into blind despotism; for in spite of all the concentration of powers the three "social persons" *pouvoir, ministre,* and *sujet* (ministers, power, subject) remain separate in de Bonald's social theory. The *Théorie du pouvoir* keeps a careful balance between the "homogeneity" and the "distinction" of the social members: it founds the inner order of its political power precisely upon the state of tension which prevails between them. Thus democracy and despotic monarchy are rejected because under them there is a *confusion de personnes.* Only *royal* monarchy is a legitimate form of state, because it guarantees both the homogeneity of *pouvoir* (through heredity) and the mutual independence of government and people. On the other hand, de Bonald continuously stresses the functional interchangeability of *pouvoir, ministre,* and *sujet* in

[50] *Démonstration philosophique de principe constitutif de la société,* Oeuvres, I, 83 ff.

society. In his *Demonstration philosophique du principe constituif de la société*, he writes:

> Ainsi le même homme qui est sujet dans la société, y peut être ministre, s'il remplit des fonctions politiques, et il est pouvoir dans sa famille: et les rois eux-mêmes sujets, comme les autres hommes de la Divinité, ne sont, comme les chefs de la société, que les premiers ministres du pouvoir divin pour faire le bien, minister Dei in bonum, dit l'Apôtre (Rom. 13:4), et ils sont comme rois, pouvoir dans la société civile, et comme homme, pouvoir dans leurs familles.[51] [Thus the very man who is a subject in society can be a minister if he fulfils political functions and a power within his family. And kings, themselves subject like other men to the Divinity, as heads of society are nothing more than prime ministers of that divine power to do good, *minister Dei bonum* as the Apostle Paul says in Rom. 13:4, and as kings they are a power in civic society and a power in their families.]

The orders of family, state, and religion are like concentric circles, encompassed by the ring of the threefold natural law which is structured as *original cause, means,* and *effect*. This law is but philosophical shorthand for the Holy Trinity.[52]

The glance which sweeps from this universalist vision to French history sees only the spirit of schism at work, as de Maistre had before, a schism which destroyed the original unity of politics and religion. Like de Maistre, de Bonald considers presbyterianism the precursor of revolutionary democracy, and he,

---

[51] *Loc. cit.*, p. 88 ff.

[52] On the theological doubtfulness of a "political theology," cf. E. Peterson, "Der Monotheismus als politisches Problem," in *Theologische Traktate* (Munich, 1951), pp. 45–147, against C. Schmitt, *Politische Theologie* (Munich, 1922). As to the further continuation of de Bonald's "trinity positivism" in the philosophy of Comte see H. de Lubac, *Le drame de l'humanisme athée* (Paris, 1945), II, 3.

too, points out the connection between the humanitarian salva-
tionist mood of the revolution and the apocalyptic mood of its
clerical defenders. *"Les hommes qui ont voulu faire revivre les
temps de la primitive Église, ont toujours ramené les sociétés
politiques à leur enfance."*[53] ["The men who wanted to revive
the times of the primitive church always brought political societies back to their infancies."] Return to the primitive church is
impossible because the social preconditions of primitive Christianity no longer exist. Attempts at restoration, as made by Fauchet and Grégoire, signify for de Bonald only the state of crisis
in society.[54] An ordered society does not seek change, nor does it
need a constitution in order permanently to establish its momentary political state. *"Une nation qui demande une constitution à
des législateurs ressemble . . . à un malade qui prierait son méde-
cin de lui faire un tempérament."*[55] ["A nation which demands
a constitution from its legislators resembles a sick man who begs
his physician to give him a new body."]

De Bonald is blind to all historic connections except the sequence of traditional motivations by which the revolution is
explained by the Enlightenment and the Enlightenment by the
Reformation. His desire to preserve the political and religious
mission of France induces him, like de Maistre, to assume an
attitude which exclusively looks outside and to others on whom
to lay the responsibility for the fate of France. Occasionally,
however, there is a glimpse of recognition—as for instance in
the intelligent essay on the *Peace of Westphalia*[56]—that the
ésprit du schism had its origin, not in the Reformation, but in-
side France itself, the kind of France which, in alliance with

[53] *Pensées, Oeuvres,* III, 1351.
[54] *Le Traité de Westphalie, Oeuvres,* II, 491 f.
[55] *Pensées, Oeuvres,* III, 1339.
[56] *Le Traité de Westphalie, et celui de Campo-Formio, Oeuvres,* II, 479–516.

Turks and Swedes, destroyed Catholic ecumenicity. But de Bonald quickly passes over these things. Likewise, he is not at all susceptible to the idea of the political functionalization of Catholicism in the *ancien régime* and its fatal consequences for religion. In contrast to de Maistre, he hardly criticizes Gallicanism. His concept of church is as static as his theory of society: neither state nor church develop; their form is fixed according to eternal designs. And the system of social harmony which unites the two was the state of things under the old monarchy.

LAMENNAIS

Lamennais's *Essai sur l'indifférence en matière de religion*[57] is a synthesis of the thoughts of de Maistre and de Bonald. This four-volume work is the theological side of traditionalism. The precedence of society to the individual, of collective reason to individual reason, is posited as the leading principle of Catholic dogma: the truth of dogma rests entirely upon the *sens commun* of humanity. The *quod semper, quod ubique, quod omnibus* is, for the Catholic religion, proof of truth. There is no other. In this appeal to society and the *raison générale*, Lamennais sees the only possibility of refuting Cartesian individualism: "*Si l'on rejette mes thèses, je ne vois aucun moyen de défendre solidement la religion.*"[58] ["If my thesis is rejected, I see no other way of defending religion forcefully."]

The basic ideas of Lamennais' theological system are developed in *Défense de l'Essai*, a response to his critics published in 1818.[59] Here Lamennais examines the question of whether and

---

[57] F. de Lamennais, *Oeuvres complètes*, (12 vols.; Paris, 1836/37), Vols. III and IV.

[58] As quoted by Bellamy, *op. cit.*, p. 15.

[59] *Oeuvres*, Vol. V.

how philosophical thinking can arrive at the truth. His point of
departure is the contrast between philosophy—especially in its
modern garb—and what he calls the traditional verities.

En remontant à l'origine de la philosophie, et en l'obser-
vant à toutes les époques de sa durée, nous avons constaté un
fait important, c'est qu'en enseignant à l'homme à chercher
la vérité dans sa raison seule, elle a partout ébranlé les vérités
traditionnelles, et perdu les peuples en les précipitant dans le
doute et dans l'erreur.[60] [By returning to the beginning of
philosophy and studying it in all the epochs of its history, we
are able to derive an important fact: by teaching man to seek
the truth only in reason, philosophy has shaken the traditional verities and lost the people by throwing them into
doubt and error.] Cherchant ensuite la raison de ce fait, nous
avons vu que toute philosophie qui place le principe de certitude dans l'homme individuel ne peut en effet donner de
base solide à ses croyances, ni de règle sûre à ses jugements.
[Consequently, in seeking the reason for this we have seen
that any philosophy which places the principle of certitude
within individual man cannot really give his belief a solid
basis or a ruling for his judgment.]

Cartesian philosophy—toward which this is chiefly directed—
cannot serve as a basis for belief. It leads only to skepticism and
error. Man is brought to truth, not through his individual reason,
but through the needs of his human nature.

En effet la nature force tous les hommes de croire mille
choses dont il est aussi impossible de démontrer la vérité,
qu'il est impossible d'en douter. [Actually nature forces man

[60] Lamennais does not mean just philosophy. As can be judged from the following sentence, he refers to a specific school of philosophy. "*En enseignant*" therefore is to be understood conditionally.

to believe a thousand things for which it is impossible either
to prove their truth or to doubt.]

Just as belief is a fundamental need of human nature, it is also
the presupposition of all intellectual perception. Sure knowledge,
therefore, can be gained only on the ground of a common religious conviction.

> Nous sommes donc convenu d'admettre comme vrai ce
> que tous les hommes croient invinciblement. Cette foi invin-
> cible, universelle, est pour nous la base de la certitude; et
> nous avons montré qu'en effet si on rejette cette base, si on
> suppose que ce que tous les hommes croient vrai puisse être
> faux, il n'y a plus de certitude possible, plus de vérité, plus
> de raison humaine. [We have therefore agreed to admit as
> true what all men believe to be unarguable. This universal,
> invincible faith is our basis of certitude; and we have actually
> shown that, if this basis is rejected, if one thinks that what all
> men believe to be true may be false, certitude is no longer
> possible, nor is truth nor human reason.]

Thus, faith becomes the logical precondition of knowledge. It
precedes perception. It lends to the efforts of thinkers the proof
which they need to earn the title of philosophy: that sum of undoubted and generally recognized statements together form what
is called truth. In the universality and cogency of these statements, Lamennais finds the actual character of truth; lacking
these characteristics they are nothing but the monstrosities of
individual reason, without binding power on people, nation, or
society. The truth, basically, is only what is recognized as truth
by everybody.

> L'uniformité des perceptions et l'accord des jugements est
> le caractère de la vérité; cette uniformité et cet accord, qui
> nous sont connus par le témoignage, constituent ce que nous

appelons la raison générale ou l'autorité: l'autorité ou la raison générale est donc la règle de la raison individuelle. [The
uniformity of perceptions and the harmony of judgments
make up the character of truth; this uniformity and this harmony, known through testimony, constitute what we call
general reason or authority: authority or genearl reason is
therefore the rule of individual reason.]

When philosophy—and again Lamennais has Cartesian philosophy in mind—departs from the principle that what individual
reason recognizes as being reasonable is also true it must first
bring proof of this thesis in the form of some new, binding
authority; in other words, it must show that the innumerable
individual authorities for reason, into which it dissolves even general thinking, necessarily arrive at an inner accord even when
they lack the common ground of the *vérités traditionelles*. Yet
modern philosophy has not yet succeeded in demonstrating this
kind of authorization. The anarchism of the revolution gave birth
to no truth recognized by everybody. Thus, the defenders of religion have easy going: by pointing up the self-contradiction of
a philosophy which postulates the truth as the creation of the
individual but which cannot create it itself and splits up into
various sects and schools, it upsets the apparent security of philosophical thought and smoothes the way for a return to the traditional foundations of faith.

   Appliquant . . . aux controverses contre les athées et les
déistes le principe d'autorité, on force tous les énnemis du
christianisme à en reconnaître la vérité ou à nier leur propre
raison.[61] [By applying the principle of authority to the contro-
versies between atheists and deists, all the enemies of Christi-

[61] *Défense de l'Essai*, pp. 171–73.

anity are forced to recognize its truth or to negate their own reason.]

Lamennais defended this apologetics passionately against all attacks, including those from the Catholic side. Thus he remarks at the place already cited in *Défense de l'Essai* (1818):

> C'est donc bien vainement, qu'on attaque; elle n'est pas moins inébranlable que la vérité catholique elle-même: et nous sommes arrivés à des temps où, contraints de ramener de loin, et comme des extrémités de l'erreur, un grand nombre d'esprits à cette vérité sainte, on a dû mieux reconnaître la voie qui y conduit, et s'assurer qu'il n'existe qu'une.[62] [It is therefore vain to attack it, for it is as unshakable as a Catholic verity itself; we have come to the point when, forced to call back a great number of spirits to this holy truth from the extreme borders of error, we had to recognize better the path which leads there and to assure ourselves that there is only one.]

Only one path can lead from agnosticism back to faith, only one sufficiently strong proof can be produced against unbelief: the very proof which the *raison générale* itself delivers against the *raisons particulieres*, splintered into their thousand fragments. It is love's labors lost to found an apologetics on the tottering foundations of individual reason. Lamennais sees in such attempts only a Cartesian bias.

> [He] flings the accusation into the face of his adversaries that in fighting the revolutionary spirit they hold to a method which puts the reason of the individual in the place of a "*sens commun*" and, which since it is not sufficient, it must logically lead to a skepticism in no way capable of successfully

[62] Loc. cit.

defending religion. He believed that his apologetics of the sens commun would lead to a recognition, not only of the indissoluble unity between faith and knowledge, church and society, authority and freedom, but that it would also provide the secure basis for progress and human liberty.[63]

In fact, Lamennais had good reason to defend his system as the cornerstone of traditionalism against all attacks; for if Christianity's claim to truth was in doubt, not only would the motivation for his apologetic efforts disappear but so would the key to the political and ethical restoration demanded by de Maistre and de Bonald.

The church, however, did not make the apologetics of the traditionalists her own. It certainly was not political prejudice which prevented her from doing so. For the program of monarchic restoration which Lamennais shared in the beginning with de Maistre and de Bonald had some sympathy in clerical circles: the royalist attitude of a majority of the clergy after 1815 is undoubted.[64] It was considerations of theology that militated against the acceptance of Lamennais' proposals. The criticism of reason, which the author of the Essai sur l'indifférence took over from de Maistre and de Bonald, was in sharp conflict with Catholic dogma itself. According to Catholic teaching, the individual reason is able to recognize religious truth and, above all, the existence of God by its own light. For such a perception there is considered to be no need for fideistic submission of the intel-

[63] Gurian, Ideen, p. 114.
[64] On these questions, which here can be dealt with only marginally, see Ch. Pouthas, "Le Clergé sous la Monarchie Constitutionelle 1814–1848," in Revue d'histoire de l'Église de France, XXIX (1943), 19–53, and his "Histoire politique de la Restauration" (mimeographed paper). The best introduction to this period is given by G. de Bertier de Sauvigny in his dissertation, "Un type d'Ultra-Royaliste: le comte Ferdinand de Bertier (1782–1864) et l'énigme de la Congrégation (Paris, 1948), and in his description, La Restauration (Paris, 1955).

lect to a mere fact of revelation to be accepted but not analyzed. Even when revealed truth is not quite comprehended by reason, this not-grasping is a "not yet"; it will eventually give way to a purer cognition. In the meantime the rule says that faith precedes reason but that this sequence is in keeping with reason proper. According to Augustine's famous dictum, it is a precept of reason that faith precedes reason; where this is not the case, he continues, "there, without doubt, even that little bit of reason which teaches us so, precedes faith."[65] There is no room in Catholic thought either for a complete co-ordination of the difference between faith and knowledge or for a sharp contrasting of these two ways of perception. Rather, man's reason remains the natural point of contact with and the precondition for faith: to deny its efficacy is to destroy the foundations of revelation.[66]

Lamennais, thus, remains far from the modern concept that only the reasonable form of the truth of salvation has made possible Christianity's transmission and its historical existence.[67] At the same time we cannot deny that the beginnings of an historical approach are to be found in Lamennais. Thus the embattled theology of the *sens commun* originated not least in a desire to bring the church closer to the historical movements of mankind than had been possible in the perspective of the teachings which separated world history from salvation history. It was thus that the leading position of Christianity in the historical process of the development of truth would show itself. How this is done, however, is characteristic of Lamennais, whose theological thinking is always above all sociological. Lamennais' common religious spirit always remains detached from the personal existence of the individual. It is a collective being which comes into relation with

[65] *Epistula CXX*, c. 1, 3.
[66] Bellamy, *op. cit.*, p. 15.
[67] W. Kamlah, *Christentum und Geschichtlichkeit*, (2d ed.; Stuttgart, 1951).

the individual only insofar as it imprints the general direction of
the *sens commun* upon his individual reason. It is true that Lamennais later expressly declared the church to be the guardian of
that *sens commun*, because in this way he might protect truth
from the vicissitudes of the spirit of the times. But the coincidence of popular religious spirit and the teaching office of the
church gave the question of the place of the individual and his
liberties in such a theological system greater urgency still. For
did the church not consist of individuals? Did it not lose its significance if understood merely as the external norm of personal
liberty? Was historical reason, which was to be administered and
articulated by the magisterium of the church, independent of
individual religious decisions? It is impossible to disregard the
dynamic consequences implicit in this doctrine of the church. If
the possibility of a personal recognition of truth is done away
with, if truth is recognizable only in the outward order of things,
the character of the church changes with it: from a community
of those united in the faith it becomes a purely positivist instance
of order. This had already become apparent in de Maistre and
de Bonald, whose fideism was basically pure positivism.[68] One
believed in religion because its order was indispensable to a permanent society. This is repeated in Lamennais, if not quite so
obvious. If the form of the church developed in the one case
from the exigencies of the political and social order, in the other
it originated in the historical movement; it was bound to change
as the social forms in which it lived changed. We must not be
deceived about this by Lamennais' seeing in the church itself
something unhistoric, something independent of history, an institution which caused change but did not suffer change. In fact,
the unification of the popular spirit and the church's magiste-

[68] Gurian, *Lamennais*, p. 78.

rium signified a far-reaching secularization of religion by which the individual, already passive before the ecclesiastical common spirit, lost any possibility of independent action in the face of the historical *sens commun* which completely determined him.[69]

Such a concept of history could lead to a purely conservative attitude, for fideism and conservatism have an inner kinship.[70] But it also could lead the individual toward the path of revolutionary action, since individual resistance was senseless in the face of the inevitability of historical movement and a voluntary enlistment might seem useful and promising. As a matter of fact, there is a revolutionary element hidden next to the conservative one in traditionalism. We have already seen how de Maistre condemned the revolution, on the one hand, as the work of satan, but justified it on the other as a divine necessity. It is rather difficult to justify the demand for a restoration of pre-revolutionary conditions from this position. The longer the revolution lasted, the more the followers of traditionalism were forced to recognize the salvific function of evil in history and its significance as an "apocalyptic moment,"[71] and thus to accept an idea which had to rupture the compactness of their system.

Lamennais, who appeared at the end of the traditionalist movement, recalled Saint-Martin and de Maistre when, in *De la religion*,[72] he interpreted the revolution as a divine judgment.

---

[69] In his introduction to the new edition of the book *"Einheit in der Kirche,"* J. R. Geiselmann refers to similar traits in J. A. Moehler's theory of church (*Kirchenlehre*), which reveals a similar one-way relationship between man's true nature under God and the social structure of the church, understood as a people's church (*Volkskirche*). J. A. Moehler, *Die Einheit in der Kirche*, ed. by J. R. Geiselmann (Cologne-Olten, 1957), pp. 81–82. *Mutatis mutandis* this is also true of Lamennais.

[70] Cf. H. Friedrich, *Montaigne*, pp. 132 ff.

[71] Term used by Gurian, *Ideen*, p. 77.

[72] *De la religion considérée dans ses rapports avec l'ordre politique et civil* (Paris, 1825/26)., cf. esp. chap. v.

But since he also held with de Bonald that the divine order had to have its visible counterpart on earth he was forced to give theological sanction to the political forms that developed out of the revolution. Lamennais' later turn toward democracy was thus only a logical development of his traditionalist thinking. His sentence, *"La Révolution a été une brèche providentielle ouvrant l'avenir au catholicisme"*[73] ["The revolution was a providential breach opening the future for Catholicism"], corresponds to Saint-Martin's description of the revolution as a *decret formel de la Providence.* In this sense it may be said that Lamennais' later condemnation by the church was a condemnation of traditionalism; at the same time the passage through traditionalist teachings was necessary to the growth of Christian Democracy.

The quarrel about traditionalism was not only a dispute between theological schools of thought. It shook the entire French church. In Christian Maréchal who wrote on Lamennais, we can follow the course of the theological disputes in detail.[74] In the political struggles of the times too—and not only in France— one constantly encounters the polemics surrounding traditionalist teachings. This astonishing fact can be explained in that traditionalism, although originally a theory of cognition and a system of fundamental theology, became identified in time with certain conclusions which shifted it from the religious to the political and social spheres. Behind its theological concepts lurked sociological problems. The re-orientation of Catholicism in the post-revolutionary world was at stake. What de Maistre, de Bonald, and Lamennais developed, basically, was nothing but the theological form of an attempt to define the position of the church in post-revolutionary society, a society no longer Christian and not quite de-Christianized. Seen in this double perspective,

[73] *Avenir,* June 29, 1831.
[74] Ch. Maréchal, *La dispute de l'Essai sur l'indifférence* (Paris, 1925).

we can understand the political resonance which the theologumena of the traditionalists, apparently so far removed from the world, found in French public opinion and far beyond: they were accepted because they gave expression to the content of the situation.

Two questions crystallize in this dispute: Gallicanism versus Ultramontanism on the one side; and the constitutional church versus ecclesiastical freedom on the other. The position of French Catholicism had to be defined anew on these two fronts separating the French state and the Catholic ecumene. The questions were intimately connected; ever since the revolution, a change in the degree of liberty of the state immediately signified a correspondingly stronger or weaker link with Rome. The number of open alternatives was narrowed in the situations created by the revolution.[75] Two possibilities were eliminated immediately for French Catholicism: any alliance between the Ultramontane direction and the old constitutional church system or an alliance between Gallicanism and political democracy. Whoever would defend papal power could do so only by simultaneously fighting state influence on the life of the church. Whoever supported the old Gallican constitution of the church was forced to deny, together with the papal claim to sovereignty, the demands of the Catholic laymen who composed the core of the Ultramontane party. Politically, Gallicanism found itself in a similar dilemma: a church delimited in territory, as corresponded to its concept, would have no choice in the age of the national state but to become the tool of the secular power. This secular power was no longer, as it had been under the monarchy, linked to the church by consecration and coronation. For the religious presuppositions of Gallicanism, too, had been destroyed by the

[75] Rhoden, *op. cit.*, p. 272.

revolution: since the *roi trés chrétien* had become a thing of the past, the state itself had become profane.[76] Thus the Gallican church could find its unifying center only in the pope, unless it should decide to be absorbed in political society as a sort of spiritual power.

The Napoleonic concordat left unresolved Catholicism's position in post-revolutionary society. It formulated no definitive solution but created a compromise between the old "establishment" church and the new conditions created by the revolution by assigning Catholicism a position which was weaker than the one it had occupied within the framework of the *ancien régime* but stronger than one it might have obtained in a democratic order. The concordat system was, as Gurian puts it, buoyed by the conviction "that even if the old belief in the Catholic church no longer was the foundation of the state, it was still widely diffused in French society and represented an important factor for the securing of order and peace. This compromise became ever more questionable as its foundation, the fact that the great majority of Frenchmen were Catholic, became more of a fiction."[77] The concordat secured only the external position of the church; with the advance of the democratic movement the social presuppositions which formed the basis of this position changed and with it the questions raised by the revolution returned in new guise.

In the form which de Maistre and de Bonald gave it, the traditionalistic program of reform was tailored to the *roi très chrétien*. It hardly suited the kingdom of the Restoration. At the same time de Maistre had smoothed the path for a return of the French church to the papal order. Should the renewal of the old

---

[76] As the Charte and Louis XVIII's and Charles X's bearing in the course of the coronation demonstrate, this is true even for the restored Bourbon monarchy.

[77] Gurian, *op. cit.*, p. 52 ff.

monarchic order fail, the only remaining guarantee of the future of French Catholicism lay in the papacy.

This orientation back to Rome was the chief legacy left by the author of the book on the pope to French political Catholicism. It outlasted both the Restoration and the philosophical vitality of traditionalism. Whereas traditionalism became a rigidly positivist system after 1830, de Maistre's religious and church-political ideas would continue effective in the changed environment. Religious traditionalism passed through its first metamorphosis in Lamennais' liberal Catholicism.

4: LIBERAL CATHOLICISM AND CHRISTIAN DEMOCRACY (1830-50)

The family tree of the Christian Democratic movement has many branches and a variety of sources, many of them quite divergent.[1] Liberal and socialist Catholics, the scattered adherents of the former constitutional church, descendants of the Saint-Simonists, and romanticists of all religious and political varieties in France have advocated the reconciliation of democracy and the church. Such movements appear as early as the Restoration and take on clearer outline under Louis Philippe between 1830 and 1848. The two revolutions—the bourgeois and the socialist—form the cornerstones of the movement, and they provide a kind of mirror in which the multicolors of the *Démocratie chrétienne* first begin to be revealed.

In the early period we cannot speak of a political movement, unless Lamennais, whose influence on French Catholicism lasted

[1] The connections between Fauchet's and Grégoire's revolutionary Catholicism and the movements of the so-called *Démocratie chrétienne* have so far only been glanced at. Threads run especially from Fauchet and the group of the *Cercle social* to the religious early socialism of Blanc, Buchez, and Leroux. Cf. references in Karl Marx in *The Holy Family* and of Buchez in the "Preface" to Vol. X of the *Histoire parlementaire*. Louis Blanc's chapter on Fauchet and Bonneville (*Histoire de la Révolution française* [Paris, 1847–62], III, 24 ff.) impressively shows to which historical models the religious socialism of 1848 referred. While Fauchet derived socialist teachings from the Gospels, for Blanc socialism was *l'évangile en action*.

only a few years, is considered as such. As a rule we are confronted with circles more or less tightly grouped about a prominent personality; with associations of friends who share the same attitude; with groups who come together to philosophize —united by opposition to the regime and by partly religious, partly political interests. All share the idea—the philosophical starting point—of a crisis created by the revolution in the relationship between Christianity and society. They also share a strong ethical impulse, a desire to co-operate in overcoming the conflicts between revolution and church and re-establishing *communes croyances*, common beliefs, as moral foundations of social life. They thus play the dual role of analyst and prophet, diagnostician and therapist, critic of the revolution and activist motivated by revolutionary idealism. The instability and insecurity of French society impels them to a tireless projection of new plans: the darker their image of French reality, the stronger their utopian will to overcome it.

The leitmotif of their writings is the reshaping of society by the help of a renewed Christianity. A Christianity renewed, however, is not simply the old Christian belief, but rather a philosophic analysis of the content of that belief, a precise evaluation of its social value, and a choice of those elements in it which are apt to assist the building of a new society. The Christianity of the Christian Democrats lies somewhere between orthodox Catholicism and the secularized *nouveau christianisme* of Saint-Simon.[2] It called, if not for a new religion, for a renewed religion cleansed of all impurities.

[2] H. de Saint-Simon, *Le nouveau christianisme* (Paris, 1825), in *Oeuvres complètes de Saint-Simon et d'Enfantin* (Paris, 1865 ff.), Vol. XXIII. On the influence of this book on Lamennais and Buchez, cf. F. Muckle in the "Introduction" to the German edition (in the series: *Hauptwerke des Sozialismus und der Sozialpolitik*, Vol. XI, edited by C. Grünberg (Leipzig, 1911), pp. 28 ff.

This sociological approach to Christianity is characteristic of early Christian Democratic movements. It points to their connections with Catholic traditionalism. We mentioned earlier the inner connection between de Maistre and Lamennais, de Bonald and Buchez. In one as in the other, there is an inclination to find the essence of religion in its social relations, in its socially formative and state-preserving powers. At the same time, the differences in their thought should not be lost sight of: *Démocratie chrétienne* is not the simple linear development of Catholic traditionalism. Where traditionalists wished to renew Christianity in the historic shape it had achieved under the Catholic kings of France, liberal Catholics and Christian Democrats rather dreamt of an alliance between the church and an irrepressibly advancing democratic movement. In both cases, nonetheless, we have to do with a "sociological Catholicism,"[3] one looking to the past, the other to the future, or, in political terms, one inclined toward the right and the other toward the left. The kinship of the two movements is less in their political aims than in ideological style: traditionalism and Christian Democracy, as the latter name implies, seek a place for the church in an integral polity; this idea is bracketed with the Christian conception of the equality of all men before God, which justifies and elevates it above democratic egalitarianism.

Christian-Democratic ideas came to focus for the first time in 1830 in France, radiating widely thereafter through the Catholic countries of Europe.[4] There were no lasting effects at that time,

[3] Cf. *supra*, p. 67.
[4] Impact on Germany: F. von Baader, *Rückblick auf de Lamennais*, 1838 (*Sämtliche Werke*, V, 385 ff.). A summary is given by F. Schnabel, *Deutsche Geschichte im neunzehnten Jahrhundert* (2d ed.; Freiburg, 1947 ff.), IV, 189 f. On the impact on Belgium, H. Haag, *Les origines du catholicisme libéral en Belgique* (1789–1892) (Louvain, 1950), pp. 127 ff. and 163 ff., and K. Jürgensen, *Lamennais und die Gestaltung des belgischen Staates* (Wiesbaden, 1963). On the

at least not in France. The anticlericalism of the July Revolution was not favorable to an alliance of democracy and church.[5] Moreover, the overwhelmingly Gallican episcopate and Rome itself refused to support the new political ideas.[6] The strength of Lamennais's liberal Catholicism was tested by the conflict of duties occasioned by the juxtaposition of his politics and his obedience to the church; it failed the test. It was the Revolution of 1848, which saw the beginnings of a romantic and social Christianity,[7] that created a favorable climate for the moods evoked by the phrase *Démocratie chrétienne*. It gave the first and for a long while the only example of a Christian Democratic school in France able to unite a considerable part of the Catholic public behind it.[8]

LAMENNAIS

We have accompanied Lamennais, in the analysis of his *Essai sur l'indifférence*, to the point where his apologetics shifts from a conservative to a revolutionary position. We meet him again at the moment that he is preparing to draw out the consequences of this shift. Without detaching himself from traditionalism and thus continuing the philosophy of *sens commun*, Lamennais had moved further and further away from his original opposition to

impact on Poland, J. Leflon, *op. cit.*, p. 456, and R. P. Lecanuet, *Montalembert* (3d ed.; Paris, 1900–2), I, 354 ff.

[5] Leflon, *op. cit.*, p. 419.

[6] See *infra*, p. 196.

[7] On that see J.-B. Duroselle, "L'esprit de 1848," in *Révolution créatrice* (Paris, 1948).

[8] The term *démocratie chrétienne* appears frequently as late as 1848. In the *Journal de Saône-et-Loire* of February 3, 1848, F. Morin, for instance, speaks of an *École da la Démocratie chrétienne*, of which the *Européen* and the *Revue Nationale* were parts; both were publications of Buchez' school (Duroselle, *Catholicisme social*, p. 344).

liberalism in the years before the July Revolution. Encouraged by
the examples of the Catholic movements in Belgium and Ireland, he began to approach the concept of an alliance between
church and democracy. Thus, he slowly emerged from the narrow circle of his philosophic and scholarly interests into the light
of politics; he immediately became an important factor in attempts to reconcile church and revolution.[9]

Lamennais said of himself: "*On m'accuse d'avoir changé.*" ["I
am accused of having changed."] "*Je me suis continué, voilà
tout.*"[10] ["I have only continued as before."] This is more than
apologetics; it gives us a glimpse of something essential in the
personality of Lamennais. In fact, his enormous labor, expressing
itself in innumerable essays, letters, and other writings heaped
one upon another, has an architectural unity and compact effect,
in spite of the variety of stylistic influences which it betrays. His
utterances are all part of one great apologia for Christianity, deriving from the mind of a sociologist. Thus, his contemporaries
were not wrong when they compared him—a slight exaggera-

[9] On Lamennais, see the fundamental work of Ch. Boutard, *Lamennais, sa vie
et ses doctrines* (3 vols.; Paris, 1905 ff.). F. Duine gives a bibliography up to
1922 in his *Essai de bibliographie de Félicité Robert de La Mennais* (Paris,
1923). Since then there have appeared, among others: R. Vallery-Radot, *Lamennais ou le prêtre malgré lui* (Paris, 1931); V. Giraud, *La vie tragique de Lamennais* (Paris, 1933); C. Carcopino, *Les doctrines sociales de Lamennais* (Paris,
1942). L. de Villefosse, *Lamennais ou l'occasion manquée* (Paris, 1945), draws
the Lamennais picture of the *chrétiens progressistes;* see also the special edition
of the periodical *Europe,* February–March, 1954. From an American point of
view, J. C. Murray, *Theological Studies,* X (1949), 177 ff. and 409 ff., gives a
balanced judgment. Recently there appeared a book by M. Mourre, *Lamennais
ou l'hérésie des temps modernes* (Paris, 1955), which is in some respects daring
but very stimulating; and the very thorough study by B. A. Pocquet du Haut-
Jussé, *La Mennais. L'évolution de ses idées politiques jusqu'en 1832* (Rennes,
1955).

[10] Leflon, *op. cit.,* p. 481.

tion—to Pascal.[11] It is true that, apart from the difference in station, the focus of Lamennais's apologetic endeavors seems to have shifted from anthropology to sociology; the place in Pascal's thinking which is occupied by man is given to society. The social crisis that followed the French Revolution was the real impetus of his reflections. Moreover, Pascal and Lamennais have in common the passion with which a genuine Christian attitude arrogates the means of contemporary thinking in order to overcome the indifferent and even the non-religious—and last but not least they are both possessed by a volatile fierceness and a stubborn self-consciousness toward everything they defended. Lamennais could have used the words of Pascal: "Si mes lettres sont condamnées à Rome, ce que j'y condamné est dans le ciel: Ad tuum, Domine Jesu, tribunal appello.[12] He not only uttered these ideas; he lived by them.

Lamennais's personality is full of contradictions. These were not only a consequence of his falling away from the church later in his life, dividing it, so to speak, into two halves, Catholic and freethinking. His political views oscillated. Contrasts, even apparently incompatible views, are to be found in the line of thought which reaches from the young cleric's faithful royalism to the liberal and democratic views of the mature man. There is, of course, a continuity in this line, as there is in Lamennais's religious development (*je me suis continué*); but the typical, the thematic, in his existence is hidden behind countless variations, by changing and often contradictory attitudes, which can be made consistent only with difficulty. Seen from the outside, his life is as adventurous as it is impenetrable. This is why he has always

---

[11] The expert on canon law history, Picot, wrote to Lamennais: "Soyez bien certain que votre ouvrage vous met a côté de Pascal." Similar views are expressed by Boutard, *op. cit.*, pp. 131–32 and pp. 151 ff.

[12] *Pensées*, ed. Brunschvicg, 920.

exercised a strong attraction upon biographers.[13]

Born June 29, 1782, the son of a wealthy middle-class family in St. Malo, distinguishing himself early through journalistic and scientific writings,[14] destined for the priesthood and ordained at the age of 33, Félicité Robert de Lamennais[15] made his name chiefly through his monumental *Essai sur l'indifférence en matière de religion*, the first volume of which appeared in 1817.[16] This book was Lamennais's personal answer to the philosophy of Enlightenment and to the French Revolution. Moreover, he gave traditionalism its long-sought and long-needed theological base. As a result, it aroused enthusiastic approval from within French Catholicism.[17] Following de Maistre, who had justified Christianity politically, and Chateaubriand, who had done so from the aesthetic point of view, Lamennais seemed to present philosophic proof of the truth of Christianity and to lay the groundwork of a massive assault on the rational school philosophy and the apologetics influenced by it. As the work progressed, however, it became increasingly clear that Lamennais had not forsaken Cartesian rationalism. By linking Christianity's truth to the judgment of humanity as a whole, rather than to the opinion of individual reason, and to the historic test of time and duration, the supreme judiciary position in the system remained the *raison générale*. Yet, in conceiving reason to be an

[13] For Lamennais' psychology, cf. Sainte-Beuve's testimony in *Portraits contemporains I* and *Nouveaux Lundis XI*. However, we have to be careful concerning his emphasis on *prêtre malgré lui*. On that cf. W. Gurian, "Lamennais," in *Perspektives U.S.A.*, III (1953), 79–96.

[14] See *supra*, p. 64, n. 111.

[15] This is the spelling of his name in his "pre-democratic" (*vordemokratische*) period.

[16] The second appeared in 1820, the third in 1822, the fourth in 1823.

[17] See Boutard, *loc. cit.*, I, 151 ff. Chateaubriand, Frayssinous, and the young Montalembert were, among others, admirers of Lamennais. In Germany his essay especially influenced Görres and Baader; also Hegel mentioned him.

historical process, rather than an individual capacity, he distinguishes himself in a basic manner from his apologetic precursors in the Enlightenment. It was precisely this attitude of his that made him appear as the great adversary of Enlightenment in the eyes of his contemporaries. As a matter of fact, Lamennais can in part be counted—though he has little in common with the romantic movement—as belonging to the anti-rationalistic, historicizing current of thought which gained influence in France during the Restoration and which substituted the experiments of history for authoritative criticism by reason and which measured religious truths, not by logical evidence, but by their affirmation in history.[18]

The first volume of the *Essai* brought quick fame to Lamennais. The second volume encountered opposition, less for its apologetic tendencies than for the philosophical presuppositions on which it was based. True to the traditionalist doctrine, Lamennais appealed from the individual conscience to the *sens commun* of humanity; he anchored proof of the truth of Christianity in a *consensus omnium*, which would find its expression in the infallible magisterium of the church. Contemporary philosophers, such as Hermes and Bautain, used similar methods; historical proof had always had its place in apologetics. In Lamennais, however, the dynamic consequences of this theological recourse to the past became immediately apparent. By extending in a gesture of sweeping integralism the power of the magisterium to the whole breadth of political and social life, he precipitated the truth of Christianity again into, (and it had hardly been rescued from criticism by the Enlightenment) the stream of historical events. This triggered the dispute which was to determine the course of Lamennais's life: did the church have a duty to make

[18] See P. Stadler, "Politik und Geschichtsschreibung in der französischen Restauration," *Historische Zeitschrift* CLXXX (1955), 265 ff.

itself the leader of great historical movements, or did it stand above them in an attitude equally independent of existing dogma-like forms of state as from the excesses of democratic spiritualism? Should it take an active part in history or be content with the role of passive onlooker, pilgrim? The critics reproached Lamennais that the demand he made in the *Essai sur l'indifférence* would necessarily entangle the church in all kinds of secular disputes and force it to a dangerous conformism; in its political weakness it would have to follow the movement which at any given time was the strongest. Lamennais replied that the task of the church was not to sanction power, but to defend the weak; therefore the church should hurry to the aid of the masses and should assume political leadership of democracy. This thought was probably best expressed in *Les affaires de Rome* (1837), written at the time of his breach with the church; but it was latent in the writings of the Restoration period and continued to determine more and more his whole political theory; the frequent protests of his contemporaries only made this more obvious.

But we do no justice to the religio-sociological thinking of Lamennais if we first inquire about his attitude toward actual politics. For Lamennais's will toward a renewal was deeper and broader in scope than the average political Catholicism of his times. He is not interested in momentary solutions, in a momentary restoration; if he is more critical of the Bourbon monarchy than a superficial reader of the *Essai* would expect, it is because the Restoration had foundered in superficial politics, as de Maistre and de Bonald had already seen. What really moved Lamennais, what he repeatedly expressed in ever-new terms, was the demand for a spiritual-political unity, an organic linking of religious and political society which came very close to theocracy: "*reconstituer la société politique à l'aide de la société religieuse,*" as he put it in the famous introduction to the second volume. This should not be understood in a political sense, as a view of the church's duty to give moral assistance to the state, or in the sense of an alliance between throne and altar. Political and religious society, for Lamennais, are not equal partners which mutually support and assist each other: between them there is a clear state of dependence. The polity can constitute itself only with the help of religious society. The former receives from the latter authority, legitimacy, and permanence. A people's religious constitution is older than the changing political forms of their states. Lamennais's philosophy of authority, therefore, does not start in the political sphere nor is it in contrast to early traditionalism one-sidedly royalist, nor, by the same token, is it one-sidedly democratic. It is *theocratic* and its theocratic content can be allied with a Catholic democracy as easily as with a "monarchy by the grace of God."[19]

This kind of universal view permits Lamennais to lift himself above the superficial quarrel between revolution and Restoration which then occupied the political stage. It makes possible a criticism of the times in which absolutism, Enlightenment, and revolution are seen as an identity. In Lamennais's historical judgment, everything after the revolution and the Enlightenment (or since Descartes in France) is unhistory, dissolution, decay: lament for the destruction of all political institutions, worry at the uncertainty of social conditions, runs through all his writings. He is prey to a deep sense of catastrophe. Like Karl Marx, he believed in an approaching total transformation of modern society. In 1830 he exclaimed:

> En moins d'un demi-siècle, on a vu tomber la monarchie absolue de Louis XIV, la république constitutionnelle, le direc-

[19] Cf. Gurian, *Ideen*, pp. 129 ff.

toire, les consuls, l'empire, la monarchie selon la charte: qu'y a-t-il donc de stable?[20] [In less than a half century we have seen the fall of the absolute monarchy of Louis XIV, of the constitutional republic, of the Directory, the consuls, the empire, the "monarchie de charte"—what is there left that is stable?]

Lamennais sees only one stable point in the whirl of events: the church. It outlives all catastrophes; it rises rejuvenated above all destruction. Against an apocalyptic background, its apotheosis is brilliantly limned. Does it need catastrophes to regain authority over souls? Lamennais weighed this problem as early as 1826. In his book, *De la réligion considérée dans ses rapports avec l'ordre politique et civil,* he wrote:

> Après d'affreux désordres, des bouleversements prodigieux, des maux tels que la nature n'en a point connus encore, les peuples, épuisés de souffrances, regarderont le ciel. Ils lui demanderont de les sauver; et avec les débris épars de la vieille société, l'Église en formera une nouvelle, semblable à la première en tout ce qui varie selon les temps, et telle qu'elle résultera des éléments qui devront entrer dans sa composition. Si au contraire ceci est la fin, et que le monde soit condamné, au lieu de rassembler ces débris, ces ossements des peuples et de les ranimer, l'Église passera dessus et s'élèvera au séjour qui lui est promis, en chantant l'hymne de l'éternité.[21] [After awful disorders, mighty upheavals, and such evil as nature has never known before, the people, exhausted from suffering, will again look toward heaven. They will ask it to save them; and with the scattered remnants of the old society the church will form a new one similar to the old one in everything, except what varies with the times and such as results from the elements which enter into its composition. If, however, this

---

[20] *Avenir,* October 16, 1830.
[21] Lamennais, *Oeuvres,* V. 342.

is the end and the world is condemned, the church, instead of gathering in these remnants, these bones of the people, to revive them, will pass on and lift itself up to the promised dwelling and sing the hymns of eternity.]

This text is of the utmost significance for Lamennais's concept of history. It points to the experiential roots upon which his thinking is based. At the same time it marks the point of his departure from Catholic tradition. The apocalyptic moment becomes immanent in the historical process: confusion and upheaval, sufferings such as the world has not experienced before, introduce the dissolution of society. Yet differences between the end of a culture within history (*les débris de la vieille société*) and the end of history as a whole are still distinguished (*si ceci est la fin . . .*). In fact, however, that secular tendency has begun which will lead to the idea of an intrasecular realization of the Apocalypse and to the vision of a redeemed humanitarian and democratic mankind risen from the ruins.[22]

In this context the characteristics of what has been called Lamennais's *Catholic liberalism* appear.[23] His is no religious liberalism; dogma remains untouched.[24] Nor is it a political liberalism in the accepted sense. The *parti libéral*, pushed into opposition under the Bourbons, was composed of heterogenous elements, most of them inimical to the church: Jacobins and atheists were

[22] Cf. Gurian, "*Ideen*," p. 111.: "Es sind . . . nicht nur apokalyptische Erwartungen wie etwa in den Considérations, die der ihrem Ende sich zuneigenden anarchistisch-despotischen Epoche entgegengehalten werden: Eine gesellschaftliche Realität lässt Lamennais eine Art apokalyptischer Erneuerung innerhalb der soziologisch-historischen Entwicklung als ihren Abschluss erhoffen."

[23] Boutard, *Lamennais*, Vol. II; G. Weill, *Histoire du catholicisme libéral en France* (Paris, 1909), pp. 11 ff.

[24] However, the traditionalistic motivation of the dogma remains problematic; cf. J. Bellamy, *La théologie catholique au XIXe siècle* (Paris, 1904), pp. 14–15, and F. Schnabel, *op. cit.*, p. 187.

the most influential among them. Characteristic of it are the pamphlets of Courier, the political songs of Béranger, and the writings of Thiers.[25] Lamennais cannot make common cause with this movement. His liberalism is of a different nature. His aim is not political, but religious, freedom. He seeks freedom from the state, not for the individual, but for the church. Since Lamennais believed that the house of Bourbon was intended to topple, it was necessary to make every effort to loosen its ties to the church; otherwise the church will be threatened in the fall. This is the basic idea of De la religion, and the later Des progrès de la Révolution et de la guerre contre L'Église.[26] In this primarily religious, not political, conception lies the origin of the theory of liberal Catholicism.

In the solitude of La Chênaie, his estate in Bretagne, Lamennais assembled a circle of disciples—priests and laymen belonging to the elite of young Catholic France. They were the core of a future grouping, the école mennaisienne. Among them were Lacordaire, the future founder of the new order of Dominicans in France; Gerbet and La Morvonnais, who were destined to play important parts in the Catholic social movement; and the young Montalembert, who after 1830 led political Catholicism in France. The original motive for the circle was religious: a community of Breton priests asked Lamennais to be their spiritual reformer; from this invitation there developed the congregation of St. Pierre, a community with the characteristics of an order which, according to Lamennais's plan, was to replace the Jesuits and assume the task of the religious renewal of society. The clergymen were aided by lay people.[27] Through his writings,

[25] On that see D. Bagge, Les idées politiques en France sous la Restauration (Paris, 1952), p. 24 ff.
[26] Des progrès de la Révolution et de la guerre contre l'Église (Paris, 1829).
[27] Boutard, op. cit., chap. v ("L'école de la Chesnaie"), pp. 85 ff.

his influence upon Catholic youth, and the initial favor which Rome showed him, Lamennais rose in the twenties to the position of "dictator of French Catholicism."[28] Not even a reluctant Gallican episcopate, which opposed him because of his defense of papal power, was able to disregard his influence entirely. The *école mennaisienne* continued to increase in importance; it was already a strong public force when the fall of the Bourbons in July, 1830, came about as Lamennais had predicted and gave an unexpected opportunity for the airing of Catholic-liberal ideas.

Until then, the publications of French Catholicism represented, almost without exception, the cause of the monarchy.[29] Now Lamennais clearly changed course. He founded the review *Avenir*, which appeared under the motto *Dieu et la liberté*. In it, assisted by Lacordaire and Montalembert, he espoused cooperation between Catholics and liberals. More important than this chiefly tactical political maneuver was *Avenir's*—the first political organ of modern Catholicism—systematic examination of the new situation of the church in post-revolutionary times and its development of norms of behavior that were to become decisive for a whole generation of liberal Catholics. Rightfully, Gurian called *Avenir* "until now the most important Catholic press organ."[30]

In its columns *Avenir* treated a variety of questions on religion and the state. If the essays of its many authors are arranged according to their main ideas, three schools of thought are to be found.[31] The first is philosophical and religious in nature and bears the stamp of Lamennais. Its main objective is a new foun-

---

[28] Gurian, *op. cit.*, p. 123.
[29] Especially in *"Ami de la religion"* and in the ultra-royalist *"Drapeau blanc,"* whereas the *"Correspondant"* takes a middle position.
[30] Gurian, *op. cit.*, p. 124.
[31] Boutard, *loc. cit.*, gives a detailed analysis.

dation for and strengthening of Christianity in the post-revolutionary world. The second is chiefly concerned with questions of church politics. It treats the relationship between state and church, of concordats, state control of schools, and similar things. Here, in addition to Lamennais, we find other ecclesiastical writers, among them Lacordaire. Finally, the third school advances, on a basis of religion, into practical politics; here the name of the third member of the *Avenir* triumvirate is encountered, the young Montalembert.

The philosophical foundation of the views of *Avenir* was completely the work of Lamennais. When the collaborators expressed themselves on questions of principle posed anew by the revolution, their thinking remained strictly within the limits set by Lamennais's *Essai*. Thus again in *Avenir* there are the familiar traits of state and church theory as sketched by Lamennais; the subordination of the secular (*ordre de conception*) to the spiritual (*ordre de foi*), the concept of the church as the true society which—since its essence is free and supranational—forms the model for political society. At the same time there is a turning away from the institutional thinking that had remained characteristic of de Maistre and de Bonald and from the idea of the foundation of the political order upon the voluntary agreement of the citizens and the liberties of the people. Moreover, the traditionalist concept of a primitive revelation, which in Lamennais loses its static quality, is historicized and brought into close touch with events: the revolution seems to be theologized and assumes the character of a renewal of revelation. These principles, in their abstract theoretical formulations, seem far distant from the practical political program with which *Avenir* introduced itself to the French public. Yet they are the true content of Lamennais's liberalism. It is a liberalism which weds the confrontation of state and church to the religious sphere by making society the bearer of a hidden revelation, thereby bringing it close to the church, which then articulates this revelation historically through her magisterium:

> instead of the confidence in the given institutions of the conservative traditionalists we find a boundless confidence in society which, according to its essence, in the interest of survival and development, has to recognize the authority of the church as the only spiritual and religious authority, whereas the state, in Lamennais's idealistic world, was transformed into a formal instance of settlement, a sort of clearing house of interests.[32]

This concept of state, of course, anticipated the future condition of society. At first, the content of *Avenir* was determined by attempts to distance the church from the prevailing political order, to regain for the church the independent position lost when it had entered the service of the Restoration. This effort also determines the thesis on church policy advanced by Lamennais and his collaborators. Negatively, it culminates in the proposal to abolish the Napoleonic concordat and to separate church and state entirely; positively, in all those claims for freedom in which liberal Catholicism for the first time announces the claims of the church community in defiance of the state: demands for freedom of conscience, freedom of teaching, freedom of the press, and freedom of association. Lamennais demands the independence of the church from the state. He proclaims the strict neutrality of the church in purely political questions. The state should not grow in power through the religious institutions dependent upon it. *Within* the church, however, Lamennais proposes to strengthen the religious central power. Is this a contradiction? It is decidedly not. Either can be explained in terms of

[32] Gurian, p. 133.

Lamennais's idea of the future order of society. According to him, while the state should restrict itself more and more to purely administrative tasks within the framework of the nation, the church will spread more and more universally; in the same measure, that is, in which an all-embracing social order is developing. Once this condition has been reached, the time to fuse the spiritual and secular principles has arrived. But the future theocracy will be based upon voluntary assent and will preserve as an indivisible ingredient the rights of the people. The free assent of all the people to the universal spiritual power, which is to lead them, corresponds to the spontaneity of the natural processes of society.

The third group of thoughts that constitutes the political core of *Avenir's* theories is not as clear as the religious and church-political ideas of Lamennais. Insofar as we can bring thematic order into them, a duality appears: on the one hand, a liberal criticism of the revolution, its point aimed at the atomism of modern democracy; on the other hand, a pessimistic view, already detaching itself from liberalism, of the social conditions of the times. The attitude is liberal insofar as it resists political centralizations, defends communal self-administration and the strengthening of personal initiative, and stresses the natural communities that exist between individual and state (these views *Avenir* shared with the older, somewhat more conservative, liberalism). Here, especially in the works of Montalembert, is the influence of the English model; but a natural consequence of the conservative criticism of the state as made up of atomized individuals is an inner necessity to re-evaluate the social and thus to leave liberal conceptions far behind. When, as *Avenir* does, the rights of the people are considered to be human rights and when the democratic principle of self-determination is claimed as a matter of fact, there must follow the most far-reaching social

consequences. These cast their shadows in Belgium and Ireland
in 1830 in revolutionary forms; they became clearly apparent in
1848 when the census-democracy of the bourgeoisie was transformed into a democratic government by all; for the first time
the revolution added social rights to the code of human rights.

It was this third approach above all which brought violent
opposition from Europe's conservative governments and gave
Avenir its reputation as a revolutionary and demagogic publication. "*L'Avenir confond l'égalité sociale avec l'égalité évange-
lique,*" Metternich wrote to the Austrian ambassador in Rome;

> il défend les théories les plus subversives de l'ordre social
> avec la même chaleur avec laquelle il défend la hiérarchie
> de l'Église.[33] [*Avenir* mistakes social equality for evangelical
> equality; it defends the most subversive theories of the social
> order with the same warmth as it does the hierarchy of the
> church.]

As Luise Ahrens has proved, contrary to the earlier opinion represented by Dudon, it is to the intervention of the Austrian state
chancellor in Rome that a great part of the later condemnation
of *Avenir* by the Holy See can be attributed.[34] That Lamennais's
ideas found warm acceptance in Ireland, Belgium, Italy, and
Poland—that is, in countries where the national movement was
in part supported by Catholic tradition—was not conducive to
lessening the distrust of the governments. In Germany, despite
passing effects of his political ideas, especially in the Rhine-
land, Lamennais evoked deep understanding only in Franz von
Baader. Baader wrote to Montalembert:

> If the present complete separation of religion and secular

[33] Ahrens, *op. cit.*, Appendix, pp. 235–36.
[34] Ahrens, pp. 26 ff. Cf. also J. R. Derré, *Metternich et Lamennais d'après les
documents conservés aux Archives de Vienne* (Paris, 1964).

power is considered an evil by many, *Avenir* has shown us that God has meant it differently than men have understood, since this separation has already begun to prove to mean an emancipation of religion and its resurrection out of the dust.[35]

Unlike his French friends, Baader did not consider sudden and revolutionary undertakings useful; he often criticized the political passion, the rashness, of the team of *Avenir*; at the same time he was hopeful that the seed it planted would bear fruit in the not too distant future. "The little mustard seed has taken fresh root in the primitive pap of dissolving society and will go on growing."

The final failure of Lamennais's attempts are attributable to the impatience of the *Avenir* circle and to the obstinate resistance, in the episcopate above all, of conservative and Gallican forces in France. When the periodical was forced to halt publication, chiefly because the bishops' negative attitude curtailed its readership, Lamennais, Lacordaire, and Montalembert turned to Rome for the pope's judgment on the theories represented by *Avenir*. The ruling went against them.[36] Lamennais and his friends submitted to it, but in 1834 Lamennais began to attack Roman diplomacy and the politicians who held fast to the *Staatskirchentum* ("establishment" church). This was his revolutionary manifesto (*Paroles d'un croyant*), an impassioned plea for the liberation of the suppressed; since it could be interpreted as an attack against the Holy See, it made a breach unavoidable.[37] Since the church refused to take up the political role he assigned to it, Lamennais refused to obey the church. Hence he ceased to

[35] F. von Baader, *Über die Zeitschrift Avenir und ihre Prinzipien* (1831).
[36] See *supra*, pp. 22 ff. *Mirari vos* does not mention Lamennais. It is the encyclical *Singulari nos* (June 25, 1834) which expressly condemns him. The text of the encyclicals can also be found in *Oeuvres complètes*, II, 603–14 and 621–25.
[37] Cf. Boutard, II, 1 ff.

believe in dogma, and his Christianity became a religion of philanthropic humanitarianism. He divested himself of the cassock. In place of Christian symbols he installed a statue of Liberty in his apartment. He attempted to place Catholicism in the service of humanitarian aims by developing a positive system from it without reference to revelation. To a woman visitor he sketched a view of a Catholic priesthood *"tout à fait identique à une organisation de garde urbaine"*[38] ["identical to the organization of a civil guard"].

In turning his back on the Catholic church, however, Lamennais rapidly lost his influence upon French Catholicism. His social ideas roused little enthusiasm, since they were but a repetition of what Saint-Simon and Fourier had long since said. Nor was he able to play a part in the Revolution of 1848.[39] His death on February 27, 1854, was hardly noticed.

What did this man mean to the development of Christian Democracy in France? At first glance, his contribution seems negligible. It did not consist of anything practical, of a palpable political bequest. Lamennais was not an organizer or a diplomat; he lacked the precision and patience to transform his far-reaching concepts into political realities. Nor did he have the gift of creating programs in keeping with the political facts of his times. His ideas anticipated the times; they could become effective, therefore, only much later—in the twentieth century.

Lamennais recognized that the time was running out when the church could count on the support of the Catholic princes. The influence of democratic thought and democratic institutions was growing all over Europe. In France the revolutionary movement was accompanied by a revival of anti-religious spirit: de-

[38] *Le prêtre et l'ami. Lettres inédites de Lamennais à la Baronne Cottu* (1818–1854) (Paris, 1910), p. xlv.
[39] Boutard, *op. cit.*, pp. 402 ff.

mocracy was hostile to the church, seeing it as part of the old order. Lamennais recognized that Catholicism was condemned to complete insignificance in the future unless it could be successfully freed from alliances with the *ancien régime*. It followed for him then that the church could not remain neutral in the political struggles of the times; rather it must make common cause with victorious democracy in order to obtain those guaranties of liberty which the absolutist state denied in part out of weakness, in part out of its ties with the *staatskirchliche* (state-controlled, "establishment" church) tradition.

Lamennais was convinced that the deep cleavage of church and state created by the revolution could not last.[40] With Fauchet and Grégoire, he clung to the ideal of the religio-political unity of society: the renewed fusion of spiritual and secular principles was the aim to which his thoughts, moving on various paths, were directed. It was in this sense that he was able to say of himself: *Je me suis continué*. In fact, however, only the outward scheme of his thinking was unchanged; the background against which it was played out changed. The Catholic ideal became a humanitarian ideal, and the vision of the Church Triumphant was wholly secularized.

Lamennais marks the point where Catholic traditionalism becomes revolutionary, democracy having proved its durability against de Maistre's argument that it was by nature an ephemeral, accidental form.[41] As democracy became more stable, the traditionalist argument that time (the capacity to endure) is the measure of all historic events had to turn against its originators, forcing *de facto* recognition of the revolution, to avoid which had been the very aim of traditionalism. Lamennais's attempts to

[40] "De la Séperation de l'Église et de l'État," *Avenir*, October 18, 1830.
[41] *Considérations*, chap. iv.

ease this difficulty with the aid of a philosophy of *sens commun* can be interpreted, on the one hand, as a theological attempt to cope with a state of permanent revolution; on the other hand, it retained the formal methods of de Bonald and de Maistre. His idea conjoined conservative traditionalism with a nascent *revolutionary tradition*.[42] It makes no difference whether this combination was Lamennais's original intention or was forced upon him by prevailing conditions. One thing is certain: a system which referred to history to such an extent as his would be much harder hit by historical changes than would a philosophy alien to time and history.[43] As it had been for de Maistre and de Bonald, for Lamennais history became the final proving ground of Christianity. It was the experiment which stamped as genuine and durable what, until then, enjoyed only hypothetical validity. The church in his eyes was the institutional expression of this experiment. Beyond its character as the historical proof of Christianity, it had no separate existence, and it was therefore to be conceived as a completely positivist phenomenon: as the most perfect of the many conceivable social orders; as a type of religious association which might serve as the model for the reconstruction of political society. The characteristics found earlier in Fauchet and Grégoire—the dismemberment of Catholicism into a dualism of spirit and cult, the spiritual delimitation of the content of faith which, on the side of institutions, corresponded to the retreat to a purely sociological concept of church—are not only retained by

[42] Cf. Gurian, *op. cit.*, pp. 126 ff.

[43] The reason for the renaissance of Thomistic thinking in the nineteenth century certainly lies with the decline of the romantic-organologic and historic-positive theology between 1830 and 1870. Already the second generation of the Catholic social movement drew upon Thomistic philosophy, and it proved an indispensable instrument for orientation in the modern industrial world. Cf. now L. Foucher, *La philosophie catholique en France au XIXe siècle, avant la renaissance thomiste et dans son rapport avec elle (1800–1880)* (Paris, 1955).

Lamennais but are considerably intensified. Nor could Lamennais ever free himself from dogmatizing political forms, which was nothing but the theologically questionable reversal of the revolution's politico-religious desire for unity. Although his political ideas are quite distinct from those of de Maistre and de Bonald, they grew from the same soil of positivism: instead of monarchy, democracy was theologized.

As a thesis, this was unacceptable to the church. Yet we cannot deny that many of Lamennais's liberal ideas bore fruit, if not in theory, at least in the field of practical politics, that is, as hypotheses[44]; they thus signaled the course which Catholicism would take in the democratic world.[45] The separation of church and state, which even in Lamennais had more of a tactical than an essential character,[46] could become a lesser, and therefore a necessary, evil in the face of a state hostile to the church, as the revolution had shown. The postulate of freedom of teaching permitted liberal Catholicism to reject the alliance movement which was directed against the church, by recourse to the democratic principle of equality for all. Finally, Christian parties would con-

---

[44] The two categories of thesis and hypothesis had been introduced into theological terminology by Dupanloup in the sixties of the nineteenth century who thus tried to moderate the shock caused by the Syllabus: "A wrong theory which must be repudiated as a general principle and as in all cases a true thesis can however contain so many truths that it can lead to a materially practicable solution, if it is applied to adequate circumstances (as a hypothesis) in a prudent and cautious way" (A. Hartmann, Toleranz und christlicher Glaube [Frankfurt, 1955], pp. 273–74).

[45] Cf. the excellent book by K. Jürgensen, n. 4 above, which describes with reference to an historic occurrence (Lamennais and Belgium) the concrete intensity of not only intellectual but also constitutional effects which originated from Lamennais and influenced European Catholicism and liberal constitutionalism.

[46] Boutard, Lamennais, II, 145 ff., describes the development which Lamennais' concepts went through on this question.

sider the *Essai sur l'indifférence* as their charter.[47] *"La nouvauté hardie de Lamennais consista à faire du catholicisme un parti,"* as Renan put it.[48] ["Lamennais's courageous novelty consisted in making a party of Catholicism."]

It is true, however, that all this was completely antipathetic to Lamennais; his "liberalism" was no doctrine, no political ideal, but a brief transitional state of his thinking, the threshold of the new blending of spiritual and secular principles. It was valid only in a clearly defined historical context: in a society no longer Christian or not yet Christian again. Lamennais's disciples either overlooked this dialectic character of his liberalism or intentionally neglected it. They took over his liberal ideas without drawing their consequences or considering their presuppositions. It was precisely this, however, that gave Lamennais great historical efficacy later. It was only through this kind of deliberate inconsistency that Christian Democratic ideas could be freed from the constriction of a political theory which itself was contradictory and incompatible with Catholic dogma. Although his efforts at systematic religion after 1830 drew little attention, Lamannais's liberalism had the potential to show the way for that part of French Catholicism which aimed at reconciliation with the democratic state. It was the work of the *prêtre malgré lui* from which originated some of the strongest impulses toward the peaceful association of church and democracy.

BUCHEZ

The strange designation, *École catholico-conventionelle* (although probably meant ironically), is the label affixed by con-

---

[47] Thus the MRP, according to an expression of G. Weill, quoted by J. Roger, *Ideas politicas de los catolicos franceses* (Madrid, 1951), p. 486.

[48] E. Renan, *Étude sur Lamennais*, new edition in the series, Livre du peuple (Paris, 1872), pp. 18–19.

temporaries to the Catholic-social school of the physician and philosopher Philippe-Joseph-Benjamin Buchez who played an important part in the early history of the *Démocratie chréti-enne*.[49] The label refers to the forty-volume *Histoire parlemen-taire de la Révolution française*, which Buchez, together with Roux-Lavergne, began to publish in 1834. This work occupies a special position in the French theory of revolution, since on the one hand it passionately defended the rule of the National Con-vention in which it saw the fulfilment of the revolution (whereas the National Assembly and the Legislative Assembly were dis-missed as degenerate early bourgeois conditions) whereas on the other hand, it attempted, at least theoretically, to express a strictly Catholic view point. It may have been the unaccustomed conjunction of such disparate attitudes which startled contempo-raries and produced the term "Convention Catholics," a phrase which probably sounded in the ears of Catholics of those times as "Christian socialism" would have struck their grandchildren or "Catholic communism" those of today's Catholics. In time stretching from the immediate prehistory of the revolution to the fall of Napoleon, the *Histoire parlementaire* is a huge compila-tion of sources on the history of the revolution, mostly from the pages of the *Moniteur* but from other newspapers as well and often supplemented by extracts from the protocols and minutes of legislative bodies. As a collection of sources it has here only cursory value. Of great importance, however, are the introduc-tions to the individual volumes, where the authors develop their

[49] On Buchez, see G. Castella, *Buchez historien, sa théorie du progrès dans la philosophie de l'histoire* (Fribourg, 1909); the same author, *Bouchez* (Paris, 1911); A. Cuvillier, *P.-J.-B. Buchez et les origines du socialisme chrétien* (Paris, 1948), and, recently, W. Geissberger, *Philippe-Joseph-Benjamin Buchez. Theo-retiker einer christlichen Sozialökonomie und Pionier der Produkivgenossenschaften* (Winterthur, 1956). Cf. also Duroselle, *Catholicisme social*, p. 80 ff.

systematic conception of the revolution. One finds that the revolution is "the last and most progressive consequence of modern culture and has originated wholly in the Gospels"; its political principles, "*ces mots d'égalité et de fraternité qu'elle mit en tête de tous ses actes, et avec lesquelle elle justifia toutes ses oeuvres*"[50] ["those words of equality and fraternity with which it heads up all its actions and with which it justifies all its works"] are of Christian origin; that at the beginning of the revolution the French nation permitted itself to be led by an *esprit de réalisation chrétienne*,[51] which did not lead it to its goal, it is true, but did accompany the revolution at its high points. In the introduction to the third volume, we read:

> Le commencement et le fin de la révolution, sont, suivant nous, contenus dans ces mots: liberté, égalité, fraternité ou, en d'autres termes, dans ce but: réalisation sociale de la morale chrétienne.[52] [The beginning and the end of the revolution, as we see it, are contained in these words: liberty, equality, fraternity, or, in other terms, the social realization of Christian morals.]

It corresponds to this Christian interpretation of the revolution that Buchez and Roux should give little credit to religious freethinkers, the *libres penseurs*, in the events of the revolution, although it was well known that their influence was undeniable. But they had no part in the true content of the revolution, in the *réalisation sociale de la morale chrétienne*. The revolution, insofar as it fulfilled its destiny, was led not *with*, but *against* Voltaire. It was not an anti-Christian but a Christian movement. It follows that those who persevere in primitive anticlericalism and

---

[50] *Histoire parlementaire*, I, I.
[51] *Ibid.*, V, iii.
[52] *Ibid.*, III, v.

stale freethinking are wrong when they parade their revolutionary attitudes. Are they ignorant of the fact that the ethical and social ideas which they represent are of Christian origin?

Tous les hommes progressifs, tous les hommes généreux de nos jours, pensent, agissent et se dévouent avec une conscience de chrétien. Presque tous cependant nient cette origine; ils refusent Jésus-Christ pour leur maître, et s'indignent jusqu'aux plus pitoyables arguments, que l'on veuille le leur donner. Cependant, que demandent-ils? A réaliser la fraternité announcée par les Évangiles, la fraternité dans laquelle la première place appartiendra à celui qui sera le serviteur des autres.[53] [All progressive, all generous people of our time think, act, and devote themselves as conscientious Christians. Yet nearly all of them deny such an origin. They refuse Jesus Christ as their master; they become indignant and will use the most pitiful arguments, when one wants to give Him to them. Meanwhile what is it they want? To realize the brotherly love announced by the Gospels this fraternity which in the first place belongs to him who will be the servant of the other.]

When the revolutionaries deny they are Christians, they are so without knowing it. They are so in much stronger measure than Christians who remain faithful to the church. For the latter do not take the necessary steps from their recognition of the truth of the Gospels to their realization, whereas the others, without knowing it, realize the evangelical principle and fulfil a law of Christianity. Typical of the *Histoire parlementaire* are its stress upon the active character of the Christian message, the contrast of *invention* and *pratique*, of *révélation* and *réalisation*, the opposition of a lived Christianity to a mere knowledge of Christian-

[53] *Ibid.*, V, i.

ity. It points to the disparity between the church and the modern industrial world, which had entered the consciousness of contemporaries for the first time with Saint-Simon's *New Christianity* and was thereafter never to disappear from the world of ideas of French socialism.

In the form Buchez and Roux gave them, these thoughts did not appear as especially original. They had often been encountered in early French socialism; they are seen most acutely in Saint-Simon, Buchez' philosophical mentor, and are best simplified by Louis Blanc, his friend and disciple.[54] But the original contribution of Buchez, the actual author of the introductions to the *Histoire parlementaire*, is the adroit use of the theory of secularized Christianity, developed in the *Nouveau Christianisme*, to bridge the abyss which had opened between the revolution and Catholicism. Buchez, in contemplating the revolution, shifted from reality to ideal, just as Saint-Simon had when he contemplated Christianity. He substitutes the better future for the bad present, a future in which the idea will be realized. The *New Christianity*, too, compared with the old one, is still developing, in a state of half-finished planning. If the revolution is considered as a step toward the *New Christianity*, as Buchez and Roux believe, the failure of the revolutionaries will not be judged too harshly, considering the magnitude of their task. It is sufficient to see that the revolution aimed to realize true Christian principles: with this intention in mind, actual achievement recedes into the background.

As a matter of fact, Buchez was not blind to the differences between the ideal and the reality of the revolution. He does not at all attempt to deny the horrors of the Terror. He excuses

[54] On Saint-Simon's influence on his intellectual development, see Buchez' report in the "Introduction" to his *Essai d'un traité complet de philosophie du point de vue du catholicisme et du progrès* (Paris, 1838 ff.), pp. 19–20.

them, however, by the greatness of the ideal, an ideal which surpassed human capacities. When ideal principles are applied to
worldly conditions, some friction and some failures are bound to
appear—and how much more so when we have to do with the
realization of the Gospels. For Buchez it is an unquestionable
fact that the men of 1793 aimed at realizing the Gospels. As a
result, he does not shy away from excusing the greatest crimes
of the revolution by the good faith of their perpetrators: against
this background of a sophistic historical theory of justification,
Robespierre appears as the true Christ and his adversaries are de-
picted as not only political failures but enemies of Christianity.

The stress on the providential meaning of history, the resignation of moral to theological judgment, and the subordination of
the fate of the individual to the social process, these are all ideas
which Buchez shares with de Maistre and de Bonald. It is easy
to see that Buchez, like Lamennais, moves within the framework
of traditionalism, but under a negative sign, so to speak; unhin-
dered by humanitarian qualms, he draws the ultimate consequences of the view, upheld by Saint-Martin and de Maistre,
that the revolution was a decree of providence. History is a logical development of progress. This, in turn, develops from revelation.[55] This alters completely the question of good and evil and
the problem of human freedom of choice. History is not something from which man can choose what he likes; it is not the
formal framework of moral choices; as an outcome of God's will
it has at first to be accepted as a whole. There are only two possibilities for historical action: to assent to the historical process
and, thus, to the will of providence or to revolt against historic
necessity and thus to choose evil. The revolution as a whole, independently of the judgment of single phases, has to be seen as
a positive phenomenon.

[55] Buchez develops this thought in his *Traité de philosophie*, III, 108 ff.

But how precisely do we recognize that providence has expressed itself in the revolution? Buchez answers with de Maistre: in the revolution's opposing, like an independently effective power, the egotistical individual will. *"De Maistre disait avec raison,"* the *Histoire parlementaire* reports, *"que nul homme avait mené la révolution, et qu'au contraire tous ceux qu'elle avait élevés, avaient été des instruments entre ces mains."*[56] ["De Maistre rightly said that no man led the revolution and that actually all those whom it elevated were only instruments in its hand."] The consequences drawn by Buchez from this differ entirely from those drawn by de Maistre: since the revolution appears to him to give evidence of Christian principles, its justification is simultaneously an apologia for Christianity. Buchez thus approaches Lamennais, for whom the revolution (but only 1789) appeared as the starting point of a primitive revelation, historically accentuating its character. The idea of progress links the revolutionary development of the *New Christianity* with the history of Christianity and to its original core in the primitive church.

Buchez' life was full of changes of fortune. Born March 30, 1796, in Matagne-la-Petite in the province of Vallone, he was the son of a civil servant who was devoted to the revolution and who lost his position upon the return of the Bourbons. Living in Paris, Buchez soon entered politics and was active as a revolutionary and anarchist. With a few friends, he founded the French *Carbonaria*.[57] Arrested twice on the suspicion of instigating a military revolt and having barely escaped execution, he was freed, studied medicine in Paris, and finally joined the lodge of

[56] *Histoire parlementaire*, IV, ii. Cf. on that, J. de Maistre, *Considérations*, chap. i.

[57] "La Charbonnerie, par Trélat," in *Paris révolutionnaire*, II, (Paris, 1838), 277–341 (report of a partner).

the Amis de la Verité, where an entirely new field of political activity opened to him.[58] For many years he had led the hectic double life of a revolutionary with philosophical inclinations and a natural scientist with political inclinations; then one day, reading of Saint-Simon's New Christianity, he was jolted from his spiritual anarchy, the way to socialism was opened for him, and he was filled with the spirit of a moralistic-social, unchurchlike, and undogmatic Christianity.

Every theoretician of early French socialism was affected by the spirit of Saint-Simon. This nobleman of the ancien régime, who had been uprooted by the revolution, held fast in the depths and heights of his life to a plan to reorder the world unhinged by 1789 according to his own spiritual ideals. This sociologist, who felt himself called upon to be the architect of a new, post-revolutionary society, was for the generation of Buchez the great spiritual leader, the master spirit. He appeared to be the anointed guide into the unknown land of the new industrial world. His optimism and his belief in progress were links binding him to the older movement of eighteenth-century philosophers; he assented to the technological revolution and considered the transition from peasant and artisan culture to the age of the machine as progressive. Yet he was the first to be aware of the costs of such progress. Saint-Simon recognized very clearly that an extraordinary moral effort would be necessary to control egotistic energies and private strivings for happiness that would be released. As a result he deliberately fell back upon the moral reserves of Christianity. It was not the old Christianity which he held up to his contemporaries. He described the New Christianity in his famous book; it was to be a Christianity of pure love, without

[58] On Buchez' relations to the Carbonari and Freemasons, see Trélat, loc. cit., pp. 282 and pp. 304 ff., and Cuvillier, op. cit., pp. 10 ff. Bonneville had also been a member of the lodge of the Amis de la Vérité.

fixed ecclesiastical forms, a religion of the inward man which was to permeate every sphere of life as a fine, spiritual breath. By seeing this Christianity as a product of progress, Saint-Simon broke the antithesis of revolution and Christianity at a decisive place. The conflict of the two powers was bound to dissolve as soon as the old Christianity had taken its proper form in the new industrial age.

His encounter with Saint-Simon changed the Buchez of the early writings (according to Cuvillier's judgment, a *"Buchez matérialiste et sans illusions sur les croyances morales courantes"*[59] ["a materialistic Buchez who had no illusions about current moral beliefs"], into a believing theist who let no occasion pass for stressing the indispensability of religion to social life. Buchez's sociological attempts are inconceivable without Saint-Simon. The ideas of *physiologie sociale*, the search for the laws governing the social body by the methods of natural science, derive from Saint-Simon, as does the eclecticism of Buchez, which at times will attract and at times will confuse the reader with its odd mixture of medicine, natural philosophy, sociology, and history. But Buchez did not stop with Saint-Simon. He soon detached himself from his master (they never met personally) and his school, which was stiffening into a sect. From the moral theism of the New Christianity, Buchez found his way back to Catholicism. His systematic nature, too, forced him beyond Saint-Simon. In his *Introduction à la science de l'histoire ou science du développement de l'humanité* (1833), he attempted for the first time to base sociological theory upon a well-constructed philosophy of history, encouraged by the ideas which Comte summed up later in his *Cours de la philosophie positive*

---

[59] This is Cuvillier's opinion on the Ontognosia as published as early as 1814, *op. cit.*, p. 8.

(1842).[60] Both thinkers were similarly concerned with categorizing ideas about progress and developing them as the scientific foundation of sociology, but Buchez surpassed the author of *Philosophie positive* in his sense of history. Much more decisively than Comte, he turns from the mechanistic psychology which until then had served as the foundation of the social sciences. Buchez' idea of progress was more elastic and more subtle than Comte's; although he conceived history positivistically—that is, as a sequence of "logical ages"[61]—he left room, by not assuming a linear ascent of humanity toward civilization, for the work of decay and accident; he admitted that for a long time there had been oscillation between *périodes analytiques* and *périodes synthétiques*; only the discerning eye could read the movements of progress.[62]

Even after Buchez renounced the *Carbonaria*, his political activity continued, as did his philosophical work. It increased in energy proportionately with the establishment of his theories as an independent school, "buchezism," among the socialisms of the times.[63] In 1831, the *Européen*, the first of the many publications of the Buchez circle, still only vaguely defined the aim of the movement as the desire to explain

les moyens pratiques que réclament les besoins positifs de la

[60] On the relationship Buchez-Comte, see Castella, *Buchez historien*, pp. 81–82, and Geissberger, *op. cit.*, pp. 29–30. The priority of ideas cannot be ascertained definitely.

[61] The theory of the *âges logiques* is developed in the *Introduction à la science de l'histoire ou science du développement de l'humanité* (Paris, 1833).

[62] Cf. Castella, *Buchez historien*, pp. 67 ff. and pp. 80 ff.

[63] The foundation of an independent school coincides with Buchez' apostasy from Saint-Simonism. On the beginnings of *buchezisme*, see Cuvillier, *op. cit.*, pp. 19 ff., Duroselle, *Catholicisme social* pp. 94 ff., and Geissberger, *op. cit.*, pp. 35 ff.

société, de proposer les projets dont l'exécution nous paraît propre à faire sortir notre pays de l'état de malaise où il se trouve[64] [the practical means called for by the positive needs of society for projects whose fulfilment appears likely to us to bring our country out of the state of malaise in which it finds itself.]

Yet this program soon took concrete forms in the workmen's associations (*associations coopératives de production*), whose spread was furthered by Buchez practically and by propaganda.[65] These were production cooperatives in which the workers exercised entrepreneurial activities by giving up the greatest part of any individual gain. A part of the income went into a common treasury and served as a *capital indivisible* for special kinds of social assistance: old age pensions, sickness insurance, and assistance to education. Within the associations there were no social differences: all workers received the same wages. Between 1832 and 1850 the movement of workmen's associations gained some importance in France, especially in the crafts, but Buchez' expectations of a new form of production that would help overcome class distinctions and lead to an all-embracing *organisation du travail* were not fulfilled.[66] Nonetheless, the experiment was not without effect; the associations of workers were followed by the cooperative movement, which sought to find its own way, dis-

[64] Quoted by Cuvillier, *op. cit.*, p. 22.

[65] On that Wassilieff, *P.-J. Buchez, der Begründer der modernen Associationsbewegung Frankreichs* (Bern, 1898), and Cuvillier, "Buchez, le fondateur en France de l'Association ouvrière de production," *Revue des Études coopératives*, July–September, 1922. Also cf. E. Seiler, *Die Entwicklung berufsständischer Ideen in der katholisch-sozialen Bewegung Frankreichs* (Zurich, 1935), pp. 34–35, and Duroselle, *op. cit.*, pp. 89–90.

[66] Cf. the "Introduction" to Vol. XXXII of *Histoire parlementaire* and the first chapter of the *Introduction*.

tinct from syndicalism, of overcoming class distinctions and greatly influenced social Catholicism in France.[67]

After 1830 Buchez and his school were the focus of every current that sought to reconcile Catholicism and the revolution. Buchez' followers saw Christianity chiefly as a moral and social force, a counterweight to bourgeois individualism. We have already mentioned that Buchez sharply criticized the work of the Constituent Assembly in his *History of the Revolution*. He also restricted and completed his justification of the revolution with a sharp criticism of the liberal principles of human rights.[68] Like Fauchet and Grégoire, he demanded that the rights of individuals be complemented by a listing of civil duties. The revolution he saw as unfinished, for it had not achieved the demands for the equality of all men that it had raised. What had been neglected in 1789, socialism was now to bring about: an *equalization of bourgeois democracy*. This is the bridge between the Great Revolution and the February Revolution, between Fauchet's revolutionary Catholicism and Buchez' "Christian socialism." This development, too, is closely related to the revolution. It does not pretend to be anything but a rethinking in Christian terms of the order aimed at by the revolution.

The essence of this—and it is true of nearly all of the authors of the Buchez circle—is the idea of the equality of all men, a concept which appears in part as a form of natural law and in part as an interpretation of the Christian New Testament. In Buchez it has a threefold aspect: First, according to *natural*

---

[67] On that, see Seiler, *op. cit.*, p. 56, n. 20. In his *Traité d'Économie*, Buchez' pupil, Ott, gave the theoretical directions to the Catholic social movement of de Mun. In contemporary France Cooperatism is being represented especially by Hyacinthe Dubreuil and the circle publishing the periodical *Fédération* to whom also belongs Gabriel Marcel. Cf. H. Dubreuil, "L'organisation du travail et le système des équipes autonomes," in *Revue internationale du travail*, October, 1951. In Germany Eugen Rosenstock and Ernst Michel have developed similar ideas.

[68] *Histoire parlementaire*, Vols. V and XXXII (introductions).

science, there is the equality of gifts which every person possesses. Buchez departs here from the principle that heredity can be deliberately influenced and which holds that differences in talents are the results of influences of the environment and are not attributable to unvarying natural gifts.[69] Second, *socially*, the social equality of opportunity, which was first demanded and proclaimed by Rousseau and began increasingly to be realized after the revolution; here Buchez is reminiscent of Condorcet, the first to recognize the "progress toward equality" as the leading tendency of the modern period.[70] Finally, in Buchez' Christian period, there is the evangelical *equality of all men before God*, which affects history as *morale d'égalité* and poses the duty in the interpersonal realm of bearing the other's burden. In Buchez' opinion, insofar as practical and social Christianity dominates over a purely contemplative understanding of the Gospels, the shorter will be the distance between the revolutionary and the Christian world view.

Atelier (1840–50), founded by Buchez, the first French newspaper edited and published by working men, proclaimed Christianity to be a "unifying bond." It held:

> Si les laïques voulaient se donner la peine d'examiner sans prévention, d'étudier, de suivre le mouvement des idées, ils comprendraient bientôt la grandeur du dogme chrétien; ils verraient la puissance qu'il peut donner même à des intelligences aussi peu cultivées que les nôtres; ils verraient que là est la vérité universelle, et ils s'y attacheraient, parce qu'ils comprenderaient qu'il n'y a d'unité possible que par un lien spirituel, que par la reconnaissance d'un principe commun, obligatoire pour tous.[71] [If lay people would take the trouble

---

[69] Geissberger, *op. cit.*, p. 17, n. 58.

[70] On Buchez' student-master relationship to Concordet and Rousseau, see Geissberger, *op. cit.*, pp. 20 ff.

[71] No. 1, September, 1840.

to examine it without prejudice and to study the flow of its ideas, they would soon understand the greatness of the Christian dogma; they would see the force which it can give to even lesser endowed intelligences such as ours; they would see that here is universal truth, and they would cling to it because they would understand that no other unity is possible save the spiritual, through the recognition of a common principle binding on all.]

A manifestation of this spirit of Christian socialism is to be found in the dedication of a popular edition of the Bible that was issued by the printers of the Buchez circle. It read:

> Dédiée à la nation française par des ouvriers imprimeurs, avec une introduction par les auteurs de l'Histoire parlementaire. [Dedicated to the French nation by the printing workmen, with an introduction by the authors of the *Parliamentary History*.]

As in his other writings, Buchez here mixes religious, social, and national feelings.[72]

Buchez' role as mediator between Catholicism and socialism seemed to promise an important political position for him in the Revolution of 1848. While he did become vice-mayor of Paris and the first president of the National Assembly, he was only a radical in terms of theory but rather too ready to compromise in practical politics to be a match for the difficult tasks

---

[72] On Buchez' nationalism, see Cuvillier, *op. cit.*, pp. 23–24. Much evidence can be found in the historical part of the "Introduction," which was added in the 2d edition of 1842. For instance, p. 476: "L'humanité fut sauvée (sc. de l'Arianisme) par le pape, évêque de Rome, et par la France." Or, p. 509: "Le salut de l'Europe sera assuré le jour ou le clergé lui aura donné un nouveau Grégoire VII, et la France un nouveau Charlemagne." H. O. Sieburg, *Deutschland und Frankreich in der Geschichtsschreibung des 19. Jahrhunderts* (Wiesbaden, 1954), misinterprets Buchez' national messianism when he classifies him as a forerunner of the modern European unification movement.

posed by the actual and increasingly radicalized revolution. During the stormy May days he capitulated to the demonstrators who stormed the National Assembly.[73] Moreover, the course of political events itself quickly cut the ground from under *buchezism*. After the June battle there was no longer any thought of an alliance between Catholicism and the workers' movement. The middle class, frightened by the revolution, began to move closer to the church. One expression of this new alliance was the *Lex Falloux* (1850), which assured Catholicism a controlling influence in education.[74] So hard hit was *buchezism* by this double turn that it failed to survive the revolution. Both its journal and the group dissolved. Buchez, whose last years were devoted to travel and science, died alone and completely forgotten on August 11, 1865.

Like Lamennais, in Buchez we must distinguish between the rigid claims of the system and the living effect of the man's personality. If the system alone is under consideration, one's judgment is simple: a *Catholic Jacobinism* was a contradiction in itself. If the spirit and the political attitude of the school are taken into account along with the doctrine, then it appears that the desire to reconcile Catholicism and revolution corresponds, not only to the *juste-milieu* tendencies of the middle class, but to the wishes of many Catholics including members of the hierarchy, as well. Archbishop Affre of Paris, later a victim of the revolution, expressly sanctioned Buchez' intentions.[75] Certainly, the head of the *école catholico-conventionelle* contributed much toward *rapprochement* of church and workers through his unself-

---

[73] Cuvillier, *op. cit.*, pp. 62–63, undertakes an apology.

[74] Cf. H. Michel, *La loi Falloux* (Paris, 1906), and J. Lecler, "La loi Falloux," *Études*, CCLXVI (1950), 3 ff. On the political consequences, also P. R. Rohden, "Zur Soziologie des politischen Katholizismus in Frankreich," *Archiv für Sozialwissenschaft und Sozialpolitik* LXII (1919), 498 ff.

[75] Cuvillier, *op. cit.*, p. 60.

ishness, his many-sided scientific interests, and his publishing activities. If the Revolution of 1848, in contrast to that of 1830, was distinguished by unusual religious tolerance, this is in great measure due to him.[76]

In terms of sociology Buchez found his way to Catholicism via the New Christianity of Saint-Simon.[77] Later Buchez turned his back on the theory of a secularized Christianity and sought a way to return to the dogma of the church. Lacordaire, among others, befriended him. Buchez became closely linked with the newly awakened religious movement. His circle produced some of the first Dominican followers of Lacordaire in his restoration of the order in France.[78] One of them, later Bishop of Nimes, described Buchez as "un moyen dont Dieu s'est servi"[79] ["a means of which God had made use"]. Ozanam, too, stressed the beneficial influence of buchezism on Catholic laymen.[80]

The lives of Buchez and Lamennais cross and separate at this point: Buchez turned to the church where Lamennais began to leave it. A similar contrast exists in their politics: Buchez, critic of the Constituent Assembly and defender of Robespierre,[81] developed what might be called the socialist alternative to Catholic liberalism.[82] Both thinkers sound the theme of Christian Democracy, but in positive and negative formulations. Later we shall

[76] In his Vie du Révérend Père Besson, E. Cartier writes: "La différence qui existe, sous le rapport de la tolérance religieuse entre la Révolution de Juillet et celle de 1848, vient en grande partie de l'influence qu'eut l'école de Buchez sur le parti du National." Quoted by Cuvillier, op. cit., p. 60.

[77] Cf. the "Introduction" to his Traité de philosophie, pp. 19 ff.

[78] "Introduction," 2d edition, pp. vii–viii.

[79] Cuvillier, op. cit., p. 58.

[80] In a letter to Lacordaire of August 26, 1839, Oeuvres completés de A. F. Ozanam (Paris, 1881 ff.), I, 334 ff.

[81] Histoire parlementaire, Vol. V, "Preface." Cf. Cuvillier, op. cit., p. 33 ff.

[82] The Traité de politique et de science sociale, which appeared after Buchez' death (1866), however, moderates the anti-liberal criticism.

see the effect of this tension on theoretical and practical politics.

The political contradictions of the early stages of *Démocratie chrétienne* were not decisive, however. More important by far was the conflict of sociological and religious Catholicism. Despite his rejection of Saint-Simon, Buchez stopped halfway, and barely went beyond the position taken by Lamennais later. Seeing religion mainly in the light of its importance to society and valuing it sociologically, he justified it as a unifying force. He no longer redesigned it as self-glorification but took it over unchanged from the tradition of the church. His was a positivist belief without a sense of personal involvement. In spite of his relationships with the religious movements following 1830, Buchez, as *"portier de l'Église,"*[83] stopped all his life at the threshold of the church. He never was a practicing Catholic.

1830–48

Avenir was the first Catholic periodical in France to accept society as non-Christian. The proposals and demands which were put forward out of this understanding can be summed up in the dual principle: On the one hand, the church was called on to dissolve the covenant binding it to the state; on the other hand, it was expected to go along with the new democratic power insofar as the interests of church liberty allowed. Opinion divided on how far *rapprochement* could go: where Lamennais wished to make democratic state forms obligatory for Catholicism, Lacordaire and Montalembert were more cautious. While they considered democracy inevitable, they saw in it neither the gift nor the punishment of God. All agreed, however, on the principle that Catholics were to be shaken out of their lethargy and encour-

---

[83] One of his students gave him this name; see Castella, *Buchez*, p. 15.

aged to choose, since it depended solely on them to defend the position of Catholicism in a new state and amidst an indifferent society, to whom the protection of the church was no longer a duty.

When Lamennais broke with Rome and left the church, both Lacordaire and Montalembert turned against him. The formal break was preceded by a long process of alienation. In the correspondence between Montalembert and Lamennais, published by Georges Goyau,[84] it is clear that the image of the master slowly faded for the romantic and enthusiastic young man: Lamennais's struggle with Rome was only a prelude to the final breach. Lacordaire expressed the reasons for his break with Lamennais in a programmatic essay. In this he assigned to the philosophic obstinacy of the Breton and to his insistence upon logical explanation and analysis of the elements of faith the responsibility for his failure:

> La grande erreur de M. de Lamennais . . . a été de vouloir fonder une école philosophique et d'espérer que cette école serait le lien des esprits, la base de la religion, le salut de la société.[85] [The great mistake of M. Lamennais . . . was to found a philosophical school and to hope that this school would be a spiritual link, the basis of religion, and the salvation of society.]

In Lacordaire's view Lamennais was a disciple of the traditionalists, and historically this is true. When traditionalism, however, led to such consequences as appeared in Lamennais's work of 1830, the restoration of the old monarchic and legitimist ideol-

[84] *Lettres de Montalembert à La Mennais* (Paris, 1932).

[85] H.-D. Lacordaire, *Considérations sur le système philosophique de M. de Lamennais*, (Paris, 1834), in *Oeuvres complètes* (Paris, 1872 ff.), VII, 1 ff. This quotation is on p. 107.

ogy was no longer possible: it raised not only political, but theological, doubts. Thus, Catholic liberalism was not dead when *Avenir* was condemned: it now turned to more practical and palpable aims. It fought for the freedom of the press, freedom of association and education, and began to develop its own tactics for its encounters with democratic society.

Montalembert kept at a distance chiefly from Lamennais's dogmatization of democracy.[86] A liberal aristocrat whose Catholicism was an inherited tradition and an emotional necessity, he distrusted democracy and occasionally looked upon it with open contempt.[87] An apocalyptic belief in the coming of democracy was alien to him. On the other hand, he was too clever an observer of the political scene to go along with the legitimist bent of his aristocratic friends. He appraised the chances of French Catholicism realistically; as a practical politician, he would use whatever means the constitution offered to Catholics. Like Louis Veuillot, his opposite number on the right, he was a democrat by political method but not by conviction.

---

[86] On Montalembert the fundamental work is the already-mentioned biography by Lecanuet; since then, P. de Lallemand, *Montalembert et ses amis dans le romantisme (1830–1840)* (Paris, 1927), A. Trannoy, *Le romantisme politique de Montalembert avant 1843* (Paris, 1942), and by the same author, "Responsabilités de Montalembert en 1848," *Revue d'histoire de l'Église de France*, XXXV (1949), 177–209.

[87] On Montalembert's aversion to democracy, cf. Lecanuet, *loc. cit.*, II, 383 ff. In a letter to the editor of the *Ami de la religion* in October, 1848, Montalembert protests against the identification of democracy and Christianity which Lacordaire and Ozanam tried to realize in the *Ère nouvelle*: "Je ne puis me défendre de sourire quand j'entends déclarer que le Christianisme c'est la démocratie. J'ai passé ma jeunesse à entendre dire que le Christianisme était la monarchie . . . J'ai lutté vingt ans, et non sans quelque succès, contre cette vieille erreur aujourd'hui dissipée. Je lutterais vingt ans encore, si Dieu me les donnait, contre cette nouvelle prétention; car je suis convaincu que ce sont deux aberrations du même ordre."

Montalembert chiefly attacked the state's monopoly of education. Unlike many Catholics, he desired to leave the Napoleonic system of universities untouched; but he claimed for Catholics the right to have their own schools and universities. In his work, *Du devoir des catholiques dans la question de la liberté de l'enseignement* (1843), he stresses the incompatibility of liberalism and the state's claim to a monopoly in education.[88] His campaign for freedom of education, begun in the upper chamber, was later taken to the public by the founding of the *parti catholique*, a development stimulated by the examples of Belgian and, to a lesser extent, German Catholicism.[89] In his attempts, however, at educating French Catholics to more conscious political action, he encountered resistance where he least expected it: from Rome. While he, leader of Catholicism in France after 1830, toyed with the thought of "direct action," the official church clung to the methods of secret petitions and consultations among governments. The *parti catholique* was finally disavowed by Rome in its unflinching defense of the Jesuits.[90] Its position only gained strength when Montalembert received help from among the bishops, mainly from Parisis and Dupanloup, and when Rome conceded the Catholic movement a restricted freedom of action.[91]

In view of the difficulties in the path of developing a Catholic party at that time, it is not surprising that the *parti catholique* could hardly move beyond limited individual action and that it was held to a minority role in its parliamentary and pub-

[88] Lecanuet, II, 169 ff.; Gurian, *Ideen*, pp. 159 ff.

[89] On the occasion of the occurrences in Cologne in 1837, Montalembert had expressed his solidarity with the German Catholics. Lecanuet, II, 35 ff.; Gurian, *Ideen*, p. 161.

[90] Lecanuet, II, 245 ff.

[91] In a letter of the cardinal secretary of state, Lambruschini, to Montalembert of March 26, 1846, from Lecanuet, II, 289 ff.

lishing activities. Its position was complicated for various reasons. Considered ultramontane by the liberals, its liberalism raised suspicions in church circles. On the one hand, it had lost the sympathies of the Orleanistic bourgeoisie through its struggle against the state monopoly of education and against the vulgarized Voltairianism of the liberal press; on the other, it was considered a bothersome middle group by the Roman curia as well as by the Gallican wing of the episcopate, a bothersome obstacle to smooth communications between the spiritual and temporal powers. The most disparate elements united to thwart the establishment of a Catholic party. There were the Catholics who remained faithful to the house of Bourbon and who clung to legitimism; on the other side, there were the liberals who could not fit the program of the *parti catholique* to their own aims, who conceded the truth of Montalembert's criticism of existing state institutions but did not approve of his defense of the church, let alone of Rome. Thus, the *parti catholique* for religious and political reasons was unable to find a place in French public opinion. Theories which would look to *rapprochement* of church and revolution were still to come; people were little inclined to abandon the firmly established reform program of traditionalism for uncertain political improvisations.

It was Montalembert's tragic fate to abandon the traditionalism program of reform, to which he was originally close, for political reasons, without being able to strengthen the theoretical foundations of Catholic liberalism. There was a contradiction, not unnoticed by his contemporaries, in the man: the political aristocrat whose writings suggest a romantic knight was at odds with a parliamentary tactician who went about his political work with cool empiricism and frequently employed means which he rejected in theory. Even later, the great Catholic lay leader was regularly accused of giving too little attention to principles and too much to tactics. As Trannoy has shown, this interpretation is incorrect, for Montalembert was always true to his religious and political convictions, despite his flexibility in practical politics.[92] As a member of a romantic generation fascinated by the "cult of freedom," his aristocratic desire for liberty was permeated by his Catholic liberalism; he was as passionately in revolt against the state absolutism which faced him in state-controlled church and schools, as against the vulgar Catholicism, so despotically insistent upon equality, of such men as Louis Veuillot.

The difficulties with which Lacordaire, the spiritual renewer of French Catholicism after 1830, had to contend were even greater.[93] Here, too, his rejection came not only from the church but from the state. Nothing better characterizes the painful slowness with which French Catholicism became accustomed to the new political conditions than the endless delays, procrastinations, and obstacles raised against Lacordaire's preaching at Notre Dame. The attempt to address a broad lay public in a style that evinced an awareness of the problems of the day stirred the mistrust of both sides. When Lacordaire finally decided to renew the Dominican Order in France, there were both religious and personal reasons at work: as an order priest, he hoped to be less hampered in his fight for public recognition of Catholicism than as a dependent upon the instructions of an episcopate whose majority was still of Gallican "establishment" persuasion.[94] Under his leadership the restored order became the focus for a daring spirit that strove against the official, *juste milieu*, Catholi-

---

[92] According to Trannoy, *op. cit.*, pp. 491 ff.

[93] For earlier literature on Lacordaire, see G. Ledos, *Morceaux choisis et bibliographie de Lacordaire* (Paris, 1923), especially Montalembert's book *Vie du Père Lacordaire* (Paris, 1862). The best biography is by Foisset: *Lacordaire* (Paris, 1870). Since then, especially, Guihaire, *Lacordaire et Ozanam* (Paris, 1933).

[94] Gurian, p. 119.

cism. It remained so both in religion and in politics.[95]

It must be admitted that the episcopate's distrust of Lacordaire was not altogether unfounded. The passionate and impulsive rhetorician had been the loudest and most radical of the triumvirate of *Avenir*. In his zeal he had demanded the abolition of the budget for public worship and had advocated the complete separation of church and state. The bishops, however, failed to recognize that Lacordaire's views altered after 1830 and that he had distanced himself from his earlier radical demands. Likewise, his temperament and words could not conceal that he was actually rather a moderate, *"démocrate par sentiment plutôt que par raison"* ["a democrat rather from emotion than from reason"], as Aubert said of him.[96] His attitude to the February Revolution is very significant in this regard: just as he greeted it with enthusiasm, he as quickly turned away when its political radicalism surfaced. Indeed, it was his generous nature, inclined to enthusiasms, that made Lacordaire the ideal mediator of liberal and democratic currents in French Catholicism. Beyond all his contradictions his thinking aimed always at achieving reconciliation with the adversary.

The aim of Montalembert and Lacordaire was to reconcile Catholicism and modern society. Unlike Lamennais's, theirs was a practical, political goal. To achieve it, they used liberal means and methods. It was Montalembert's belief that only Catholicism could do justice to the aspirations of liberalism. He wrote to Lamennais:

Rien ne peut se faire sans la liberté, et la liberté ne

[95] In politics the Order ranged itself with the left. Cuvillier, *op. cit.*, pp. 57 ff., attributes this fact to the relations of the first Dominicans to the Buchez school.

[96] R. Aubert, *Le pontificat de Pie IX* (Vol. XXI of the *Histoire de l'Église* by Fliche-Martin), p. 46. Lacordaire's article is in *Avenir*, October 27 and November 2, 3, and 5, 1848.

peut exister que par le Catholicisme et avec les Catholiques.[97] [Nothing can be done without liberty, and liberty cannot exist except through Catholicism and with Catholics.]

And there is a similar expression, using a daring simile, in Lacordaire:

> Dieu avait traité l'homme avec respect, en lui donnant la liberté morale, il a traité les nations avec respect en leur donnant par son Fils la liberté politique.[98] [God has treated man with respect by giving him moral free will. He has treated the nations with respect by giving them political freedom through His Son.]

Despite the echoes of Fauchet, this call for liberty of political action excluded the dogmatization of democracy as a state form. This is the difference between the second generation of Catholic liberalism and Lamennais. In practice, concessions to the political exigencies of the day could be very marked, as Montalembert later showed in his Malines speeches (1863).[99] They were the conclusions, however, of sober reflection on the politically acceptable and possible and not of a political theology.

Events after 1830, however, made it clear that there could be no stopping with the liberal pragmatism of Montalembert or with the purely verbal formation of the concept of liberty in Lacordaire. Above all, French Catholicism was forced to a new orientation by new social problems. Montalembert, who distinguished himself in fighting against child labor and for the pro-

---

[97] *Lettres à Lamennais*, p. 21 (November 22, 1832).

[98] *Oeuvres*, IX, 202–3.

[99] Comte de Montalembert, *L'Église libre dans l'État libre. Discours prononcés au Congrès Catholique de Malines* (Paris, 1863). The complete edition of Montalembert's works does not contain his Malines speeches. On them see Lecanuet, III, 348 ff.

tection of the workingman, was still able to hope to control unbridled industrialism through a new class order in which the Catholic elite, especially the French nobility, would assume the role of leader and protector. Lacordaire was far more skeptical about such plans, although he, too—through the Buchez circle— sought contact with contemporary ideas about corporations and associations and reflected the spirit of industrial society. However, neither man can claim to have deeply altered the sensitivity of French Catholicism to changed social conditions. The credit for this goes to a younger man, a member of the third generation of the Catholic movement in France: Antoine-Frédéric Ozanam.[100] Uninterested in the political problems which had rent French Catholicism since 1819, he paid little attention to the thorny question of monarchy vs. republic, yet became the inspiration of the philanthropic lay movement in France and gave Christian Democracy, whose name he coined, its own form distinct from Catholic liberalism.

Ozanam experienced the first wave of industrialization in his native city of Lyons. He witnessed the misery of the working class and the moral and physical decay caused by industrialization. He had also seen and felt the attraction of various religious socialisms on the proletarian masses. His first literary achievements were won in his fight against Saint-Simonism, which had become something of a church itself with its own fathers and a strictly regulated ritual.[101] Later in Rome and Paris where he

[100] On Ozanam, E. Galopin, *Essai de bibliographie chronologique sur Antoine-Frédéric Ozanam* (Paris, 1933) and G. Goyau, *Ozanam* (Paris, 1925) (also German). Then M. Rischke, *Ozanam* (Cologne, 1927); F. Méjecaze, *F. Ozanam, Essai de synthèse des idées et des jugements littéraires*, Thèse (Paris, 1932); L.-Y. Camus, *Frédéric Ozanam* (Paris, 1953) and A. R. Carranza, *Ozanam et ses contemporains* (Paris, 1953) (with a newer bibliography which has to be used with caution; cf. *Études*, April, 1954). Excellent L. Celier, *Ozanam* (Paris, 1956).
[101] G. Goyau, *op. cit.* (German edition), pp. 29 ff.

studied law and languages, he founded the first St. Vincent Conference, an institution which spread throughout the Catholic countries. Although Ozanam did not devise a social theory,[102] his example to his contemporaries as an apostle of untiring loving action contributed toward arousing in French Catholics the sentiment of social responsibility without which even the best of theories was bound to wither. He did not spare himself in his self-appointed task. In addition to his social and propagandistic work, he was professor of foreign literature at the Sorbonne. He exhausted himself early and died at barely forty years of age.

With Ozanam there arose a new spirit, opposed to pragmatic liberalism, which passionately sought the realization of the social kingdom of Christ. Ozanam started not from empirical theory, as had Montalembert and Lacordaire, but from an ideal: the community of brotherly love of the primitive church at Jerusalem, to him the highest realization of a *societas perfecta*.[103] This was the spirit with which he wanted to inform the present. At the same time, he was not an exalted romantic who believed in a new spiritual church and in a mankind transformed by it, as Lamennais; though he believed in the perfectability of society, he was no blind follower of a progressive enthusiasm.[104] He was separated from Catholic conservatives, not so much by his higher degree of optimism and faith in human nature, as by a more radical religiosity combined with well-founded doubts at all attempts to regenerate the church that stopped with externals and remained mired in politics.

It is remarkable, however, that in spite of his distance from

---

[102] Some starting-points can be found in the notes for a lecture on commercial law which he gave at the University of Lyon in 1839. (*Oeuvres completès*, VIII, 471 ff.).

[103] *Les origines du socialisme*, Oeuvres, VII, 218.

[104] *Du progrès par le christianisme*, Oeuvres, VII, 107 ff.

Lamennais the apocalyptics of the master of *La Chênaie* show up again in Ozanam. Filled by the vision of an impending age of the "Barbarians," he prophesied the destruction of the old world by the proletarian masses. At the same time, like Lamennais, he hoped for the triumph of the church. He was deeply moved by the problem of cultural decay and barbarization. He paid unusual attention to the fate of the church during the migration of peoples.[105] Again and again, he was fascinated by the spectacle of the raw force of barbaric peoples who had overrun the old cultures being slowly tamed and reformed through the church. The church as the educator of barbarians—this is a repeated motif of his work, the echo of the social criticism in which his historic studies would culminate.[106]

When the development of the political ideas of French Catholicism between 1830 and 1848 is examined, there is at first discerned an apparent increase of democratic tendencies, a turning away from the liberal views which were characteristic of the early Catholic movement; a deepened concern for social problems, frequently on the lines of a socialist thinker, Saint-Simon or Fourier, for instance. We have only to compare *Avenir* with *Ère Nouvelle*, the outstanding Catholic leftist paper of the Revolution of 1848,[107] to feel the whole impact of the difference between 1830 and 1848: while the social problem is only marginal

---

[105] *La civilisation au cinquième siècle*, Oeuvres, Vols. I and II.

[106] "J'ai toujour cru à l'invasion des barbares; j'y crois plus que jamais. Je la crois longue, meutrière, mais destinée tôt ou tard à plier sous la loi chrétienne, et par conséquent à régénérer le monde." Letter to Comte de Champagny, July 31, 1848, Oeuvres, XI, 247 ff.

[107] It was the second great newspaper (besides the *Avenir*) of the French Démocratie chrétienne. It existed from April 15, 1848, to April 1, 1849. For an exact analysis, see Duroselle, *op. cit.*, pp. 249 ff. Cf. also P. Fesch, *Lacordaire journaliste* (1830–1848) (Lyon, 1897), and P. Guihaire, *Lacordaire et Ozanam* (Paris, 1933).

in the July Revolution, it has become eighteen years later the
focus of attention. The political forces instituting French Catholicism had also changed. In the February Revolution it was no
longer Montalembert and his friends who had the upper hand
but men like Ozanam, Buchez, Maret,[108] Cormenin,[109] joined
later by Arnaud de l'Ariége,[110] republicans and sociologists who
no longer recognized the validity of the liberal program of the
constitutional monarchy and who considered social problems
more important than political problems; in command, next to
Buchez, was Feuguerrey,[111] Cheve,[112] La Morvonnais,[113] and
others. Characteristic of this general change in attitude is Montalembert's pessimism at the beginning of the 1848 Revolution.[114]
He felt that his life work was endangered by the impact of the
revolutionary masses; at the same time Lacordaire delivered a
paean from the pulpit of Notre Dame to the people of Paris,
who spared the altars in their plunderings, while he refused Oza-

[108] On Maret, see G. Bazin, Vie de Mgr. Maret (2 vols.; Paris, 1882).

[109] On Cormenin, P. Bastid, Cormenin (Paris, 1948).

[110] He took over the leadership of the Christian Democratic movement in 1848.
Duroselle describes him as a man who is predominantly theoretical; in: "L'attitude
politique et sociale des catholiques français en 1848," Revue d'histoire de l'Église
de France, XXXIV (1948), p. 49–50. Duroselle's typewritten study, "Arnaud de
l'Ariège et la démocratie chrétienne (1848–1851)" (Paris, 1949), was not accessible to me.

[111] He was Buchez' most important pupil; together with Ott he earned special
merit for the revival of the Thomistic social teachings. Cf. his Essai sur les doctrines politiques de Saint-Thomas d'Aquin (Paris, 1857), which was edited by
Buchez.

[112] According to Duroselle, Catholicisme social, p. 346, "le plus fécond, le plus
hardi aussi des journalistes catholiques sociaux sous la Seconde République."

[113] He belonged to the circle of La Chênaie; orginally he had been a pupil of
Fourier and had tried to attune Fourier's teachings to Catholicism. On him see
Fleury, Hippolyte de la Morvonnais (Paris, 1911).

[114] Cf. Montalembert's diaries and letters of the years 1848–52, edited by A.
Trannoy, in Revue historique, CXCII (1942), 253–89, and CXCVI (1946),
408–42.

nam, the embattled leader of liber Catholicism, his help, with
these words in *Ère Nouvelle*: "*C'est impossible, tu es un vain-
cu*"[115] ["It is impossible: you are defeated"].

This picture of a sudden general change seems to contradict
a widespread view of the events of 1848 and the role of the
French Catholics, upheld chiefly by Marxist historians but also
by some Catholics.[116] This view holds that French Catholicism,
intimately linked with the social interests of the middle class,
joined the revolutionary movement only temporarily and only in
appearance; that it awaited deliverance from its uneasy alliance
with republican forces in order to go its own way with Cavaignac
and Louis Napoleon; that it did not hesitate to attack the Parisian workers from the rear by instigating the dissolution of the
atéliers nationals, thus creating an impasse which could only lead
to open revolt. This very revolt, then, gave it the welcome opportunity to call in the militia and to achieve the bloody suppression
of the whole revolution. The *rapprochement* after the June battle
between the Orleanistic middle class under Thiers and the Catholic party under the leadership of Montalembert is seen in
Thiers' assisting the fulfilment of Catholic demands for school
reform. The Catholic movement is supposed to have come under
the influence of bourgeois reaction; the price paid by the Catholic bourgeoisie for the liquidation of the revolution[117] is assumed
to have been the dissolution of the republic and the refusal of
the justified demands of the workers.

Under close examination this view appears to be based on the
axiom of the indivisible connection between social position and
political action, which fails completely when applied to the polit-

[115] Quoted by P. Guihaire, *op. cit.,* p. 86.
[116] See Duroselle's article in the *Revue d'histoire de l'Église de France* (n. 110),
"Introduction," p. 44.
[117] Especially, H. Guellemin in his *Histoire des catholiques français au XIXe
siècle;* cf. Duroselle, *op. cit.,* p. 45.

ical Catholicism of 1848. First of all, class differences had little influence upon politics at this stage of parties still bound together by ideology. This circumstance is reflected in the fact that the Catholic leaders of the time came from the most diverse social backgrounds. On the other hand, it should be remembered that the religious tensions and fights for control in the church also had consequences in French Catholicism, where the lines of religious-ideological group formations often intersect the mosaic of social forces. The Catholic bourgeoisie, constantly mentioned in this connection, was not a unity: it included legitimists and liberals. Nor does the cool equation of social-progressiveness and leftist politics apply. There were in 1848 numerous republicans who were blind and unresponsive on the social question, while after 1850 the Catholic social movement was strongest and most clearly articulated by the school of Le Play, which was politically conservative. As for the alliance between Thiers and Montalembert, the initiative came from Thiers as a consequence of the failure of the Second Republic and when the political forces of the July monarchy, which remained unscathed, gained new momentum after 1849. If we agree with Paul Bastid's judgment that there has hardly ever been a political regime that contributed so much to undermining itself as the Second Republic,[118] why should Catholics not have acted logically in this situation; their loyalty to the February, 1848, republic could not remain unaffected by the fact that this republic, as was shown in the following months, was unable to contribute anything to the solution of even the most pressing political and social problems.

And, still, some questions remain. If it is admitted that the republican and socialist leaders of the 1848 Revolution were the victims of their own ideology, how was it that liberal Catholi-

[118] P. Bastid, *Les doctrines et institutions de la Seconde République* (2 vols.; Paris, 1949), *passim*.

cism, with its far greater experience, did not take over and that
the energy of the renewed Catholic-social religiosity contributed
next to nothing to the Second Republic? The reference to the
bourgeois or aristocratic class ties of the Catholic middle class
and of the episcopate misfires in view of the evidence of such
men as Ozanam, Cormenin, and Buchez, and in view of the
nearly unanimous assent of the French bishops to the new republic.[119] If republican-social Catholicism, the true démocratie chrétienne, formed only a minority among French Catholics, how
can that explain the ineffectuality of their political as compared
to their ideological impulses, so that they had no effect worth
mentioning on practical pólitics or how can it explain their
inability to alter events after 1849?

The reason may lie in the near total absence of contact between the working class and the majority of French Catholics
and, especially, in the deep-seated antagonism of active, religious
lay circles (forming the core of the religious socialists) with the
Parisian proletariat. Using latest French research, Jean Baptiste
Duroselle has repeatedly pointed to the near de-Christianization
of the French working class in the forties.[120] Thus, it remained
outside the influence of the religious renewal which began after
1830 and which was limited to intellectual and aristocratic
circles. The great difficulty that even Buchez faced in spreading
ideas in the working class is clear in many instances.[121] In 1844,
Monsignor Affre, the Bishop of Paris, had to trust Catholic laymen to proclaim the church in workmen's circles because the
framework of normal parochial pastoral care was too narrow for
the newly forming proletariat. His successor, Sibour, even envisioned the founding of an inner mission, carried on by "worker

[119] For an impressive documentation, see Duroselle, op. cit., p. 46.
[120] Op. cit., pp. 54 ff.
[121] See infra, p. 246, n. 158.

priests."[122] The weakness of the Catholic-social forces in 1848 was not least caused by the fact that they operated without real knowledge of the world of working men; their proposed reforms were still connected with the traditionalist class-corporative ideal which to the traditionalists had seemed the only effective defense against the individualism of 1789. A solution to the social question was thus not sought in an extension of the democratic rights of freedom but in their restriction through corporations. But precisely this solution was made impossible by the Revolution of 1848: a world of its own had been forming among the developing proletariat which no longer fit the framework of either church or state concepts.

How was it possible to achieve access to this world? It would not happen without deep-going religious reform. It was no longer sufficient to liberate French Catholicism from the ghetto of being a state-controlled "establishment" church and to give it its independence; it was much more important to renew it internally and make it a force to be reckoned with in the spiritual dialogue of the times. Catholic liberalism had exhausted its creative powers with the destruction of Gallicanism and the securing of rights to set up Catholic schools. Its organizational means were inadequate for the remaining tasks. The penetration of society by a new Christian spirituality was work for monks; and it was monks, together with laymen, who took over the painstaking work of translating the worldly experiences of the political and social struggles into new religious forms.

The tasks which faced Catholic laymen were entirely new. They called for an ability to detach one's self completely from its hitherto closed world (or the one which it believed it had occupied); it demanded realism in weighing the changed social

[122] Duroselle, op. cit., pp. 48 ff.

possibilities of Catholicism and sophisticated political thinking. In the face of a secularized society, the methods that had been valid in a politico-religious order so closed that it permitted individuals to retire into the ethics of individualistic striving after virtue were outdated. In the religious crisis that began with the Great Revolution, it became apparent that a Christianity ordered by a goal of personal perfection was insufficient in solving the new tasks. Yet if lay political activity remained outside the religious perspective, it threatened to become a rigid, merely tactical activity, as shown in the example of Catholic liberalism. From this view of the situation sprang the alliance between the newly founded and reformed orders and the Catholic laity, a noteworthy sign of the times after 1830, the encounter between conventual and lay forms of life which found expression, for example, in the friendship of Buchez and the first Dominicans and in the close connection of Lacordaire and Dom Guéranger (the renewers and reformers of the Dominican and the Benedictine orders), with La Chênaie, and in Montalembert's participation in the Solesmes. This movement took the shape of secular institutes, a form which, starting in France, was to conquer all of modern Catholicism.[123] Lacordaire's and Montalembert's religious writings sprang from this situation as a consideration both of the religious rank and the characteristics of orders and also of laicism in the church. With them a new image, "holiness in the world," took a place side by side with the ascetic-mystical ideal predominant until then.[124] In this sense a book like Montalembert's Vie de sainte Elisabeth can be considered to symbolize the

---

[123] On the newly founded order and the secular institutes, see Aubert, op. cit., pp. 457 ff. On the present situation of the secular institutes, see Dokumente, Vol. IV, (1953), and H. Urs von Balthasar, Der Laie und der Ordensstand, (Freiburg, 1949).

[124] Y. Congar, Lay People in the Church (London, 1957), pp. 341 and pp. 380 ff.

sociological event: it mirrors the emergence of Catholic laity in post-revolutionary Catholicism. Most of the expressions of the new lay consciousness are to be found between 1830 and 1848. For this a review of the development from *Avenir* to *Ère Nouvelle* is pertinent.

Christian Democracy from 1830 to 1848 was not a complete system but a variety of political types and temperaments. Its ability to co-ordinate contradictions and blend similarities into a unified whole reaches from Lamennais to Arnand de l'Ariége, from liberal to democratic Catholicism, from the remnants of the traditionalist and the Saint-Simon schools to the renewal of religious forces as manifested in Lacordaire and Ozanam. It is not a doctrine but a political attitude which unites Christian Democrats. Their trust is in the development of democracy. In the Revolution of 1848, according to Lacordaire, the *Démocratie chrétienne* is the "*parti de confiance.*"[125] It puts its trust into reconciliation of church and revolution.

What unifies spirits so different from each other as Lamennais, Buchez, and Ozanam? Chiefly, it was the experience of the revolution and the state of uncertainty and crisis created by it, a sense of general political instability, a foreboding of catastrophes.

> Tous les esprits élevés annoncent que nous sommes arrivés à une période de catastrophes et de déchirements universels [the nineteen-year-old Ozanam writes to his friend Le Jouteux]. Telle est du moins l'opinion de MM. de Chateaubriand, de La Mennais et de Lamartine.[126] [All the best spirits proclaim that we have arrived at a period of catastrophe and general agony. This at least is the opinion of Messrs. de Chateaubriand, La Mennais, and Lamartine.]

[125] Later this was also the name of the republican wing of the *parti catholique* in the National Assembly.
[126] Letter of July 23, 1832, in Oeuvres X, 59 ff.

Lamennais, who loved the apocalyptic colors in his palette, forecast a darkening image of modern Europe:

> There is no real link between states which are separated by the old politics of interest now complicated by thousands of new interests; and in every single state a spirit of independence, more or less developed, more or less favored by the events of the times, leads to revolutions or is secretly undermining the foundations of order. Everywhere, or nearly everywhere, peoples are breaking free of their leaders. Fed up with obedience because they have been told that obedience means slavery, they consider themselves to be oppressed as long as they do not command. A generation is rising, filled with anarchistic theories, passionate, and ready to construct a world according to its own ideas. This is the spectacle which Europe offers.[127] [He forecast a new revolution:] Never before were such passions unleashed for a new order of things, the whole world cries for it and thus, without admitting it cries for revolution![128]

Everywhere there is decay, dissolution, decline of religion, victory of unbelief:

> A cry of despair rises in the East and reverberates in the West: What is happening on earth? What is the meaning of the distant death knell, of weeping, of mourning, of general anxiety? Are we destined, as some think, to assist at the funeral of a superannuated Christianity? Is it destined to devour itself like everything else? Will there come a time when even this will be nothing but a memory?[129]

There then follows the charge which is so characteristic of

---

[127] "De la religion," chap. x, Oeuvres complètes (Paris, 1836 ff.), V, 339–40.

[128] "Des progrès de la Révolution" as quoted by M. Leroy, Histoire des Idées sociales en France, Vol. II (Paris, 1950), p. 371, n. 1.

[129] Affaires de Rome, p. 198.

Lamennais: Revolution not only destroys; it prepares the way for
the new. Under the influence of the Catholic emancipation in
Ireland and Belgium, Lamennais discovers the positive possibilities of democracy:

> Are these not actually the Catholic peoples everywhere,
> who rise as if they were the first to receive the revelation of
> future events which are withheld from mankind? Something
> as sweet as hope is attracting them; something that is as
> mighty as God spurs them on.[130]

It is unquestionable: God speaks in the revolution. The early
Lamennais knew this, even when he was still enmeshed in traditionalism: "The impulse for the events which shake society
always originates above."[131]

In view of the democratic movement, the church, too, had to
decide if it wants "to be reborn more beautiful and stronger
through liberty, or expire in shameful and incurable servility":

> époque . . . unique dans son histoire et dans l'histoire d'au-
> cune autre Église; époque fatale qui décidera de la vie ou de
> la mort du catholicisme parmi nous.[132] [A unique epoch in
> its history and the history of any church, a fatal span which
> will decide the life or death of Catholicism among us.]

These sentences, written in 1831, are echoed in Ozanam:

> I believe in an imminent civil war whose battlefield will be
> all of Europe, entwined as it is in the nets of Freemasonry.
> But this terrible crisis may eventually bring a decision, and
> from the ruins of the old, exhausted nations a new Europe
> will rise; then Catholicism will be understood; then the mo-
> ment will have come to carry civilization to the old Orient; it

[130] Avenir, June 26, 1831.
[131] De la religion, chap. v, loc. cit., p. 169.
[132] "Position de l'Église de France," Avenir, as quoted by Boutard, op. cit.,
II, 143.

will be a great epoch; but we shall not live to see it.[133]

With great relevance to the political sphere are the expectations of other Christian Democrats, who, like Marets, wrote:

> To us the principles of 1789 and 1830, the ideas of the French Revolution, once shorn of the evil attached to them by passions which were and still can be attached to them, seem to us the beginning of the political era of Christianity and the Gospels. In them we always see the possibility of a perfect application of the spirit of love and justice, the basic idea of human dignity which divine revelation has given to the world.[134]

Finally, Lacordaire, in his speech on the Irish Catholic leader O'Connell, inadvertently equates the interests of the church and humanity: "Modern society is an expression of human needs and consequently an expression of the needs of the church."[135] Thus, there is a bridge from Lamennais' liberal ideas that God is present in all the changes of the world to the republicanism of the younger generation which recognizes with Ozanam the *avènement temporel de l'Évangile* ["the temporal coming of the Gospels"] in the revolution.[136] In Montalembert's Mecheln speeches, which constitute the closest *rapprochement* of liberal Catholicism and democracy, we find the echo of these moods:

> I look around and everywhere I see only democracy. I see the Flood mounting higher and higher. As a man I would be frightened; but I am not afraid as a Christian, for as I see the Flood I also perceive the Arch.[137]

[133] In the letter cited in n. 126.
[134] Quoted by G. Bazin, *op. cit.*, I, 225.
[135] Éloge funèbre de Daniel O'Connell, Oeuvres, VIII, 192.
[136] Message Aux électeurs du département du Rhône of April 15, 1848, as quoted by Duroselle, *Catholicisme social*, p. 301.
[137] *Discours de Malines* (Paris, 1865), pp. 14–15.

The religious inspiration of the *Démocratie chrétienne* could not last long. It was a spurious excitement, an impetus which came to an end with the June battle and the advent of the third Bonaparte. After the resignation of Lacordaire, the *parti de confiance* in parliament was a rudderless ship. *Ère Nouvelle*, in whose pages various political tendencies had wrestled with each other, became moderate, its democratic verve continually weakening. It ceased publication in May, 1849.[138] The attempts to build a stronger organization afterward, as Arnaud de l'Ariège tried in his *Cercle de la Démocratie catholique*, were doomed to failure, as were the various publications founded following the demise of *Ère Nouvelle*. It became obvious that the majority of French Catholics remained conservative and wanted nothing to do with an alliance with democracy such as Ozanam suggested. Yet French Catholicism, as shown in the first general elections, was well equipped to defend itself by democratic means. The addition of many bourgeois and peasant votes, however, did not result in the reconciliation with the republic that the Christian Democrats had hoped for; rather it stiffened the tendency in the country to resist change. After the bloody quelling of the workmen's riots in Paris, the *parti catholique*, again under the leadership of Montalembert, approached the Orleanistic party of Thiers to form the coalition which carried the third Napoleon to power. His reign ended not only the Christian Democratic movement of 1848 but the experiment of the Second Republic.

Thus, the years 1848–52 form an era in the history of French Catholicism that signifies the end of the attempt to reconcile the church and modern society on the basis of a democratic socialism and at the same time smoothed the way for the return of the middle class to the church. The *Lex Falloux*, which con-

---

[138] See *supra*, n. 107.

ceded to Catholic congregations a decisive influence in primary and secondary education, were only fulfilling an old demand of Catholic liberalism that would hardly have had a chance for passage in the chamber had not the liberal right, on grounds of *défense sociale* (and contrary to their real condition) come to the aid of Montalembert. Faced with a choice between the Catholic curé and the laicist teacher, Thiers, the follower of Voltaire, decided for the curé, "*parce que je compte beaucoup sur lui pour propager cette bonne philosophie qui apprend à l'homme qu'il est ici-bas pour souffrir*"[139] ["for I much count upon him to further that fine philosophy that teaches man that he is upon earth to suffer"]. Burdened with this mortgage of cynicism, the *édit de Nante du dixneuvième siècle* of Lacordaire ["the Edict of Nantes of the nineteenth century"] passed the parliamentary stage. It is small wonder in the face of this purely tactical use of religion and in view of the jubilation a little later over Napoleon III as the savior of the church and a new Constantine that the mocking phrase *alliance du sabre et du goupillon* ["the alliance of the sabre and the incense sprinkler"] gained currency. Anti-clericalism found new fuel in the workmens' circles which until then had not openly been hostile to the church. Great numbers of these circles now joined the camp of socialism, their hopes in Catholicism disappointed. After 1850 the paths of the church and the working class separated in France. This has remained so until our own days, despite efforts by the church. This was another way in which the February Revolution was epoch-making for French Catholicism.

The failure of apocalyptic hopes triggered deep disillusion among the *chrétiens démocrates*; they suddenly felt their isolation within French Catholicism. Most of them, following Lacor-

---

[139] Aubert, *op. cit.*, p. 50.

daire's example, retired from politics. Those who had not already
gone over to the *parti de l'ordre* had their democratic enthusiasm
dashed by events: Buchez moved toward liberalism during the
last years of his life.[140] Some of those forced into political retire-
ment took the occasion to contemplate the problems of church
and democracy from a perspective detached from the actual
struggle. It was precisely during the years of the Second Empire
that French Christian Democrats wrote and published volumi-
nously.[141]

Here we have to be reminded that the history of *Démocratie
chrétienne* is closely linked to the intellectual trends which led
to modern French sociology.[142] What had occupied Lamennais
and Buchez, Maret and Ozanam, was exactly that crisis which
overtook France in the Great Revolution, the unhinging of the
structure of state as a result of which the hitherto valid order was
ripped apart and nothing left of the *ancien régime* but a heap
of scattered stones whose regrouping greatly attracted the play of
sociological fancy. Lamennais wished to see society restored on
religious foundations; Buchez attacked the obstacles in the way
of providential progress by a scientific kind of criticism; Lacordaire pressed for the recognition of a reconciliation between
church and modern society which, according to his view, had
already taken place; Ozanam looked forward to such a reconciliation in the future. These are variations of a common theme: a
view of Christianity as containing the seeds of social progress.
Lacordaire could say:

> In the three great epochs in which modern society was
> formed, we have extended our hand to it. In 1789 it was the

[140] Cuvillier, *op. cit.*, pp. 78 ff.
[141] Duroselle, *op. cit.*, pp. 657 ff.
[142] On that N. Sombart, "Vom Ursprung der Geschichtssoziologie," *Archiv
für Rechts- und Sozialphilosophie* XLI (1955), 469–510.

majority of the Clerical Chamber which first made common cause with the Third Estate and substituted a vote by estates for the head vote, the equivalent of the *coup de grace* for feudalism. . . . There was the Concordat, which broke the old church, the deposition of the whole episcopate, which represented a past society; the successor of St. Peter crossed all of Europe to lay a crown on the head of the new man. In 1830 the most important and celebrated French priest since Bossuet took up the fight and challenged the nation: he failed less because he had surpassed the aim, but because he could not do full justice to it.[143]

There is, then, a revolutionary tradition in French Catholicism. It reaches from the spiritual Constituent Assembly of 1789 to Lamennais. Catholics had a hand in every upheaval in the formation of modern society. Moreover, Catholic participation had not only a political but a religious, a church, aspect. We can hardly overlook the satisfaction with which Lacordaire pointed to the deposition of the whole of the French episcopate in the course of the negotiations for the concordat between Napoleon and the pope:[144] this revolution, too, this revolt of papal power against Gallican particularism is a stage in the formation of modern society. From this point of view we can understand Lamennais and Lacordaire's fight against the state-controlled church of the Restoration and of the bourgeois monarchy. More sharply than the high prelates who had grown up with the ideas of Gallicanism, they felt that Bossuet's church system could not be revived, since the revolution eliminated the feudal episcopate and the *roi très chrétien.*

---

[143] *Oeuvres*, IX, 82–83.

[144] However, he suppresses the fact that this operation was very embarrassing for Rome; cf. J. Schmidlin, *Papstgeschichte der neuesten Zeit* (Munich, 1933 ff.), Vol. I, p. 53, n. 69.

Lamennais considered the fall of Gallicanism to be a judgment of God. He wrote:

> Lorsque Dieu voudra que le monde change, il changera tout le système des rapports qui lie son Église aux souverainetés temporelles.[145] [Since God wanted to change the world, He will change every system of relationships which binds His Church to the temporal powers.]

He fought vigorously against a political Gallicanism founded on the organic articles of the Concordat, with the abuse of the appeal power connected with it, and the submission of the Roman decrees to the government's "*placet.*"[146]

> Religion administered like customs and taxes, the priesthood degraded, discipline sinned against, revelation suppressed, the church bereft, so to speak, of the independence necessary to it, communicating under progressively more difficult conditions, with its head every day more subject to the moods of the temporal power, used by it for everything, receiving everything from it, priests, laws even the teaching: what is this if not death?[147]

He concentrated his efforts to making the *église salariée* a free church again, even at the price of complete separation from the state. Lacordaire and Arnaud de l'Ariège, like him, demanded the separation of church and state.[148] Lamennais administered

[145] *Avenir*, June 28, 1831.
[146] Further regulations were: prohibition of episcopalian synods or travels to Rome without governmental permission; abolition of all exemptions; priority of civil over Christian marriage; the obligation of professors at seminaries to adhere to the Gallican Declaration of 1682, etc. On the organic articles, cf. Leflon, *op. cit.*, pp. 194 ff., and F. Mourret, *Histoire générale de l'Église* (Paris, 1917 ff.), VII, 329.
[147] *Avenir*, October 18, 1830.
[148] Concerning Lacordaire, see *supra*, n. 96, p. 223; concerning Arnaud de l'Ariège, cf. his book, *La Révolution et l'Église* (Paris, 1869).

the decisive blow to Gallicanism in France and contributed to the victorious movement of what was, polemically, labeled ultramontanism in the nineteenth century because of its subordination of the national churches to the universalism of Rome. He was helped by the lack of strength in the state-controlled church of the Restoration, by its having already become a system "on call," entirely dependent on politics and not viable after the fall of the Bourbons. After the July Revolution, which saw the exile of the last anointed king of France and the elimination from the charter of the provision that Catholicism was the dominant religion, state interference in inner-church matters was already an anachronism. Had the Gallican self-maintained its alliance with the political power against Rome despite its bad experiences, it would not have had support in either a laicist or a neutral state. Thus, the inner condition of the church gave the pope's monarchic power new impetus. Lamennais recognized and furthered this process where he could. Like de Maistre he was recognized as an advocate of papal infallibility. Like the former, he too saw in the pope not only the *principium fidei* but the

> principium societatis: Sans pape, pas d'Église, sans Église, point de christianisme, sans christianisme, point de religion et point de société, de sorte que la vie des nations européennes a sa source, son unique source, dans le pouvoir pontifical.[149]
> [Without pope, no church, without church, no Christianity, without Christianity neither religion nor society of the kind for which the European nations draw upon as its source, its unique source, the papal power.]

As from a solid rock within the whirl of revolutionary changes, new orders issued from the papacy on the new structure of society. In this, Lamennais's programs, *reconstituer la société poli-*

[149] *De la religion*, as quoted by Leflon, *op. cit.*, p. 480.

tique à l'aide de la société religieuse, is reduced to its shortest institutional formula.

Renewed by papal authority, the church would have an authoritative effect upon society. In this, Christian Democrats, especially the generation of 1848, continued the work begun by Lamennais. Ozanam had recognized that social problems outweighed political problems: *"Derrière la révolution politique, nous voyons une révolution sociale"*[150] [Behind the political revolution we see a social revolution"]. Buchez developed the theme: society is split into two classes; one owns the means of production, the other has nothing; it works for the former to eke out a living. This is the universal condition of the liberal state: equalization, established only halfway, is immediately followed by a setback, a new and more acute division of the social structure along the lines of money and property.[151] There are similar observations in Ozanam: in a letter to his friend Lallier, the class struggle is described as the most moving event of the times:

> If this is the struggle between those who have too much and those who have nothing, it is our duty as Christians to stand between these irreconcilable enemies and to see that the ones give up, as if they fulfilled a law, and that the others receive, as if they received a benefit; that the ones cease to demand and that the others stop refusing; that equality becomes reality as far as it is humanly possible, that voluntary community takes the place of forced taxes and loans; that love creates what justice alone cannot create.[152]

As can be seen, Ozanam had faith in the free operation of Christian love, while Buchez attempted to reorganize work by legislation.

---

[150] "L'attente et l'action," *Correspondant,* March, 1848.
[151] *Introduction,* I, 8–9.
[152] Letter of November 5, 1836, *Oeuvres,* X, 213 ff.

It is no coincidence that the consideration of social problems by Christian Democrats again has its source in criticism of the revolution. In Buchez proletarization is seen as the end result of the negative, individualistic spirit of 1789 which destroyed the old corporations without replacing them. It thus deprived workmen of the possibility of protecting themselves against exploitation and fraud.[153] The bourgeois revolution, which improperly started with the rights and not the duties of men,[154] opened wide the door to social anarchy. With this the theme is sounded that will later be taken up by conservative Catholicism, that is, the necessity of establishing a well-ordered community to back up the structure of society and without which, as Lamennais said, the state would be nothing but a *"vaste agrégation d'individus dépourvus de lien"*[155] ["a vast aggregation of individuals bereft of any link"]. Here Buchez' thoughts point far into the future. The rise of the union movement, which may be conceived as the invasion of corporate principles into the individualism of *démocratie pure*, developed in France under the protection of the conservative social Catholicism of the school of de Muns. It is mostly because of the efforts of conservatives that the *Lex Le Chapelier* which prohibited any professional or unionist organization of interests, was repealed.[156] The social teachings of Leo XIII (and those of Pius XI even more) are embedded in the conception of a corporate order which closely approaches what Christian Democrats understand when they speak of a "structured society."

---

[153] *Histoire parlementaire*, XXXII, "Preface."

[154] "Le droit émane du devoir," says Buchez, with Fouchez and Grégoire. Castella, *Buchez*, p. 57.

[155] *De la religion*, chap. v; *Oeuvres*, V, 169.

[156] On the *Lex Le Chapelier*, see E. Soreau, "La loi Le Chapelier," *Annales historiques de la Révolution française*, VIII (1931), 288–314. The law was mitigated under the reign of Napoleon III and finally abolished by the syndicate law of 1884. On that H. Rollet, *L'action sociale des catholiques en France 1871–1901* (Paris, 1947), pp. 218 ff. and pp. 469 ff.

Of course, Buchez did not conceive of unions in the modern sense. We have mentioned the quite different conception that was at the bottom of his workmen's associations: the effort to neutralize the conflict between capital and labor in an all-embracing *organisation du travail*. The workmen should themselves become entrepreneurs. Workmen's association, therefore, unlike the later unions, are not the organs of the workmen in the fight between economic interests; on the contrary, they were supposed to transform industrial society, which seemed to be governed by egotistical interests, by a kind of republican *vertu* projected onto the social sphere. Buchez was speaking about a situation that preceded the class struggle.[157] His warnings are therefore directed with like insistence to all *industriels*, workers or owners. Both are threatened by materialism.[158] Buchez hoped to counteract the deleterious effects of the bourgeois revolution through education in the Christian-social spirit, convinced that the social order had to change sooner or later: "*Cette inégalité est une monstruosité odieuse dans une société chrétienne*" ["This inequality is an odious monstrosity in a Christian society"].[159]

If for Buchez Christianity and socialism are of the same metal, Ozanam was much more cautious. He distinguishes between the true and false in socialism: some of its teachings have Christian origins; others are un-Christian. Not all can be accepted by the church.[160] Directed against Fourier and Saint-Simon, this is also

---

[157] A class-conscious proletariat arose in France as late as 1840; cf. E. Dolléans, *Histoire du mouvement ouvrier* (Paris, 1936 ff.), I, 227 ff. Rohden "Zur Soziologie des politischen Katholizismus in Frankreich" (cf. *supra* p. 215, n. 74), p. 497.

[158] Buchez' followers complained that it was easier to raise 100,000 francs than to find a worker who would agree to become a member of a workmen's association, for he would thereby waive his chance of becoming a master. *Histoire parlementaire*, XXXII, VIII.

[159] *Ibid.*, pp. x–xi.

[160] *Les origines du Socialisme*, in Oeuvres VII, 211 ff.

aimed at Buchez and his social perfectionism. Ozanam, too, believed in progress in social life. But he had no confidence, as Buchez had, in an all-embracing program of self-help backed by the state, nor did he consider direct state intervention the proper means to overcome the difficulties caused by industrialization, as the conservative Villeneuve-Bargemont[161] did. Laws will never solve the social question, and caritas, personal help, will always be needed. Like the socialists of the Buchez circle, Ozanam also wished "that the love and faith of the first centuries would return: *"ce n'est pas trop pour notre âge"*[162] ["This is not too much for our age"]. While the neo-Catholic Buchez thinks of a revival of primitive spirituality, Ozanam wishes to oppose Christianity in the visible, historical form of the church, in which he sees the *esprit d'association,* to egoism as a civilizing factor. Thus his social thinking flows naturally into the first great antithesis of Lamennais:

> On the one side revolutionary individualism, on the other ecclesiastical solidarity. While modern legislators strive for the ideal of political order, which apparently has more reason than ever to detest such resistance, the church, this great society, was not afraid to authorize within its bosom all sorts of communities in constantly increasing numbers: from the national, provincial, and diocesan churches whose special rights it recognized, to the orders which she honored and the last fraternities which she blessed.

But the church wants only voluntary association.

---

[161] Beside Le Play he was the most important theorist of conservative Catholicism; his principle work was *Économie politique chrétienne* (Paris, 1835). On him cf. Théry, *Villeneuve-Bargemont* (Nancy, 1911); M. I. Ring, *Villeneuve-Bargemont, Precursor of Modern Social Catholicism* (Milwaukee, 1935); and Seiler, *op. cit.,* pp. 57 ff.

[162] Letter to X——, February 23, 1835, in Oeuvres, X, 146 ff.

Never did Christianity agree to the enforced community which grasps man even before birth, pushes him from the state-controlled school to the state-controlled factory, and therefore reduces him to a will-less soldier in the industrial army, to a mindless little wheel in the machinery of the state.

Thus, the Christian social concept lies between the extremes of individualism and collectivism; it seeks an agreement "*en prê-chant l'association, mais en la prêchant volontaire*"[163] ["by preaching association, but voluntary association"].

The polarity of the views held by Buchez and Ozanam is only an especially striking form of the old tension between freedom and law, charitable action and state welfare, caritas and justice, which permeates the whole history of Catholic social ethics.[164] We may here point out that the path taken by the *démocratie chrétienne* was insufficient and ineffectual in the search for a solution: that of Ozanam, because private charity was not sufficient to meet social tasks; that of Buchez, because he violently pushed toward a harmonizing, total economic solution, for which the time had not yet come. But for us it is decisive here that we find in the essential elements of the Catholic social teachings as they developed anew in the nineteenth century the demand for an auxiliary structure of society and the rejection of the class struggle.

Although the *Démocratie chrétienne* of 1848 sprang from the Catholic socialism of "purified" schools of Saint-Simon and Fourier, it was not a socialist movement in the accepted sense of the word. It is true that its demands were the same as the socialists: universal suffrage, a shortening of the work day, and a con-

---

163 *Les origines du Socialisme, op cit.,* pp. 245 ff.

164 On that, W. Schöllgen, *Die soziologischen Grundlagen der katholischen Sittenlehre* (Düsseldorf, 1953), pp. 373 ff.

stitutional right to work. But all this was in a different context and served different aims than those of the socialists. The *Démocratie chrétienne* was less concerned with the liberation of the proletariat than with its *education*. It strove for the participation of the people in power, but it was Christian people who were destined to govern; educated by the church, the "barbarians" would govern through democracy. From them Ozanam hoped for the strength to overcome the moral laxity of the old liberalism and to bolster political and social morals. There is no doubt in his view that private egoism, unbridled competition, divorce, and legalized prostitution were incompatible with democracy; here if nowhere else he continues the tradition of Fauchet.[165] Above all, he aimed to destroy the belief that the aim of the state was the greatest happiness of the greatest number. Buchez, too, fought against the modern idea of mass happiness. He saw in it a step toward slavery and the omnipotence of the state. Not happiness but *vertu*, civic virtue, should become the aim and impulse of economic man.

> Ainsi tous, en quelque lieu que nous soyons placés, riches ou pauvres, nous devons tous, dans l'intérêt de l'avenir, dans l'interêt de nos enfants, nous devons repousser loin de nous les enseignements qui s'annoncent par ce signe: le but de l'homme sur la terre est le bonheur.[166] [Thus all of us, no matter where we are placed, must in the interest of the future, in the interest of our children, reject the teachings which are announced by the sign: the aim of man on earth is the attainment of happiness.]

Similarly, Ozanam scourged the "egotistic teachings" of Helvetius and of Diderot;[167] the belief that the aim of man on earth is

---

[165] On that, cf. his article "Du divorce" in *Ère nouvelle*, as in *Oeuvres*, VII, 355.

[166] *Histoire parlementaire*, Vol. XXXII, "Preface," p. xv.

[167] *Réflexions sur la doctrine de Saint-Simon*, in *Oeuvres*, VII, 355.

happiness was nothing but the cause of extravagance, envy, war, revolution: *"mais nous ne croyons pas au bonheur sur la terre"*[168] ["but we do not believe in happiness on earth"]. In spite of their criticism of the eudemism of the revolution and the Enlightenment, the *démocratie chrétienne*, unlike conservative Catholicism, did not support counterrevolution. The reason for this lay in the often repeated view of the natural development of democracy. For Lacordaire, the revolution was not evil, as it was for de Maistre, nor unsuccessful, as it was for Buchez: it was unfinished. Thus all possibilities remained open for the church of the future. He wrote optimistically:

> L'esprit moderne ne touche en rien aux dogmes, à la morale, au culte, à l'autorité du christianisme; il lui retire seulement le secours du bras civil pour rechercher et punir l'héresie, se fiant à la force intime et divine de la foi, qui ne saurait faillir faute d'un glaive matériel levé contre l'erreur.[169] [The modern spirit touches nothing in the dogmas, morals, worship, and authority of Christianity; it only removes the help of the civic arm in the seeking out and punishing of the heretic and relies on the intimate and divine power of faith which will not fail because of a material sword raised against error.]

The modern spirit is not against the church; it demands only that it fulfil its office without help from the state, alone and supported only by freedom of conscience. This is to be found in Lamennais; Lacordaire goes far beyond Lamennais' sharp antithesis. With him, the thought of development enters into the consideration of the state-church relationship and reduces the

---

[168] "Aux insurgés désarmés," in *Ère nouvelle*, July 8, 1848, as quoted by Duroselle, *op. cit.*, pp. 305–306.
[169] *Discours sur la loi de l'histoire*, in Oeuvres, VIII, 277 ff.

acerbity of the historical clash of church and revolution. This results in new opportunities and areas to be reconciled. Detached from its messianic claim and limited to the political sphere, democracy can become a partner of a church which has freed itself from alliance with the monarchic form of state. The secularized state and the spiritualized church—this, for Lacordaire, is the end of the process which began with the revolution.

Thus, Christian Democrats enthusiastically greeted and celebrated the Revolution of 1848 as the longed-for continuation of the Revolution of 1789. That Pius IX was an interpreter of the liberal spirit of the times only increased their optimism. Ozanam wrote in March, 1848:

> Il me semble que ce plan de Dieu dont nous apercevions les premières traces se deroule plus rapidement que nous n'avons cru, que les événements de Vienne achèvent d'expliquer ceux de Paris et de Rome, et qu'on entend déjà la voix qui dit: Ecce facio coelos novos et terram novam.[170] [It seems to me that the plan of God whose first traces we saw developing is coming about much faster than we expected and that the events of Vienna will succeed in explaining those of Paris and of Rome and that one hears already the voice which says: See I have made a new heaven and a new earth.]

He pointed to the mission of the church in the midst of revolutionary renewal. Revolution as theophany! No doubt, Lamennais would enthusiastically have endorsed such a thought, although he would have given it a more general turn in the direction of a humanitarian reign of justice outside and above the church. Orthodox Ozanam, however, was convinced that he was only articulating the intention of the church when he entreated Cath-

---

[170] Letter to Foisset, March 22, 1848, in Oeuvres, XI, 230–31.

252 CATHOLICISM AND CHRISTIAN DEMOCRACY

olics to make peace with victorious democracy: *Suivons Pie IX et passons aux Barbares.*[171]

In these words there is a kind of apocalyptic optimism and confidence, so to speak, in the theological virtues of democracy. Although Christian Democrats after 1830 retraced their steps with ever-increasing conviction toward the church and away from a politically and sociologically colored Christianity—and Lacordaire and Ozanam testify to the transformation—in their opinion there remained an absolute theological claim for democracy which does not fit any Catholic dogma. It was precisely this audacious combination of liberty and equality with the "temporal reign of the Gospels" (Ozanam) that constituted the peculiar character and, beyond all differences and contrasts, the inward unity of the early *Démocratie chrétienne*.

[171] "Les dangers de Rome et ses espérances," *Correspondant*, February, 1848.

5: CHRISTIAN DEMOCRACY IN THE
RALLIEMENT (1891–1901)

Lex *Falloux*, the last parliamentary achievement of liberal Catholicism, constituted a pyrrhic victory. Its result was that there remained no room for Montalembert and Dupanloup to operate between church conservatism and doctrinaire socialism, the line between which stiffened considerably after 1850. In addition, the encyclicals *Quanta Cura* and *Syllabus* showed that Rome's political views were very different from those of the liberal Catholics.[1] The Second Empire in France saw a vehement anti-liberal reaction in French Catholicism.

It was the time of the rise of Louis Veuillot, the brilliant, merciless polemicist who excoriated modern trends in his newspaper *Universe*; liberal Catholicism in particular drew his grim fire.[2] In clerical circles an intransigent trend came to the fore led by Monsignor Pie and Dom Guéranger. It broke with the conciliatory tactics of Dupanloup and bluntly promoted the claims of the church.[3] In politics, too, conservative forces and conserva-

---

[1] On the extensive literature on the *Syllabus*, cf. Bishop Dupanloup's book, *La convention du 15 septembre et l'encyclique du 8 décembre* (Paris, 1865). The text of the encyclical is in Acta Pii IX, vol. III, pp. 701 ff.

[2] On Veuillot, see E. Veuillot, *Louis Veuillot* (4 vols.; Paris, 1902 ff).

[3] On Pie, see Baunard, *Histoire du cardinal Pie* (Paris, 1893); on Guéranger, the founder of Solesmes who originally proceeded from Lamennais, see Delatte, *Dom Guéranger, abbé de Solesmes* (Paris, 1919–20), and E. Sevrin, *Dom Guéranger et Lamennais* (Paris, 1933).

tive views dominated, except for the period of the *empire libéral*, the last years of the empire. *Christianism démocratique et social*, as envisioned by Ozanam and Arnaud de l'Ariège, seemed a thing of the past.

As much as Catholic conservatives rejected democracy and socialism, they could not be deaf to pressing social problems. Many were seriously and passionately concerned with the new socio-political tasks, and some showed much more earnestness in these matters than liberal Catholics, only Montalembert among the latter seriously cared about the workers.[4] Veuillot and his associates lacked a deep understanding of social questions. But men like Villeneuve-Bargemont, Villermé, and Le Play influenced modern French social politics both through practical activities and by pioneering scientific research.[5] French social legislation was the result of the initiative of the conservative Comte de Melun.[6]

The kind of pioneering work that had earlier been the secret work of individual Catholics came before French public opinion increasingly after the war of 1870–71 and the revolt of the communes. Again a political-social catastrophe had posed the question of the *lien moral* to a shaken community. Again it was French Catholicism which searched for a formula to permit it to participate actively in society. Frightened by the bloody spectacle of social anarchy during the civil war, many Catholics turned to legitimist and counter-revolutionary ideas and sought salvation through a conservative social program. It is small wonder then that the Catholic social movements which formed in

---

[4] Cf. his intervention against child labor on March 4, 1840, in the chamber of Paris; *Oeuvres* I, 138 ff.

[5] On that, see Duroselle, *Débuts*, pp. 198 ff. and 413 ff.

[6] *Ibid.*, pp. 498 ff.

reaction to the communes initially showed strong authoritarian and paternalistic features.

Only gradually did social Catholicism adapt to the conditions imposed by the republican state and industrial society. Pope Leo XIII could already rely on it when he initiated the *Ralliement* with the pastoral letter *Au milieu des Sollicitudes.*[7] The second *démocratie chrétienne* in France originated in the turn of the Catholic social movement toward the republic. Our task is to describe its most important stages.

THE CATHOLIC SOCIAL MOVEMENT

The Catholic social movement which arose in France after 1870 was above all the work of three men: Comte de Mun, the Marquis de la Tour du Pin, and Léon Harmel,[8] the manufacturer. Its first phase was under the influence of the *ordre moral*, when it had the support of Comte de Chambord and President Mac Mahon, then considered a representative of the monarchy. After his resignation and the initiation of the actual *républic républicaine*, the movement divested itself increasingly of its anti-revolutionary origins. This was chiefly manifested in the turn from a paternalistic socialism that relied on the cultural privilege of the ruling classes and left the workmen little independence, and the turn toward democratic forms of organization in the relationships between capital and labor. In time the leadership of the movement passed from de Mun and de la Tour du Pin to Léon Harmel, reflecting the general political development of the

[7] *Acta Leonis Papae XIII*, vol. V, pp. 36 ff.

[8] On the Catholic social movement, see the fundamental work by H. Rollet, *L'action sociale des catholiques en France (1871–1901)* (Paris, 1947). Cf. also G. Hoog, *Histoire du Catholicisme social en France, de l'encyclique "Rerum Novarum" à l'encyclique "Quadragesimo Anno"* (Paris, 1942). For further literature, see Rollet.

elimination of the power of the nobility.[9] Maignen wrote:

> Si le marquis de Mun, le châtelain sans droits féodaux, mais seigneur quand même, a la population sous la main, c'est M. Harmel qui a hérité des droits féodaux du marquis de Mun; c'est lui, le marquis du XIXe siècle, il tient la population corvéable à lui.[10] [Although the Marquis de Mun, Lord of the Manor without feudal rights but a grandseigneur nevertheless, has the people in hand, it is M. Harmel who has inherited the feudal rights of the Marquis de Mun; he is the marquis of the nineteenth century, and the populace is liable for statute labor to him.]

As young officers, de Mun and de la Tour de Pin had become acquainted with Ketteler's writings when they were prisoners of war in Aachen, Germany.[11] Later, as a military attaché in Vienna, de la Tour du Pin was to make contact with the Catholic-social school of Freiherr von Vogelsang. The decisive experience for both men was the revolt of the communes. It suddenly rent the veil over the true condition of French society and revealed the depth of the separation between bourgeoisie and workers. To his horror, de Mun wrote, he saw the existence of an abyss between *communards* and the *société légale*, and he saw that Catholics did little or nothing to bridge it.

> Qu'avait fait cette société légale, depuis tant d'années, qu'elle incarnait l'ordre public, pour donner au peuple une règle morale, pour éveiller et former sa conscience, pour ap-

---

[9] After 1830 French nobles restricted themselves mainly to the administration of departmental and municipal affairs; however, they had great influence there. The breakdown of the *ordre moral* and the victory of the radicals in the eighties caused the loss of these positions and of any possibility of influencing politics directly; cf. Rollet, *op. cit.*, p. 507.

[10] Quoted by Rollet, p. 66.

[11] A. de Mun, *Ma vocation sociale* (Paris, 1911) p. 22.

aiser par un effort de justice la plainte de sa souffrance? Quelle action chrétienne les classes en possession du pouvoir avaient-elles, par leurs exemples, par leurs institutions, exercée sur les classes laborieuses? Ces questions se posaient avec force à nos ésprits, dans le trouble des événements.[12] [What has this legal society, which for so many years has been public order incarnate, done to give the people moral rule, to rouse and form their conscience, to appease with justice their complaints of suffering? What Christian action did the classes which held the power undertake through their example, through their institutions, for the laboring classes? These questions trouble our spirit in the midst of these disturbing events.]

Thus de Mun and de la Tour du Pin decided to try anew to solve the social question. They fell back upon older forms of Catholic social work, mainly upon the so-called *Cercles d'ouvriers*, which had already appeared in various places during the Second Empire. These were extra-professional associations of workers and apprentices within a parish that served religio-charitable ends.[13] In the ensuing years they were organized afresh and extended throughout the country; a central committee in Paris was in charge of new organization and directed the individual members of the movement. In the workmen's societies, the workmen were supposed to conduct free dialogue with members of the *classes dirigeantes*—entrepreneurs, politicians, officers—on questions of common interest. Each was supposed to learn from the other, and both groups were to educate each other in understanding and mutual consideration. Some sentences by de Mun,

[12] *Ibid.*, p. 29.
[13] On the beginnings of the Oeuvre des Cercles, see Ch. Maignen, *Maurice Maignen, Directeur du Cercle Montparnasse et les origines du mouvement social catholique en France (1822–90)* (Luçon, 1927).

taken from a founding manifesto, may be used to characterize the spirit of the *Oeuvre des Cercles Catholiques d'ouvriers*, as the movement was called. He begins:

> La question ouvriére, à l'heure présente, n'est plus un problème à discuter. Elle se pose devant nous comme une menace, comme un péril permanent. Il faut la résoudre. Autrement, la société, semblable aux pouvoirs qui agonisent et ne peuvent plus se sauver même en abdiquant, s'entendrait dire ce terrible arrêt: Il est trop tard.[14] [The workers' question at present is no longer a problem that can be discussed. It stands before us like a menace, a fixed danger. We must solve it. Otherwise society, like powers which agonize but cannot save themselves even by abdication, will hear the terrible final words: "It is too late."]

This manifesto is resonant with the experience of the communes; the people are characterized as easily manipulated, *enfant sublime ou égoiste*. Thus, education is in the foreground of concern. De Mun was most concerned to re-establish the influence and the authority of the *classes dirigeantes*; the organization of the workmen's circles was completely geared to this practical aim.

Obviously, this kind of social concept was hardly likely to effect a drawing together of the Catholic working class or to make any inroads on those proletarians influenced by socialism. In the newly founded workmen's homes, the workers were cared for but remained dependent. As a result, very few workingmen, all in all, joined the Oeuvre. Compared to similar organizations in Belgium and Germany, the membership, even at peak times, remained relatively low and never surpassed 35,000.[15]

It was not lack of ability or bad faith which hampered the

[14] *Ma vocation sociale*, pp. 72–73.
[15] Rollet, op. cit., p. 690.

spread of the Catholic social movement, but rather the lack of consideration for the strivings for independence of the workmen. Moreover, de la Tour du Pin and de Mun tied their social programs to counter-revolutionary attitudes which were unacceptable to the working class. At the same time, the clergy distrusted the workmen circles as extra-parochial and supradiocesan organizations.[16] Thus, the situation of the movement was a difficult one from various points of view. In the beginning de Mun and de la Tour du Pin relied on state help. Yet the state's readiness to help turned into open antagonism after the victory of the Republicans and the end of the *ordre moral.* After 1880 the government initiated proceedings against the Oeuvre; it saw in it a focus of counter-revolutionary activities. Influenced by this turn of events, de Mun decided upon a tactical change in order to be able to keep the workers together after the closing down of the Oeuvre. A professional structure, assimilation in the structure of economy, was to replace supra-professional organization. The circles became corporations. Though the principle of a mixed membership of capital and labor was maintained, this too would change when the corporate ideal began in practice to assume syndicalist forms.

It is remarkable that de la Tour du Pin, the theoretician of the movement, should have arrived at the very conclusions which were later forced on the movement by the political situation. The findings of a committee of studies under his direction, published in *Association catholique,* the official publication of the Oeuvre, outlined a corporate economic order which would culminate in

---

[16] In 1863 the Committee of the Oeuvre decided to call for clerical assistance. The archbishop of Paris, Mgr. Guibert, welcomed this decision but stressed that the clergy should have a moderating influence in the movement; he also expressed certain criticisms of the Oeuvre: "emballement dans son action, exaltation dans le sentiment de sa mission religieuse, mysticisme;" cf. Rollet, pp. 18–19.

a renewal of medieval guilds in the form of corporations privileged by the state. All this was inspired by the revolutionary criticism of La Play and the idea of the corporative state of the Austrian reform party led by Vogelsang. This social program, however, was not without its utopianism, since it seemed indissolubly wedded to the idea of the restoration of the monarchy. Contrary to de la Tour's hopes, there was no chance for this after the defeat of the Catholic conservatives and the death of Comte de Chambord. Still, the program had the salutary effect of giving a great shock to the development of the Catholic social movement. It was the final break with the ideology of social charity. To quote de Mun, this had made Catholic activity in the social sphere a mere *convoi d'ambulance en arrière*.[17]

If we shear the corporative program of its merely contemporary elements and its secondary political objectives, what remains is an attempt to establish the principle, until then expressed purely in charitable practices and so viewed, in the social legislation of the state. Such an idea lent itself readily to democratic interpretation. It was certainly no contradiction then that Léon Harmel, a member of the Oeuvre since 1872,[18] developed the ideas of the "reactionary" de la Tour into the new formative idea of the Catholic social movement: *action de l'ouvrier sur l'ouvrier*. With this the preparatory stage of patronage of the working class ended. The original concept, *dévouement de la classe dirigeante à la classe ouvrière*, gave way to a solidarity that embraced all classes and showed the way to new political solutions.

LÉON HARMEL

Léon Harmel repeatedly criticized the development of the

[17] Rollet, p. 57.
[18] On Harmel, cf. G. Guitton, *Léon Harmel* (2 vols.; 1925). Also Rollet, pp. 222 ff. and Hoog, *op. cit.*, pp. 31 ff.

Oeuvre des Cercles Catholiques d'ouvriers. He saw that the circles were usually recruited from those who were not "genuine" workers,[19] who were isolated from their companions and therefore unable to exercise great influence. This meant helping a group that needed protection rather than supporting a core of able shock troops. The complete dependence of the circles on the directives of superior committees, in which the *classes dirigeantes* were the main influence, would indeed immediately stifle any initiative of the workers. Meantime, the conservative circles backing the *Oeuvre* continued to refuse every attempt to give the workmen more freedom. They were afraid that the workers, once permitted to air opinions freely in assemblies, would not hesitate to criticize the capitalists and the *Oeuvre* itself, which would lead to scandalous disclosures. The workday, even in Christian enterprises, was still twelve hours or more and Sunday work was no rarity.[20] The tensions between Harmel and the conservative group of the *Oeuvre* intensified when de Mun and de la Tour staged a *Contre-Centenaire* in 1889 on the anniversary of the revolution during which Catholic workers from every part of France presented the unmet demands of the *Cahiers* of 1789 and tried to prove the bankruptcy of the revolution and democracy's failure in the face of the social questions of the times. Harmel saw that the whole spectacle had gone up in smoke when it met with indifference from the broad classes of the population. He wrote then to la Tour:

[19] "Ce n'étaient le plus souvent que des attardés de l'industrie, les cancres de l'usine, braves gens par ailleurs et d'une piété extérieure suffisante ou encore des employés des librairies cléricales, des bedeaux en rupture de hallebarde, des sacristains retraités, des concierges des communeauté, des garcons de bureaux des oeuvres" (E. Barbier, *Histoire du catholicisme libéral et du catholicisme social,* as quoted by Rollet, p. 36).

[20] Rollet, pp. 268 ff.

Mais le peuple, il n'y a rien su, il n'a pas été atteint. Or pour moi, c'est lui qui est à la fois l'enjeu et l'atout.²¹ [But the people knew nothing and were never reached. Now, for me, it is the people who are both the stake and the trump of the game.]

The patron situation which until then had been the means of the Catholic social movement was opposed by Harmel's new method, which in contrast to the paternalistic "everything for the worker, nothing *through* him" was based on transferring responsibility to the worker and the principle of *Laissez-faire*. The method had first been tried out and developed in Harmel's own enterprise, *Harmel frères*, a woolen mill, in Warmériville near Reims.²² Here in the sheltered valley of the Val-des-Bois an utopian industrial situation had been developed; for the first time in France there were industrial units organized to recognize the importance of the individual worker and allowed for decentralized responsibilities. The essence of the method consisted in the education of worker initiative:

le bien de l'ouvrier par l'ouvrier et avec lui, autant que possible jamais sans lui, et à plus forte raison jamais malgré lui.²³ [the good of the worker, through the worker and with him, as much as possible, never without him and with good reasons never against him.]

The workers here were not guided and patronized as were those in the workmen's circles but had opportunities for activity within a group or organization linked with the plant, such as consumers'

---

²¹ As quoted by Rollet, p. 250.
²² On Val-des-Bois, see L. H. A. Geck, *Die sozialen Arbeitsverhältnisse im Wandel der Zeit* (Berlin, 1931), pp. 79 ff., and Guitton, *passim*.
²³ Geck, op. cit., p. 80. Concerning Harmel's methods, cf. his *Manuel d'une Corporation chrétienne* (Tours, 1879).

cooperatives, welfare assistance, schools, and kindergartens. Nor did Harmel exercise any pressure in the religious sphere, although he was a practicing Catholic. But with the help of religiously and ethically high-minded workers he discreetly tried to influence those who had fallen away from the church.[24] His was one of the first plants in France which introduced a plant council,[25] he also permitted independent workers' associations, beginning with a *syndicat mixte* which united capital and labor, as was usual in the Catholic social movement.

Harmel's ideas gained ground in the social Catholicism of France in spite of opposition from the older generation. They found their first expression in the so-called *Sécrétariats du peuple*, voluntary assistance associations which looked for lodgings for destitute workers, aided the sick, and provided legal counsel. In addition, Harmel also tried to attract Catholic workers outside the *Oeuvre* and to organize them; this turned out to be the first stage in the development of Christian trade unions. These efforts were successful: while, on the one hand, the workmen's circles dissolved or were prohibited by the government, the *Réunions d'études ouvrières*, which Harmel organized first in Reims and later in other places, developed quickly.

But, as Harmel recognized, an important obstacle to the spread of the Catholic social movement lay in the indifference and distrust of the clergy. He had already tried, therefore, in assemblies of clergymen held in the Val-des-Bois, to alert the clergy to social problems. This resulted in the young priests' accepting his ideas with great enthusiasm, but the episcopate expressed

---

[24] On the religious education of the workers and the function of the priest in the plant, see Harmel, *Manuel*, §§ 241–43.

[25] A plant committee (*Comité corporatif*, later *Conseil professionel*) had been founded as early as 1875; a plant council (*Conseil d'usine*) existed from 1893; Rollet, p. 229.

disapproval of such unusual activity for a layman.[26] Harmel, however, was fortunate in that he won the confidence and the support of the pope, whom he saw several times in order to keep him informed about his plans. He organized French workmen's pilgrimages to Rome, a sensation not only in France but all over Europe.[27] Henri Rollet, the historian of social Catholicism in France, has pointed out the strange mixture of a democratic popular movement and the spirit of medieval pilgrimage which characterized these excursions. For it was Harmel's intention to show the pope to the workmen as "the prisoner of the Vatican" and to encourage them to make expressions of solidarity, since the Catholic governments of Europe failed to protest the confiscation of papal state properties. These *Pèlérinages ouvriers*, especially the great "pilgrimage of the ten thousand" of 1889, prepared the way for the social teachings of Leo XIII and anticipated the *rapprochement* of the Holy See and French democracy, which later bore fruit in the politics of *Ralliement*. The spectacle of workmen feted in the Vatican, greeted by the pope, and wined and dined by cardinals, left an indelible imprint on contemporaries. Melchoir de Vogüé wrote in this typically florid way:

> Les spectateurs sentaient confusément que ceux-ci n'étaient point des pèlerins comme les autres: Ce qu'on introduisait solennellement dans Saint-Pierre, c'était le nouveau pouvoir social, les nouveaux prétendants à l'empire. Ces ouvriers venaient là comme y vinrent Charlemagne, Othon et Barberousse pour y chercher le sacre et l'investiture.[28] [The spec-

[26] Rollet, p. 225.

[27] On that, Cardinal Langénieux, *Les pèlerinages des ouvriers français à Rome et la question sociale* (Paris, n.d.).

[28] In: *Les Débats*, as quoted by M. Turmann, *Le développement du Catholicisme social depuis l'encyclique "Rerum Novarum"* (Paris, 1901), p. 187. Cf. also de Mun, *Discours et écrits divers d'Albert de Mun, avec des notices par Ch. Geoffroy de Grandmaison* (Paris, 1893 ff.), V, 179.

tators felt somehow that these were not ordinary pilgrims. What was being introduced so solemnly into St. Peter's was the new social power, the new pretenders to the empire. These workmen came there as had Charlemagne, Otto, and Barbarossa in search of the Holy, in search of investiture.]

LEO XIII AND CHRISTIAN DEMOCRACY

In an atmosphere thus prepared there came in 1891 the encyclical *Rerum novarum*. It had a twofold effect upon the Catholic social movement. First, it moved the clergy, which had so far stood aside, to act; second, it strengthened and supported the intentions of Catholic laymen. Structural economic conditions were given precedence over purely charitable assistance; the intercession of the state, which Catholic liberalism had always rejected unconditionally, was termed a practicable, in some cases an unavoidable, ingredient in the solution of the social question.[29] It can be assumed that Harmel and his friends saw borne out in the encyclical, especially in the passages which invited workmen to help themselves, their own methods as tested in Val-des-Bois.[30]

In Reims, where at the end of 1891 Harmel convened a group of workers in order to explain the encyclical to them, the first study circle of the future *Démocratie chrétienne* was born. Carried mainly on the shoulders of the younger clergy, the movement expanded quickly through the rest of the country. Lille and Charleville in the north; Blois, Tours, Angers, Nantes, Rennes, and Brest in the center; and the Bretagne and Lyons in the south became the main points of support for the Christian Democrats. Paris followed later. The term *Démocratie chrétienne*, which

---

[29] *Acta Leonis XIII*, vol. IV, pp. 177–209. On the duties of the state, see pp. 193–202.

[30] *Loc. cit.*, pp. 202–8.

probably goes back to the Belgian Canon Pottier,[31] was chosen because of its suggestive connotation and its effect upon the broad masses of the population. Originally, Christian Democracy had a preponderantly social character, as with Ozanam, but in time it took on a political meaning that paralleled the actions of the pope, who, nine months after the worker's encyclical, sent out a pastoral letter *Au milieu des Sollicitudes*, in which French Catholics were invited to conciliation with the republic.[32]

Démocratie chrétienne was not a purely lay organization; the clergy took a significant part in it. It was the young priests, the so-called *abbés démocrates*, who took the step from social action to the *Ralliement*. They were enthusiastic over the directives of a social-minded pope and fired by the thought of a reconciliation between church and modern society. The years in which workmen first held public meetings in France also saw the first congresses of clergy. In Reims, the fourteenth centenary of Chlodwig's baptism was solemnly celebrated in 1896, and four years later there was a congress in Bourges and, subsequent to a letter of Leo XIII, there were debates on the intellectual education of the clergy and their public tasks.[33] In all these movements the *abbés démocrates* took active parts. As a result they made up much that the Catholic church missed for lack of great personalities—such as Ketteler or Manning—in the social education of the clergy. Moreover, their initiatives foreshadowed the future. They may in a certain sense be considered the forerunners of the worker priests, not because they limited themselves exclusively to social work, but because their inclination to secular oc-

---

[31] T'Serclaes, *Le pape Léon XIII* (Lille, 1894 ff.), II, 260.

[32] *Acta Leonis XIII*, vol. V, pp. 36 ff.

[33] On the *Démocratie chrétienne and the abbés démocrates*, see P. Dabry, *Les catholiques républicains. Histoire et souvenirs* (Paris, 1905), and H. Gayraud, *Les Démocrates chrétiens*, p. 197, n. 25. We do not have a comprehensive account.

cupations (some were politicians, others scientists or journalists)
prepared the soil for an attempt to integrate the Catholic priesthood into modern society by a radical adaptation to the modern
conditions of the Gospels.

While the *abbés démocrates*, and with them the younger generation of laymen who had grown up in the republic, hailed the
pope's politics of *Ralliement*, the older leaders of the Catholic
social movement found it rather difficult to free themselves from
the weight of monarchic tradition to turn toward democracy.
Leon Harmel, it is true, quickly made his peace with the republic[34]; de Mun, too, followed the call of Leo XIII, but with a
heavy heart and only after hesitation.[35] But la Tour, and many
others with him, held fast to their legitimist principles.[36] The
turn toward politics, the attempt to stress in public and in parliament the idea of *Ralliement*, became the permanent touchstone
of the *Démocratie Chrétienne*.

In 1896 in Reims, the first national congress of the *Démocratie
chrétienne* decided to establish a Christian democratic party. A
secretary-general was elected and a national council set up in
which two delegates of each of the individual provincial associations sat and voted. During the deliberations, as it turned out,
the members could not agree on a concrete political program.
There were differences of opinion mainly on the questions of
Christian trade unions[37] and the tactical attitude toward the lay
legislation of the republic. The problem was whether the fight
against the lay legislation or the participation in the social legislation of the republic should have pre-eminence; this question

[34] Guitton, I, 330 f.

[35] Rollet, p. 449 ff.

[36] La Tour declared: "Le pape a toujours eu ses grenadiers, ses voltigeurs (de
Mun!), souffrez qu'il ait aussi ses grognards—pour lui-même," as quoted by Rollet,
loc. cit.

[37] On that, see Turmann, *op. cit.*, pp. 74 ff.

was especially important because of the tactics of electioneering. There was thus some hesitancy about the step into politics, and the assembly accepted the resolution:

> Le parti démocrate chrétien, estimant que les questions sociales priment toutes les autres, laisse à chacun de ses groupements la possibilité de se placer ou non sur le terrain politique, mais si ces groupements se placent sur le terrain politique, ils doivent se déclarer nettement républicains démocrates.[38] [The Christian Democratic party, in assuming that social questions pre-empt all others, leaves to each of the groups the possibility of entering or not entering the political arena, but if they do enter, they must declare themselves strictly as republican democrats.]

Yet the *Démocratie chrétienne* never succeeded in a deep penetration of the politics of the Third Republic. It is true that a few of the *abbés démocrates* were elected to parliament, where they united with other Catholic *Ralliés* in a republican group. But since they were opposed not only by the laicist left but by conservative Catholics, their position was always difficult. During the reign of the moderate republicans of 1893 who embarked on a conciliatory course with regard to the church under the so-called *ésprit nouveau*,[39] the Christian Democrats seemed to have gained certain political opportunities. But the Dreyfus affair brought the conflict of the "two Frances" into sharp focus and thus the elections of 1898, the *Sedan électoral* of French *Catholicism*,[40] put an end to the politics of *Ralliement* and with it the attempted *parti démocrate chrétien*.

[38] Rollet, p. 388.
[39] The term "esprit nouveau" originated in a speech of Minister of Public Worship and Education Spuller, March 3, 1894. Cf. A. Dansette, *Histoire religieuse de la France contemporaine* II (Paris, 1951), 235 ff.
[40] Leo XIII to Harmel, in Rollet, p. 439.

The tendency to politicize social Catholicism had been challenged by de Mun during the founding congress of the party. He held to his concept of the hierarchical structuring of society and the role of the *classes dirigeants* as educators. To him, the possibility of an autonomous Catholic workmen's movement within the *Démocratie chrétienne* with an independent program and unionist forms appeared to endanger the development of social Catholicism and to deny the hope, held until then, of reconciliation of the classes and not their separation. There was some justice in the reproach that the *Démocratie chrétienne* threatened to become a class party, since some provisions had been written into the statutes of the *parti démocratie chrétien* at its founding which determined that only workers could sit on its national council.[41] Coupled with the tendency to theologize democracy and socialism, then current in the circles of the *abbés démocrates*, this development could doubtless lead to new schisms in French Catholicism and to a complete dissolution of the *Ralliement* party.

Harmel, too, as secretary-general of the *Démocratie chrétienne*, recognized after the defeat of the Christian Democratic party at the polls that the thrust into politics had been premature. In the years following, he tried to steer a middle course between the demands of de Mun and those of the *abbés démocrats*; yet he had to admit that political dissension among Catholics had gone too far. The *Démocratie chrétienne* had lost its initial strength. The battle seesawed for a few years between the various fronts of social Catholicism in France, when Rome intervened in 1901 and clarified in principle the concept of Christian Democracy.

The encyclical *Graves de communi* drew a balance sheet of

[41] Rollet, p. 388.

the work accomplished by Christian Democracy.[42] It paid tribute
to its successes and praised the courage of the men who dedicated themselves to the realization of Catholic social teachings
in public life. Then, continuing *Rerum novarum*, it highlighted
the contrast which existed between Christian democracy and Social democracy. The decisive sentence, however, was that Christian Democracy, far from politics, could be called a *benefica in
populum actio christiana* and expressly stated that a political
interpretation and application of the concept would falsify its
meaning.

> Nam naturae et evangelii praecepta quia suopte iure hu-
> manos casus excedunt ea necesse est ex nullo civilis regiminis
> modo pendere; sed convenire cum quovis posse, modo ne ho-
> nestati et iustitiae repugnet. Sunt ipsa igitur manentque a par-
> tium studiis variisque eventibus plane aliena: ut in qualibet
> demum rei publicae constitutione, possint cives ac debeant
> iisdem stare praeceptis, quibus iubentur Deum super omnia,
> proximos sicut se diligere. Haec perpetua Ecclesiae disciplina
> fuit; hac usi Romani Pontifices cum civitatibus egere semper,
> quocumque illae administrationis genere tenerentur. Quae
> quum sint ita, catholicorum mens atque actio, quae bono pro-
> letariorum promovendo studet, eo profecto spectare nequa-
> quam potest, ut aliud prae alio regimen civitatis adamet atque
> invehat.[43]
> [For the law of nature and of the Gospel, which by right
> are superior to all human contingencies, are necessarily inde-
> pendent of all modifications of civil government, while at the
> same time they are in concord with everything that is not re-
> pugnant to morality and justice. They are, therefore, and they
> must remain free from political parties, and have nothing to

[42] *Acta Sanctae Sedis*, vol. XXXIII (1900/01), pp. 385–96. English: *The Great
Encyclical Letters of Leo XIII*, "Christian Democracy" p. 482–83. (New York,
1903.)
[43] *Loc. cit.*, p. 387 (p. 483).

do with the various changes of administration which may occur in a nation; so that Catholics may and ought to be citizens according to the constitution of any state, guided as they
are by those laws which command them to love God above
all things, and their neighbors as themselves. This has always
been the discipline of the Church. The Roman Pontiffs acted
upon this principle whenever they dealt with different countries, no matter what might be the character of their governments. Hence, the mind and action of Catholics who are
devoted to the amelioration of the working classes, can never
be actuated with the purpose of favoring and introducing one
government in place of another.] *Encyclical Letters of Leo
XIII*, "Christian Democracy" (Graves de communi), p. 483.

With this the premature identification of church and democracy was tightly sealed off. Distinguishing between democracy as
a form of government and democracy as a social attitude, the
pope extracted *démocratie chrétienne* from the debated questions of French state politics and returned it to the social camp
from which it had originated.

How is the intervention of the pope, who until then had by
no means rejected the republicans among French Catholics but
had given them his sympathy, to be explained? To reply to this
question we have to go back to the church-policy of the beginning of the Third Republic and the start of the politics of
Ralliement.[44]

[44] The most important source on the politics of *ralliement* of Leo XIII are,
besides the papal letters, the memoirs of the papal nuncio in Paris, Dominique
Ferrata: *Mémoires* (3 vols.; Rome, 1921). The second volume appeared sepa-
rately, titled: *Ma nonciature en France*. On that, U. Stutz, *Die päpstliche Diplo-
matie unter Leo XIII* Abhandlung der preussischen Akademie der Wissenschaf-
ten. phil.-hist. Klasse (Berlin, 1926); Also important are the memoirs of the
leader of the "ralliement—Catholics" in France Jacques Piou: *Le ralliement*
(Paris, 1928). New illustration of the ralliement as it pertains to church politics
(with documents) in F. Guédon's article "Autour du Ralliement," *Revue d'histoire de l'Église de France*, XLIV (1958), 86 ff.

When Leo XIII was enthroned in the Holy See, he found a complicated and very confused situation in the French church.[45] The Catholics, who for the most part were to be found in the monarchist camp, had experienced a great defeat in the victory of the Republicans in 1876. In parliament their hands were tied, and they continued to lose more and more ground in public life. They lacked the means to defend themselves effectively against the ésprit laïc, which was preparing a crushing blow against the privileged position of the church through the school-and-order legislation of Ferry.[46] The weakness of its position also hampered the efforts of papal diplomacy. Since the church possessed only one means of pressure, bereft of the support of a strong party as it was—the threat to remove the French protectorate of the oriental churches—it could not achieve more than a temporary retreat by the republican governments to avoid an open breach of the concordat.[47] It was not ready to mitigate or revoke the laic laws. The pope sent a personal letter to President Grevy in which he asked him to curtail hostile measures against church congregations and clergy, but he received an evasive answer.[48] Attempts at peace by the conciliatory Nuncio Czacki were unsuccessful. While Catholics, less united than ever, continued to fight each other, the campaign for laicization continued, charitable organizations were secularized, crosses removed from schools and courtrooms, the clergy subjected to military service, and ecclesiastical expenditures reduced from year to year.[49]

[45] On the following, see my article, "Politischer Katholizismus, sozialer Katholizismus, christliche Demokratie," Civitas, Jahrbuch für christliche Gesellschaftsordnung I, (1962), 9 ff.

[46] E. M. Accomb, The French Laic Laws (Columbia University Press, 1941).

[47] In 1881 Gambetta made the concession to assure Cardinal Lavigerie of Algiers that anticlericalism was not to be exported. Stutz, op. cit., p. 65.

[48] Letter and Grévy's answer in T'Serclaes, I, 300 ff.

[49] Ferrata, Ma nonciature, pp. 143 ff.

Czacki saw in the disunity of Catholics the key to the church-political dilemma into which they had been forced by the decline of the *ordre moral*. Papal diplomacy, at first very cautious so as not to give the Republicans an excuse for canceling the Concordat, was suddenly enmeshed in a fight on two fronts: on the one hand, it could not stand by and see the laicist movement progress; on the other, it had to restrain Catholic monarchists, whose unbridled agitation excited more and more anti-church measures by the Republicans. Leo XIII unceasingly exhorted French Catholics to unity. He asked them to give up separatist desires for political independence and interests, but his appeal did not find any worthwhile echo. How this situation might be changed and how a unified political front of French Catholics could be established were increasingly important considerations in papal politics.[50]

It was clear that no party on the order of the Belgian Catholic Democrats or the German *Zentrum* could be expected in France. Although there were formal similarities in their general cultural situations, the position of Catholicism in these countries was quite different from that in France where the battle was waged not about the delimiting of state and church roles, but over the claim of radical Catholicism that it was the realization of the *république sans Dieu*. In Germany and Belgium the battle had not reached the level of ideology. Nor was the state form under debate, as it was among French Catholics. The question was the recognition of Catholic forces within the framework of an established constitutional system. In addition, people in Belgium and Germany were more indifferent about church interference in politics than were the Frenchmen of the Third Republic, whose ears had become attuned, through Gambetta's war cry, to the

[50] Ferrata, *op. cit.*, pp. 20 ff. (on his memorandum on the situation in France).

slightest diplomatic interventions and attempts at action by the curia: *Le cléricalism c'est l'ennemi* ["Clericalism is the enemy"].

The aims of the pope had to be, first of all, the separation of the French church from all connections with politics, especially from the concerns of the royalist party, thus laying the foundations for re-establishing a dialogue with the republic. As long as the demands for political reforms of the church and a limiting of laicist influences in cultural politics were linked with a program of violent upheaval of existing conditions and a monarchic restoration, it was unavoidable that republicans and Catholics should live as enemies. Only when Catholics recognized the existing form of state as legitimate and accepted the foundations of the constitution would a path be open by which they could return to politics and make their influence felt upon the spiritual formation of the republic.

It was with this in mind that papal diplomacy began its efforts to influence French Catholics.[51] The encyclical *Immortale Dei* (1885) established the fundamental neutrality of the church toward different forms of state as long as the rights of the church and the freedom to promulgate religious teachings (dogmas) were assured.[52] This roused the feelings of the French episcopate.[53] At the same time Leo XIII opposed the attempts of Comte de Mun to establish a Catholic party in France; he thought such an intention would only lead to new schisms within French Catholicism.[54] As the laicist republicans could not be mollified in spite of all of the attempts of the church to make

[51] Ferrata, *op. cit.*, pp. 82 ff.

[52] *Acta Leonis XIII*, vol. II, pp. 146–68, esp. pp. 147 ff.

[53] On the history of the origin of the encyclical and its effects, see T'Serclaes, I, 392 ff., and Ferrata, *op. cit.*, pp. 15 ff.

[54] On that, now see H. Rollet, *Albert de Mun et le parti catholique* (Paris, 1947), esp. pp. 106 ff.

peace and as the anticlerical current after the Boulanger adventure became increasingly acute, the pope finally found it advisable to recommend an alliance with the republic to French Catholics. He did this in his encyclical *Au milieu des Sollicitudes* (1892), after the famous Cardinal Lavigeries had prepared the atmosphere with a toast in Algiers, in which he counseled Catholics to come out for a reform of the legislative branch within the existing constitution.

> Voilà précisément le terrain sur lequel, tout dissentiment politique mis à part, les gens de bien doivent s'unir comme un seul homme, pour combattre, par tous les moyens légaux et honnêtes, ces abus progressifs de la législation. Le respect que l'on doit aux pouvoirs constitués ne saurait l'interdire: il ne peut importer, ni le respect, ni beaucoup moins l'obéissance sans limites à toute mesure législative quelconque, édictée par ces mêmes pouvoirs. Qu'on ne l'oublie pas, la loi est une prescription ordonnée selon la raison et promulguée, pour le bien de la communauté, par ceux qui ont reçu à cette fin le dépôt du pouvoir.[55] [Here precisely is the ground on which, political dissent aside, the men of substance should unite as one to fight with every legal and honest means the increasing abuse of legislation. The respect due the constituted law must not interfere with this: it cannot bring respect, much less obedience, without limits to all the kinds of legislative measures decreed by these same powers. If not obeyed, the law is a prescription ordered according to reason and promulgated for the good of the community by those who have received power for this purpose.]

The republic thus was to be recognized; at the same time the battle against laic legislation was to be continued by legal and democratic means.

[55] *Acta Leonis XIII*, vol. V, pp. 36 ff.

In order to unite Catholics in a common front, a slogan was needed which would transcend political quarrels and which rally the various factions of French Catholicism. There is no doubt that the pope here had in mind, above all, the Catholic social movement, for which he himself only a year before pointed the way in his encyclical *Rerum novarum*. It may well be that the development of a Christian Democratic movement in France in connection with this encyclical caused, or at least hastened, the beginnings of the *Politique de ralliement*. In any case the pope found in the *Démocratie chrétienne* his most solid resource for a policy whose dual aim was a constitutional influence upon legislation and a strengthening of the moral reputation of the church by increased social activity. The conservative de Mun's alliance with the *Ralliement* may have strengthened the pope's conviction that a reconciliation between monarchists and republicans could more easily be expected within social Catholicism and according to papal directions.[56]

These efforts were seriously threatened when the *Démocratie chrétienne* repeated the mistake of the monarchists and entered the political arena by making the question of state form one of fundamental religious principle. The pope opposed this attempt to deduce an integral political program from the teachings of the church as decisively as de Mun had. Thus it happened that the *Démocratie chrétienne* after 1896 passed as a class party, with or without justification and contrary to the express intentions of Leo XIII in his *Rerum novarum*.

During the great workmen's pilgrimage of 1898, again headed by Harmel, the pope for the first time used the name "Christian Democracy." His words were a tacit critique of the devel-

[56] On that, see the Breve Notre consolation of May 3, 1892, to the French cardinals, in *Acta Leonis XIII*, vol. V, pp. 66–72.

opment which the Christian Democratic movement had so far undergone. They took the form of a definition of Christian Democracy.

Si la démocratie s'inspire des enseignements de la raison éclairée par la foi; si, se tenant en garde contre de fallacieuses et subversives théories, elle accepte avec une religieuse résignation et comme un fait nécessaire la diversité des classes et des conditions; si dans la recherche des solutions possibles aux multiples problèmes sociaux qui surgissent journellement, elle ne perd pas un instant de vue les règles de cette charité surhumaine que Jésus-Christ a déclarée être la note charactéristique des siens; si, en un mot, la démocratie veut être chrétienne, elle donnera à votre patrie un avenir de paix, de prospérité et de bonheur. Si, au contraire, elle s'abandonne à la révolution et au socialisme; si, trompée par des folles illusions, elle se livre à des revendications destructives des lois fondamentales sur lesquelles repose tout l'order civil, l'effet immédiat sera pour la classe ouvrière elle-même la servitude, la misère et la ruine.[57] [If democracy will be informed by the teachings of reason enlightened by faith and if it will accept with religious resignation and as a necessary fact the difference in classes and conditions, while guarding itself against fallacious and subversive theories; if it will not lose sight, in the midst of a search for the solution for the manifold social problems which rise every day, of the superhuman charity which Jesus Christ declared to be characteristically his own; if, in other words, democracy will be Christian, it will grant your fatherland a future of peace, prosperity, and happiness. If, to the contrary, it abandons itself to revolution and socialism, if blinded by fantastic illusions it delivers itself to vindictive claims on the laws on which the whole civil order is

[57] Allocutio ad Galliae opifices of October 8, 1898, in *Acta Leonis XIII*, vol. VII, pp. 196–98.

based, the immediate effect for the working class itself will
be servitude, misery, and ruin.]

That these words were not meant as recrimination but as
guidelines becomes clear in a glossary of the pope's text by Cardinal Parocchi. On the occasion of a banquet at the Vatican, he
said to his workers:

> La question d'une saine et légitime démocratie est désor-
> mais résolue. Vous êtes vraiment démocrates chrétiens, et je
> vous en félicite. Mais votre tâche va plus loin: vous devez
> faire ce que saint Remy a fait de Clovis, baptiser la démo-
> cratie et la rendre chrétienne. Pour réussir, vous n'avez qu'à
> suivre la sagesse, l'adresse, la patience et la longanimité de
> Notre Saint-Père, le Pape Léon XIII. Gardez en votre coeur
> ses dernières paroles, précieux commentaire de ses encycli-
> ques. L'enseignement exposé dans l'encyclique Rerum Nova-
> rum, cette Magna Charta des ouvriers, se trouve embelli et
> complété par les paroles d'aujourd'hui. Faites que votre dé-
> mocratie soit si chrétienne qu'elle oblige vos amis et vos
> ennemis à devenir comme vous démocrates chrétiens.[58] [The
> question of a healthy and legitimate Christian Democracy is
> now solved. You are real Christian Democrats and I congratu-
> late you upon it. But your task goes further: you must do as
> St. Remis did with Chlodwig; you must baptize democracy
> and make it Christian. To be successful, all you have to do is
> follow the wisdom, adroitness, patience, and magnanimity of
> our Holy Father, Pope Leo XIII. Keep in mind his last
> words, a precious commentary on his encyclicals. The teach-
> ings contained in Rerum novarum, this Magna Charta of
> workingmen, is improved and completed by today's words.
> See to it that your democracy is so Christian that your friends
> and your enemies want to become Christian Democrats.]

---

[58] T'Serclaes, III, 263; English edition: Encyclical Letters of Leo XIII, "Christian Democracy," p. 482.

Although it was quite clear in this reference to *Rerum nova-rum* that social action should be and would remain the true field of activity for Christian Democrats, the encyclical *Graves de communi* unmistakably stated that this should not be understood in a political sense and thus it tried to put an end to differences of opinion regarding Christian Democracy:

> Nefas autem sit [wrote Leo XIII] christianae democratiae appellationem ad politica detorqueri. Quamquam enim dem-ocratia, ex ipsa notatione nominis usuque philosophorum, regimen indicat populare; attamen in re praesenti sic usur-panda est, ut, omni politica notione detracta, aliud nihil sig-nificatum praeferat, nisi hanc ipsam beneficam in populum actionem christianam.[59] [Moreover it would be a crime to distort this name of Christian Democracy to politics, for although democracy, both in its philological and philosophical significations, implies popular government, yet in its present application it is so to be employed that, removing from it all political significance it is to mean nothing else than a benevo-lent Christian movement in behalf of the people.] *Encyclical Letters of Leo XIII*, "Christian Democracy" (Graves de com-muni), p. 482.

Certainly, tactical reasons also played a part in this restraint. It was above all the consideration that too strict an adherence of Christian Democrats to the republic might undermine Catholic unity, the precondition for the successful outcome of the *Rallie-ment*. Also in view of French conditions, it was necessary for Catholic social action to remain outside the political arena; only in this way could the suspicion that Catholics were seeking state power be dissipated. But beyond tactical considerations the encyclical *Graves de communi* reflects the desire of the pope to

[59] *Acta Sanctae Sedis*, vol. XXXIII (1900/01), pp. 385–96.

keep matters of religion clear of any link with a party, republican or royalist. The pope's decision to take an active part in the Catholic social movement, his politics toward republican France, and his attitude toward democracy and socialism may be seen as an attempt to re-establish the presence of the church in contemporary history by bringing it close to legitimate modern needs and interests. But it is clear, too, that his teachings about social questions and Christian Democracy contributed to a strengthening of the respect and the moral sovereignty of the papacy. John Courtney Murray, to whom we are greatly indebted for new insights into the changes that have occurred in church-state relationships, has described the general nineteenth-century context to which Leo XIII's church politics belong:

> . . . that history and experience have brought the Church to ever more perfect respect for the autonomy of the state (as a form of the respect for an essential element in the "whole man") and consequently to ever more purely spiritual assertions of her power in the temporal order. Moreover, in proportion as these assertions of a power have become more spiritual, they have become more universal and searching, reaching all the institutions of human life, to conform in their idea and operation to the exigencies of the Christian conscience."[60]

In the democratic age, the pope no longer influences states, but societies, people, the civis christianus; but he does it with the same insistence with which he addressed the consciences of monarchs during the times of the closed confessional state.

The immediate church-political goal which Leo XIII pursued by his politics of Ralliement was never or at least only partially reached. The laicist offensive had gone too far and Catholics

[60] J. C. Murray, "Contemporary Orientations of Catholic Thought on Church and State in the Light of History," Theological Studies, Vol. X (1949).

were too little united among themselves for the courageous attempt at *Démocratie chrétienne* to achieve more than a temporary success.[61] In spite of the efforts of Harmel and the diligent activities of the *abbés démocrates*, the dissolution of the movement after 1900 was inevitable. Just as with conservative Catholics, anti-semitism was the undoing of Catholic republicans. Because they had for the most part condemned the Jewish captain during the Dreyfus Affair, they were open to the full force of the laicist reaction under Combes, and this ended their political chances at one blow.[62]

In the social sphere to which the *Graves de communi* restricted its activity, Christian Democracy was successful. It influenced the social education of clergy and capitalists and helped in the formation of a Christian workers' movement. From this grew both the Christian trade unions of France and the Catholic youth organizations, both of which have contributed much to the accommodation of church and workers.[63] Marc Sangnier, the founder of *Sillon*,[64] who later turned again from the social sphere to politics, came from the *Démocratie chrétienne*. For the period between the two world wars and up to the MRP, he constitutes the link between Harmel and social Catholicism. Thus, the sec-

[61] Cf. Clémenceau's remark to Jacques Piou, as quoted by Ferrata, *op. cit.*, p. 51: "Vous auriez dû adopter cette politique il y a vingt ans; il est trop tard maintenant, nous avons pris une trop grande avance."

[62] On the anti-semitism of the *Démocratie chrétienne*, especially of the Lyonese branch, see Rollet, pp. 420 ff. Gayraud, *Les Démocrates chrétiens*, p. 198, calls antisemitism "mouvement de défense nationale contre une race étrangère que l'on tient pour malfaisante."

[63] Especially the *Association catholique de la Jeunesse Française* (ACJF) founded by de Mun and later the *Sillon*, which was called a "Christian-Democratic youth movement" (Hermann Platz).

[64] On Marc Sangnier and the *Sillon*, see N. Ariès, *Le "Sillon" et le mouvement démocratique* (Paris, 1910); G. Lestrat, *Les beaux temps du Sillon* (Paris, 1926); J. Zamanski, *Nous, catholiques sociaux* (Paris, 1947).

ond *Démocratie chrétienne* in France, much less pretentious than the first, is connected with its revolutionary sister in the early history of the Christian Democratic movements of the twentieth century.

RESULT AND FORECAST

Christian Democracy, in the form it has taken in France, stands in a curious double relationship to its historical origins: it is understood both as the fulfilment and the defeat of the revolution. Theoretically, this contradiction is expressed in the tension between the Christian and the revolutionary idea of natural law which permeates the history of Christian Democratic thinking. In practice it is expressed in changing political attitudes, which oscillate between equality and liberty, between liberalism in practice and absolutism in theory, between flexible adaptation to what is possible and the temptation to regulate the game of politics dogmatically through a political theology. The difference between liberal and totalitarian democracy,[65] discerned by Talmon, may be applied to Christian Democracy, whose historical forms approach one or the other type depending on whether the political is treated empirically or theologically. The historical manifestations of this contradiction are liberal vs. social Catholicism, the democracy of human rights vs. the democracy of evangelical equality.

Christian Democracy, as it emerged in France after 1830, did not have a single root. We can clearly discern two lines of origin: one has its start in the Revolution of 1789, the other in Catholic traditionalism. The first leads from Fauchet and Bonneville to Buchez and his school; the connecting links are revolutionary illuminism and Saint-Simonism. (In this particular point the pre-

[65] J. L. Talmon, *The origins of totalitarian Democracy* (London, 1952) pp. 1–2.

ceding differs greatly from the results of J. Hours' studies, who
starts from an ideologically pre-determined concept of *Démocratie chrétienne*. He categorizes it under "reaction féodale" "con-
trerevolution" "opposition à l'histoire de la France" "organisation
corporative de la société" "aspirations vers un moyen-âge idéali-
sée" "tentatives persistantes pour construire l'union européenne
et mettre fin à la souveraineté nationale." These categories, loose
as they are, will hardly suffice to catch the historical characteristics of the *Démocratie chrétienne*, especially since the considerations of foreign policy which seem important to Hours, form a
bad methodological start. In examining the development of *Démocratie chrétienne* it bceomes clear that its character shows
clearly first in ecclesiastical and social concerns; farther reaching
political concepts developed only slowly and remained fragmentary. There can be no idea of a general concept based on foreign
policy. Rather we can trace a certain political aimlessness of
French *Démocratie chrétienne* caused by lack of practical diplomatic experience and the narrowing down of socio-political concerns during many decades. This is openly admitted by Maurice
Vassaud in his book on Christian Democracy. The "Habsburg
orientation" ascribed by Hours to the *Démocratie chrétienne* is
only a myth.) The second leads from the traditionalists to Catholic liberalism; the connecting link here is Lamennais who represents in his own person the transition from monarchism to
democracy. Both lines converge in the Revolution of 1848. Here,
for the first time for political Catholicism, a unified front forms.
Liberal Catholicism and Catholic-like Saint-Simonism meet in
Lacordaire and Buchez, Maret and Feuguerray; a Catholic socialism is developed, and Ozanam and Arnaud de l'Ariège add
republican traits to it.
    That it was possible for the two currents—the revolutionary
and the anti-revolutionary—to combine was not the result only

of the Revolution of 1848. Both currents had already moved away from their points of departure. Counter-revolutionary Catholicism underwent a *political* conversion, whereas revolutionary Catholicism underwent a *religious* conversion. In the hands of Lamennais, traditionalism became a liberal political doctrine, while the Catholic Saint-Simonists, dissatisfied with the sectarian Christianity of the school, began to move back to church Catholicism. Both currents met at first in a kind of sociological Catholicism, a way of thinking that chiefly sees dogma as a *lien d'unité*, a principle of social unity. The religious renewal after 1830 did away with the positivist remainders of political Catholicism. Buchez' disciples, in order to be Catholics, turned again to the church. While Lacordaire was led to Christianity by Rousseau and Chateaubriand, the young Ozanam grew up to a renewed orthodoxy which no longer needed sociological and emotional crutches.

After 1848 the *école démocratic-chrétienne* presents itself to our eyes in all its shadings and gradations as a special form of democracy deriving from Christian inspiration. It is sufficient to recall its most important characteristics: the primacy of the social over the political, Ozanam's contribution; the complementarity of human rights and civic duties; the limitation of state sovereignty in favor of individual and corporate rights; the demand for a subsidiary structure of society through political decentralization and a corporate economic system. It was not an action program, focusing on the claims of every day, which united Christian Democrats. The inner connection of their ideas is to be found on the theoretical plane; it is a new concept of state and society and is bitterly opposed to the Enlightened Jacobin concept. A utilitarian formulation of the aims of the state is rejected; a social ethics based on the common good is posited to replace bourgeois individualism.[66] Yet the organically structured democracy of Lacordaire or Ozanam, regulated by the principle of association, is no mere repeating of the medieval corporate society. We do not have before us a correction of the principles of 1789 inspired by a new, romantic theory of state, but a revival of communal forms of the church within the political sphere. It is a process already suggested by Lamennais in the demand: *réconstituer la société politique à l'aide de la société religieuse.* That it was possible for Catholic self-confidence to stress, together with the hierarchical structure of the church, its communal character, was indicative of the changes within Catholicism that had been caused or accelerated by the French Revolution.

The high point of Christian Democracy in France was short-lived. It collapsed together with the spurious flowering of the Second Republic. The *Démocratie chrétienne* dissolved in the June battle and Napoleon's coup. Later liberal Catholicism gave way to Syllabus-Catholics. In the following periods, church and democracy went their separate ways; the working class retired from Christian society; the Catholic social movement became conservative; political Catholicism became bourgeois.[67] France had seen the creation of a Christian Democratic theory by Lamennais but could not maintain it in practice. It was not French

[66] J. de Meyer, *De Staatsidee bij de Fransche Philosofen op den Voravond van de Revolutie* (Antwerpen, 1949), shows how the Thomistic conception of the *bonum commune* in the philosophy of Enlightenment turns into the greatest possible wordly "happiness of the greatest number," which, however, is restricted to a limited number: the *bonum commune* becomes an *intérêt général* (Helvétius) or a *volonté générale* (Rousseau). The Catholic social movement of the nineteenth century can be judged as an attempt to end this process.

[67] H. Rollet, the historian of social Catholicism in France, regards the adherence to paternalistic ideas as the main reason for the failure of the Catholic social movement after 1831: *L'action sociale des catholiques en France (1871–1901)* (Paris, 1947) p. 688.

Démocratie chrétienne but the political Catholicism of Belgium, Holland, and Germany which showed the way to the later Christian Democratic parties of Europe.

The reasons for this are obvious. In those countries Catholicism led the fight for its own integration in the national state; to achieve this aim it temporarily assumed the form of a political party. In France the question was not of co-operation within an existing political framework but of agreement or dissent to the principles of the revolution. The juridical spirit of the traditionalists linked the problem of political freedom of action of Catholicism with the question of state form. It seemed that Catholicism could come to full social effect only within a sympathetic monarchy. Conversely, the democratic theories of natural law, always alive in Catholicism, appeared in politico-theological guise during the nineteenth century: here, too, the tendency appeared of dogmatizing a form of state. To the *holy monarchy* of de Bonald corresponded the *holy democracy* of Fauchet and Buchez. Since both groups claimed to be correct theologically and yet were theologically incompatible with Catholic dogma, the church could not immediately intervene in the struggle for the revolution. It contented itself with refuting the religio-political claims of totalitarianism that were part of the process of dogmatizing political forms. Faced with political Catholicism in both its conservative and its revolutionary aspects, official Rome preserved a cautious distance.[68]

In the history of the dispute between revolution and church, liberal Catholicism and Christian Democracy initially remained without effect. They would have remained so had the church

[68] Not only was *Avenir* condemned by the church but so was Chateaubriand. And de Maistre experienced Rome's failure to "understand" his work and its astonishment at the new method. The popes did not make use of those theological constructions which attributed to the papacy a sovereignty which reached into the secular world (de Maistre, Lamennais).

under Leo XIII not become preoccupied with questions of democracy, a preoccupation caused by the anti-church politics of the Third Republic and by the splintering of political Catholicism in France. The pope's attempt at the last hour to reconcile French Catholics with the republic gave the ideas of liberal Catholicism, which had seemed long since theologically obsolete, sudden new life. The pope initiated a far-reaching revival of the Christian Democratic movement and threw new light on the efforts of men like Montalembert and Lamennais from an intra-church viewpoint. Seen in the perspective of the politics of *Ralliement*, liberal Catholicism and Christian Democracy no longer appeared to be heretical deviations but as first and principle contributions to the history of the accommodation of revolution and church which would occupy the church until well into the twentieth century and which would receive final form in the times of Pius XI, Pius XII, and John XXIII.

The *Ralliement*, the reconciliation of Catholics with the republic, which was the aim of Leo XIII, developed in ways which had been prepared by liberal Catholicism. First the pope stated the fundamental neutrality of the church toward any form of state—always assuming, however, that the liberties of the church and the freedom to promulgate religious teachings would be expressly guaranteed.[69] Then he asked French Catholics, in his encyclical *Au milieu des Sollicitudes*, to recognize the republican form of state. Differentiating between *pouvoir constitué* and *législation*, he counseled recognition of the form of state in order to be able to affect legislation. With this recognition of democratic principles as the formal rules for the expression of the people's will,[70] the basic thinking of liberal Catholicism was justified. Collaboration in a public body which did not conform to

---

[69] In the encyclical *Immortale Dei* (1885).

[70] A. Bergstraesser, *Staat und Wirtschaft Frankreichs* (Berlin-Leipzig, 1930), p. 32.

Catholic principles—permitted, after the practice of the *Syllabus*, only in states with mixed denominational populations—became possible for the Catholics of the French republic.

Yet the pope did not stop with his recognition of this formal liberal principle but took up the concerns of the Catholic social movement in the encyclical *Rerum novarum*. The "ideal exemplarism" of the papal social encyclical, as Ernst Karl Winter, the Austrian sociologist, calls it, was not linked to any definite political doctrine. But it expressed a claim of the church for a right to be present within society which was new, and it was received as such. The social order was committed to the hands of the *civis christianus*, who was to be obliged by conscience to fulfil his civic duties. The shaping of political conditions had become the task of laymen. Papal direction, rooted in the spiritual sphere, no longer was turned to the monarch as the bearer of public responsibilities in a Christian society but to the new democratic sovereign. For the position of the church in democratic society, the social encyclicals were a necessary, *material principle*.[71]

This spiritual influence of the church upon democratic society[72] could take effect only when the atomism of Jacobin democracy—the concept of an unrelated opposition of individuals and state—was overcome. Conversely, the "liberalization" of the Catholic theory of state became viable only after democracy had relinquished its claim to religious sovereignty. The parallel development of workers' movements, trade union movements, and Christian Democracy in the West European countries thus is no coincidence. The historical reason for placing the early history of Christian Democracy typologically between the liberal and social-

---

[71] C. Bauer, "Bild der Kirche—Abbild der Gesellschaft," in *Hochland*, XLVIII (1955/56), 527.

[72] Cf. J. C. Murray, "Contemporary Orientations of Catholic Thought on Church and State in the Light of History," *Theological Studies*, X (1949), 214.

istic parties should now be apparent: the church as a community (Ozanam) opens up toward democracy at the moment that democracy accepts the thought of *association*. Fulfilment and victory over the revolution can take place only within the church and thus, what Lamennais and Buchez had held up as the goal of Christian Democracy, becomes reality: *baptiser la démocratie.*

APPENDIX

"LIBERAL CATHOLICISM," "SOCIAL CATHOLICISM," "CHRISTIAN DEMOCRACY"

The concept of *libéraux catholiques, catholiques libéreaux*, appears for the first time in an article, *"Mission du peuple français c'est-à-dire des catholiques de France,"* in *Avenir* on January 3, 1831.[1] Yet the idea of a political union of liberals and Catholics is much older and appeared in Belgium in the twenties of the nineteenth century, where the majority of the Catholic population were opposed to Dutch-Protestant hegemony. The forays of the leader of the Belgian Catholics, Gerlac, in the Dutch general estates and of the liberal Devaux in the press (1825-27) aimed at setting up a common fighting front of liberals and Catholics against the government. They were the beginning of a Catholic movement in Belgium which contributed essentially to the emancipation of the country in the Revolution of 1830.[2] This "liberal Catholicism," originating in practical necessities and usually termed unionism by Belgian historians,[3] took over Lamennais and *Avenir's* theoretical weapons without tieing themselves to the theological conceptions of the Lamennais school. As a result, it outlived without much damage the papal corrective measures of 1832 and 1834 and was able to develop uninterruptedly under the protection of Bishop Sterckx in the *École de Malines*. The Belgian example

---

[1] C. Constantin, "Libéralisme catholique," *Dictionnaire de théologie catholique*, Vol. IX, No. 1 (1926), pp. 510-11.

[2] H. Haag, *Les origines du catholicisme libéral en Belgique (1789-1839)* (Louvain, 1950), and K. Jürgensen, *Lamennais und die Gestaltung des belgischen Staates* (Wiesbaden, 1963).

[3] H. Haag *op cit.*, pp. 99 ff.

—*la liberté comme en Belgique*—became obligatory for political
Catholicism all over Europe.

Characteristic of the early state of the movement was an exclusively
political, or rather church-political, aim, which separated "liberal Catholicism" from all other ideological liberalisms. This Catholicism is
"liberal" only with respect to the formal procedures of politics (participation in parliamentarianism, formation of parties, public action
through public meetings and petitions) but not with respect to the
dogmatic conception of liberty nor does it hold the view of democracy as an absolute form of state.

Even the "liberal Catholicism" of France after 1831, which separated from Lamennais, still belongs to the early stage of *unionism*. It
appears, chiefly with cultural forms, as the steward of Catholic freedom in matters of church and on questions of education. It makes
a point of keeping aloof from ideological liberalism. The flowering of
"liberal Catholicism" in France occurred between 1835 and 1848; its
last important success (and at the same time the last example of the
alliance of Catholic and liberal parties in Europe) is the school legislation of 1850, the so-called *Lex Falloux*. Pressed into opposition
during the Revolution of 1848, "liberal Catholicism" in the Second
Empire slowly gave way to a mood of intransigeancy in the French
church: the *Syllabus* appears to seal its fate theologically, too. But
precisely at this time there is another application of the liberal-
Catholic theology of mediation. Dupanloup, the spokesman of unionism in the French episcopate, separated the concept of freedom from
any link with the democratic form of state and with his differentiation between thesis and hypothesis opened a way for the integration
of liberal-constitutional elements in Catholic politics.[4] This solution,
taken over by Ketteler for German political Catholicism,[5] was later
taken up by Pope Leo XIII and further enlarged upon and refined.
The more that liberalism, in the second half of the nineteenth century, returned to its starting position in Voltaire, assuming antichurch
and Kulturkampf features, the more precarious became the founda-

---

[4] Mgr. Dupanloup, *La convention du 15 septembre et l'encyclique du 8 décembre* (Paris, 1865); cf. *supra*, p. 200, n. 44.

[5] W. E. von Ketteler, *Deutschland nach dem Kriege* (Mayence, 1866).

tions of the Catholic liberal idea of *unionism*. These were further
weakened because Liberal Catholicism after 1848 also underwent a
process of ideologization and developed its own reform ideas about
the church. The most important stages of this development are: the
schism of political Catholicism in France after 1848 into the opposing
schools of *Correspondant* (liberal) and *Univers* (conservative), in
which the latter was victorious over the former; the use of the Catholic-liberal formula *L'Église libre dans l'état libre* (Montalembert) by
Count Cavour, the political adversary of the popes; and, finally, the
Catholic-liberal opposition to the dogma of infallibility (1870) and
the later real or assumed connection between "liberal Catholicism"
and modernism. Through all these events, "liberal Catholicism" acquired a heretical hue in public opinion; it became more and more
difficult to use the phrase without controversy and to limit it to its
political meaning.

The concept of *catholicism libéral* first made its appearance in the
fight between the circles of *Correspondant* and *Univers*. It had a
polemical character from the first and served to raise the question of
the Catholicity of liberal Catholics by pointing to their assumed connection with the followers of Voltaire.[6] Subsequently, liberal Catholics (who had nothing against the designation *catholiques libéraux*)
defended themselves against such expressions as: *catholicisme libéral,
accouplement de mots qui est une insulte s'il n'est une absurdité*,
found in the July 25, 1888, edition of the *Correspondant*.[7]

The concept was introduced into scientific literature by Georges
Weill and Emmanuel Barbier.[8] Weill, who founded liberal Catholicism with Lamennais, summed up the essence of the movement in
three principles: *sympathie pour la liberté politique, sympathie pour*

[6] The leading pamphlets against liberal Catholicism are dated after 1870: Mgr.
De Ségur, *Hommage aux jeunes catholiques libéraux* (the title is a *captatio bene-
volentiae!*) (Paris, 1873), and J. Morel, *Somme contre le catholicisme libéral*
(Paris, 1877).

[7] As quoted by G. Weill, *Histoire du Catholicisme libéral en France (1828–
1908)* (Paris, 1909), p. 1.

[8] Weill, *op. cit.*; E. Barbier, *Histoire du catholicisme libéral et du catholicisme
social en France* (5 vols.; Bordeaux, 1924).

la démocratie sociale, sympathie pour la libre récherche intellectuelle.[9]
He stated that the principles did not appear simultaneously but one
after another. Weill's schema was taken over by E. Barbier.[10] In his
monumental *Histoire du catholicism libéral et du catholicisme social
en France*, he stresses the inseparability of the political from doctrine
and dogma. This dispute over the political or religious meaning of liberal Catholicism has today lost its significance. Yet modern research,
in order to avoid misunderstandings and make a sharper distinction
between political *unionism* and dogmatic *modernism* always speaks of
libéralisme catholique[11] and *libéralisme religieux*, respectively.[12]

The concept of *social Catholicism* is somewhat younger than that
of *liberal Catholicism*. It goes back to the Third Republic. Here it
appeared sometimes as a counterweight to the concept of liberal Catholicism, sometimes as its complement or special case. Joseph Folliet
traces the expression of *catholicisme social* to the three-volume work
of Paul Lapeyre which began to appear in 1894: *Le Socialisme catholique ou Christianisme intégral*. Its second volume bears the title *Le
Catholicisme social*.[13] Here the word is used as a collective name for
Catholic *social teachings* as they appeared in Leo XIII's encyclicals.[14]

In George Goyau it is found as a label for the *Catholic social movement* that followed the publication of *Rerum novarum*.[15] After the
First World War the concept of *catholicisme social* became current
in France.

But older than *catholicisme social* are the concepts of *socialisme
catholique* and *socialisme chrétien*. They flowered in France between
1830 and 1848, the period of early socialism and romanticism. Yet the
expression "socialism" is to be understood very broadly up to 1848.

---

[9] Weill, *op. cit.*, p. 283.

[10] Barbier, *op. cit.*, I, 2 ff.

[11] Cf. the already-mentioned article by Constantin.

[12] See the reports by Aubert, Duroselle, and Jemolo mentioned *supra*, p. 62,
n. 108.

[13] J. Folliet, "Catholicisme social," *Enzyklopädie Catholicisme* (Paris, 1948 ff),
pp. 703–22.

[14] Similarly, Abbé Naudet, *Le Christianisme social* (*Propriété, capital et travail*)
(Paris, 1898).

[15] G. Goyan, *Author de catholicisme social* (Paris, 1901).

Often, (especially in Buchez and Leroux) it formed the counterpart of words like *individualisme* and *libéralisme*.[16] For a long time a cryptoreligious meaning was connected with it.[17] Only with the scientific reconstruction of the concept by Proudhon and Marx (who also infused it with the content of their atheistic philosophies) did the word cease to be adaptable to a Christian social order. The social Catholicism in France that originated with Le Play and de Mun avoided the expression; only the radical group of romantic enthusiasts still called themselves *socialistes chrétiens*.[18]

The turn from political to social action which appeared in the encyclicals of Leo XIII was of profit to social Catholicism above all. In spite of this the concept was for a long time a doubtful and controversial one. Barbier was still treating social Catholicism, like liberal Catholicism, as an inner-church movement of romantics and heretics. But *catholicisme social* never was an open heresy. During the *semaines sociales*, which took place regularly after 1904, it circumscribed its teachings and created a dogmatically unassailable position. Its basic principles are spread today by means of official church policy. Though the practical successes of social Catholicism lag far behind those of

---

[16] The original meaning of the word "socialism" can be defined as "anti-individualism." In this sense it is, for instance, used in an article in the religious periodical *Le Semeur* of November 12, 1831, to contrast Catholic "social" teaching against the individualizing teaching of Protestantism. Cf. C. Grünberg, "Ursprung der Worte Sozialismus und Sozialist," *Zeitschrift für Sozialwissenschaft*, 1906, pp. 495–508, and "L'origine des mots socialisme et socialiste," *Revue d'Histoire des Doctrines économiques et sociales*, 1909, pp. 289–308. Similarly, P. Leroux, who introduced this word into philosophic terminology (*Oeuvres* [Paris, 1850], I, 21). The Italian priest Giacomo Giulani who had published a book *L'antisocialismo confutato* as early as 1803, calls socialism the existing state of individualism: Giulani's book is directed against Rousseau who wants to upset this order by means of his radical individualism (= anti-Socialism).

[17] P. Leroux, *op. cit.*, p. 161, n. 1 (quoted by Grünberg, "L'origine," p. 290): "Quand j'inventai le terme de Socialisme pour l'opposer au terme de l'Individualisme, je ne m'attendais pas que vingt ans plus tard, ce terme serait employé pour exprimer, d'une façon générale, la Démocratie religieuse."

[18] Nevertheless, the terms "socialisme chrétien," "socialisme catholique" were in use a long time; cf. Ch. Périn, *Le socialisme chrétien* (Paris, 1878), and A. Valez, *Le Socialisme catholique en France à l'heure actuelle* (Montauban, 1892).

comparable movements in Austria, Belgium, and Germany, it has led in the theoretical sphere for a long time. Thanks to the work of Duroselle, Hoog, and Rollet, its inner development is among the best thought out subjects in the social history of the nineteenth century.[19]

The expression *démocratie chrétienne* can be found here and there as early as the French Revolution but has not yet an outspoken political, only a religious, significance. It signifies the state of the Christianity of the early church, the *ecclesia paupera* as proclaimed by Christ, according to groups of romantic radical enthusiasts who were to renew it in the revolution. It can hardly be determined any more how far corporate-social and legal constitutional elements played a part in this concept of *démocratie*.[20] In order to come to the bottom of its meaning, the evidence will have to be systematically collected.

A sharper differentiation of the nuances is obtained between 1830 and 1848 where it shows up in circles of romantic socialists and Catholic republicans. The religious meaning still has the upper hand,[21] but it is no longer used exclusively to signify lost ideals for a reform of church constitution: it may stand for the state of a just *social constitution*, that is, as a sketch for a future new ordering of society. In this sense it is used by Ozanam.[22] The republican-political component is still present but no longer forms the main ingredient of the word. But the republican *Démocratie chrétienne* of 1848 already presupposes liberal-Catholic unionism.

The concept of Christian Democracy was spread in Europe after 1891 when, in the wake of *Rerum novarum*, numerous study circles and social political movements were formed all over Europe.[23] The

---

[19] J.-B. Duroselle, *Les débuts du catholicisme social en France* (1822–1870) (Paris, 1951); G. Hoog, *Histoire du Catholicisme Social en France, de L'Encyclique "Rerum Novarum" à l'Encyclique "Quadragesimo Anno"* (Paris, 1942); H. Rollet, *L'Action sociale des catholiques en France* (1871–1901) (Paris, 1947).

[20] Contrary to German usage, the French word "démocratie" cannot be used only to characterize the form of state but can also be applied to the lower classes, just as the word "aristocratie" has both a constitutional and a class-specific connotation.

[21] Cf. the references *supra*, p. 181, n. 8; and Gérando, *Le Démocrate chrétien ou Manuel évangélique de la Liberté, de l'Egalité et de la Fraternité* (Paris, 1848).

[22] See *supra*, p. 227, n. 106.

[23] See *supra*, p. 265 ff.

word itself seems to have originated in Belgium. It was taken over
later by the French Catholic social movement, by its left wing particularly. Abbé Six, one of the so-called *abbés démocrates*, in 1894
began a monthly review in Lille with the title *La Démocratie Chrétienne*. The same year saw the appearance of the first issue of *Sillon*,
whose name later became the program of a politico-social movement.
The *Démocrates chrétiens* circumscribed their politics with the words
Dieu, Famille, Propriété, Travail, Patrie. Their ideas were spread
through numerous books, newspapers, and reviews.[24] A detailed analysis of the movement has been published by Rollet.[25] In Austria and
Italy too at the same time, Christian Democratic trends appeared. A
professor of the University of Pisa, Giuseppe Toniolo, became the
leading theoretician of European Christian Democracy.[26]

The protest of Leo XIII in his encyclical *Graves de communi* restricted Christian Democracy to its purely social-charitable meaning.
With this any continuation of the political intentions of the French
Démocratie chrétienne became impossible. Later, in his condemnation of *Sillon*, Pope Pius XII rejected even more strongly the attempt
to make political deductions from any kind of religious and social conception of democracy. Consequently, the word, in an historical sense,
should be restricted to the short-lived Christian Democratic movement of 1891–1901.

It was only after the Second World War that the expression Christian Democracy (*Démocratie chrétienne, Democrazia cristiana*) became current as the designation for the religio-political, religio-social
movement of the nineteenth and twentieth centuries that aimed at
reconciliation between church and democracy or at a development of
a separate Christian form of democracy. Used in this sense, it has
replaced the older concepts of *liberal Catholicism* and *social Catholi-*

[24] Besides *La Démocratie chrétienne*, we must mention, *Le peuple français, Le
monde* (daily newspapers); *La Justice Sociale, La Vérité Sociale* (weekly papers).
Important is H. Gayraud's book, *Les Démocrates Chrétiens. Doctrine et Programme* (Paris, 1899).

[25] *Op. cit.*, pp. 339 ff.

[26] Cf. G. Toniolo, *Democrazia cristiana, concetti e indirizzi* (Vatican City,
1949). A complete edition of Toniolo's works has been appearing since 1947.

cism, especially in the countries of the romance languages (and also in England and the USA); or, rather, it had absorbed the concept within itself.[27] This extension of the concept corresponds to a historical perspective, visible only now, in which both movements reveal themselves as parts of a greater process of the accommodation church and modern democracy—a process which began with Lamennais and whose temporary form is the Christian Democracy of the twentieth century.

[27] Cf. the works of Biton, Einaudi-Goguel, Fogarty, Magre, Somma, Vaussard and others, mentioned *supra*, p. 1, n. 2.

BIBLIOGRAPHY

A) Bibliographies, Reference Books, Collections

Bibliographie critique des travaux parus sur l'histoire de France de 1600 à 1914; ed. by the Editorial Board of the *Revue d'histoire moderne.* 1933 ff.

Bulletin of International Institute for Social History. Amsterdam, 1937 ff.

Caron, P. and H. Stein. *Répertoire bibliographique de l'histoire de France.* 1923 ff.

Duine, F. *Essai de bibliographie de Félicité Robert de La Mennais.* 1923.

Galopin, E. *Essai de bibliographie chronologique sur Antoine-Frédéric Ozanam.* 1933.

Grandin, A. *Bibliographie générale des sciences juridiques, politiques, économiques et sociales.* 1929 ff.

Hatin, E. *Bibliographie historique et critique de la presse periodique française.* 1866.

Ledos, G. *Morceaux choisis et bibliographie de Lacordaire.* 1923.

Maas, G. *Bibliographie der Sozialwissenschaften.* Berlin, 1913 ff.

Martin, A. and G. Walther. *Catalogue de l'histoire de la révolution française.* 1936 ff.

Walther, G. *Répertoire de l'histoire de la révolution française.* 1941 ff.

Weill, G. "Le catholicisme français au XIXe siècle." *Revue de synthèse historique,* XV (1907) and XLI (1925).

Catholicisme-hier-aujourd'hui-demain. Encyclopedia in seven volumes; ed. by G. Jacquemart. 1948 ff.

Dictionnaire de théologie catholique; ed. by A. Vacant and E. Mangenot. 1909 ff.
Enciclopedia di scienze politiche, economiche e sociali. Bologna, 1956 ff.
Encyclopaedia of Social Sciences. New York, 1950.
Wörterbuch der Politik; ed. by O. v. Nell-Breuning and H. Sacher. Freiburg, 1947 ff.
Staatslexikon; ed. by the Görresgesellschaft. 5th Edition, Freiburg, 1926 ff.; 6th Edition, 1957 ff.
Lexikon für Theologie und Kirche; ed. by M. Burhberger. Freiburg, 1930 ff.; 2nd Edition, 1958 ff.

Acta Gregorii Papae XVI. Rome, 1901 ff.
Acta Pii Papae IX. Rome, 1857 ff.
Acta Leonis Papae XIII. Rome, 1881 ff.
Acta Sanctae Sedis. Rome, 1865 ff.
Acta Apostolica Sedis. Rome, 1909 ff.
Albertini, R. v. Freiheit und Demokratie im politischen Denken Frankreichs. Die Diskussion von der Restauration bis zur Résistance. Freiburg-Munich, 1957.
Denzinger, H. Enchiridion symbolorum, definitionum et declarationum de rebus fidei et morum. 30th Edition, Freiburg, 1955.
Duguit, L. and H. Monnier. Les constitutions et les principales lois politiques de la France depuis 1789. 1925.
Michon, G. Les textes pontificaux sur la démocratie et la société moderne. 1928.
Mirbt, C. Quellen zur Geschichte des Papsttums und des römischen Katholizismus. Tübingen, 1934.
Theiner, A. Documents inédits relatifs aux affaires religieuses de la France (1790–1800). 1857.

B) General; Introductory

Alexander, E. "The Sociological Problem of Catholicism," Church and Society. Catholic Social and Political Thought and Movements (1789–1950). New York, 1953.
Aubert, R. Le pontificat de Pie IX (1846–1878) (Histoire de l'église; ed. by A. Fliche and V. Martin, Vol. 21). 1952.

Barbier, E. *Histoire du catholicisme libéral et du catholicisme social en France.* 5 vols. Bordeaux, 1923 ff.

Barth, K. *Christengemeinde und Bürgergemeinde.* Munich, 1946.

Bauer, C. *Politischer Katholizismus in Württemberg bis zum Jahr 1848.* Freiburg, 1929.

Bauer, C. "Bild der Kirche-Abbild der Gesellschaft." *Hochland,* 48 (1955/56).

Bellamy, J. *La théologie catholique au XIXe siècle.* 1904.

Bergstraesser, A. *Staat und Wirtschaft Frankreichs.* Berlin-Leipzig, 1930.

Biton, L. *La démocratie chrétienne dans la politique française.* Angers, 1954.

Brinkmann, C. *Soziologische Theorie der Revolution.* Göttingen, 1948.

Böckenförde, E.-W. "Das Ethos der modernen Demokratie und die Kirche." *Hochland,* 50 (1957/58).

Bosworth, W. *Catholicism and Crisis in Modern France. French Catholic Groups at the Threshold of the Fifth Republic.* Princeton, 1962.

Buchheim, K. *Geschichte der christlichen Parteien in Deutschland.* Munich, 1953.

Congar, Y. Art. "Église et État" in the *Encyclopédie Catholicisme.* 1948 ff.

Curtius, E. R. *Die französische Kultur.* Berlin-Leipzig, 1930.

Dansette, A. *Histoire religieuse de la France contemporaine.* 2 vols. 1948/51.

Dansette, A. *Destin du catholicisme français: 1926–1956.* 1957.

Darbon, M. *Le conflit entre la droite et la gauche dans le catholicisme français (1830–1953).* 1953.

Débidour, A. *Histoire des rapports de l'église et de l'état en France.* 1898.

Dempf, A. *Demokratie und Partei im politischen Katholizismus.* Vienna, 1932.

Duverger, M. *Political Parties, Their Organization and Activity in the Modern State.* New York, 1954.

Einaudi, M. and F. Goguel. *Christian Democracy in Italy and France.* Notre Dame, 1952.

Fogarty, M. P. *Christian Democracy in Western Europe, 1820–1953.* London, 1957.

Friedrich, H. *Das antiromantische Denken im modernen Frankreich. Sein System und seine Herkunft* (*Münchener romanistische Arbeiten,* 4). Munich, 1935.

Guillemin, H. *Histoire des catholiques français au XIXe siècle.* 1947.

Gundlach, G. *Zur Soziologie der katholischen Ideenwelt und des Jesuitenordens.* Freiburg, 1927.

Gurian, W. *Die politischen und sozialen Ideen des französischen Katholizismus.* M.-Gladbach, 1929.

Hartmann, A. *Toleranz und christlicher Glaube.* Frankfurt a. M., 1955.

Havard de la Montagne, R. *Histoire de la démocratie chrétienne. De Lamennais à Georges Bidault.* 1948.

Hours, J. "Les origines d'une tradition politique. La formation en France de la démocratie chrétienne et des pouvoirs intermédiaires," *Libéralisme, Traditionalisme, Décentralisation.* Cahier 31 de la Fondation Nationale des Sciences Politiques. 1952.

Hürten, H. (ed.) *Christliche Parteien in Europa.* Osnabrück, 1964.

Kupisch, K. *Zwischen Idealismus und Massendemokratie. Eine Geschichte der Evangelischen Kirche in Deutschland.* 2nd Edition, Berlin, 1959.

Latreille, A. "Le Catholicisme," *Les forces religieuses et la vie politique.* Cahier 23 de la Fondation Nationale des Sciences Politiques. 1951.

Lavau, G. *Partis politiques et réalités sociales.* Cahier 38 de la Fondation Nationale des Sciences Politiques. 1953.

Le Bras, G. *Introduction à l'histoire de la pratique religieuse en France.* 1942.

Le Bras, G. *Études de sociologie religieuse.* 2 vols. 1955/56.

Lecler, J. *L'Église et la souveraineté d'État.* 1946.

Leflon, J. *La crise révolutionnaire (1789–1846)* (*Histoire de l'Église,* ed. by A. Fliche and V. Martin, Vol. 20). 1949.

Leroy, M. *Histoire des idées sociales en France.* 2 vols. 1946/50.

Lubac, H. de. "Le pouvoir de l'Église en matière temporelle," *Revue des sciences religieuses.* 1921.

Lubac, H. de. *Catholicism.* New York, 1964.

Martin, A. v. "Die Revolution als soziologisches Phänomen," *Festschrift für Jan Romein.* Amsterdam, 1953 (reprinted in *Ordnung und Freiheit.* *Materialien und Reflexionen zu Grundfragen des Soziallebens.* Frankfurt a. M., 1956).

Maritain, J. *The Rights of Man and Natural Law.* New York, 1943.

Maritain, J. *Christianity and Democracy.* New York, 1944.

Maritain, J. *Man and the State.* Chicago, 1951.

Michel, H. *L'idée de l'état. Essai critique sur l'histoire des théories sociales et politiques en France depuis la Révolution.* 1895.

Michels, R. *Zur Soziologie des Parteiwesens in der modernen Demokratie.* 2nd Edition, Leipzig, 1925 (Reprint of the 2nd edition, edited and with an epilogue by W. Conze. Stuttgart, 1957).

Monzel, N. *Struktursoziologie und Kirchenbegriff* (Fasc. 10 of the series Grenzfragen zwischen Theologie und Philosophie). Bonn, 1939.

Moody, J. N. (ed.). *Church and Society. Catholic Social and Political Thought and Movements (1789–1950).* New York, 1953.

Nell-Breuning, O. v. "Demokratie, Christliche Demokratie, Volkssouveränität," *Wörterbuch der Politik.* Freiburg, 1947 ff.

Neumann, S. (ed.). *Modern Political Parties. Approaches to Comparative Politics.* Chicago, 1956.

Nürnberger, R. "Revolution und Tradition," *Verhandlungen des 13. Deutschen Soziologentages in Bad Meinberg.* Cologne-Opladen, 1957.

Ostrogorsky, M. Y. *La démocratie et l'organisation des partis politiques.* 2 vols. 1903.

Peterson, E. *Die Kirche.* Munich, 1929.

Peterson, E. "Briefwechsel mit Adolf Harnack." *Hochland,* 32 (1932) (both reprinted in *Theologische Traktate.* Munich, 1950).

Pouthas, Ch. "L'Église catholique de l'avènement de Pie VII à l'avènenment de Pie IX" (Cours de Sorbonne, mimeographed).

Pouthas, Ch. "Le pontificat de Pie IX" (Cours de Sorbonne, mimeographed).

Rastoul, A. *Histoire de la démocratie catholique en France.* 1913.

Rémond, R. *La droite en France de 1815 à nos jours.* 1954.

Repgen, K. *Märzbewegung und Maiwahlen des Revolutionsjahres 1848 im Rheinland.* Bonn, 1955.

Ritter, G. "Vom Ursprung des Einparteienstaates in Europa." *Historisches Jahrbuch*, 74 (1955) (Festschrift für Franz Schnabel).

Roger, J. *Ideas políticas de los católicos franceses*. Madrid, 1951.

Rohden, P. R. "Zur Soziologie des politischen Katholizismus in Frankreich." *Archiv für Sozialwissenschaft und Sozialpolitik*, LXII (1919).

Rommen, H. *The State in Catholic Thought*. St. Louis and London, 1945.

Rothfels, H. "Ideengeschichte und Parteigeschichte." *Deutsche Vierteljahresschrift für Literaturwissenschaft und Geistesgeschichte*, 8 (1930).

Scheler, M. *Christentum und Gesellschaft*. Leipzig, 1924.

Schieder, Th. "Das Verhältnis von politischer und gesellschaftlicher Verfassung und die Krise des bürgerlichen Liberalismus." *Historische Zeitschrift*, 177 (1954).

Schieder, Th. "Die Theorie der Partei im älteren deutschen Liberalismus," *Aus Geschichte und Politik*. Festschrift für Ludwig Bergstraesser. Düsseldorf, 1954.

Schieder, Th. "Der Liberalismus und die Strukturwandlungen der modernen Gesellschaft vom 19. zum 20. Jahrhundert," *Relazioni del X Congresso Internazionale di Scienze Storiche*. Vol. 5. Florence, 1955 (Also printed in the collection *Staat und Gesellschaft im Wandel unserer Zeit*. Munich, 1958).

Schmidlin, J. *Papstgeschichte der neuesten Zeit*. 3 vols. Munich, 1933 ff.

Schmitt, C. *Politische Theologie*. Munich, 1922.

Schmitt, C. *Römischer Katholizismus und politische Form*. Leipzig, 1923.

Schnabel, F. *Der Zusammenschluss des politischen Katholizismus in Deutschland 1848*. Heidelberg, 1910.

Schöllgen, W. *Die soziologischen Grundlagen der katholischen Sittenlehre* (Handbuch der katholischen Sittenlehre; ed. by F. Tilmann, Vol. V). Düsseldorf, 1953.

Schrey, H. H. *Die Generation der Entscheidung. Staat und Kirche in Europa und im europäischen Russland 1918–1953*. Munich, 1955.

Shanahan, W. O. *German Protestants Face the Social Question.*
Notre Dame, 1954.
Siegfried, A. "Le protestantisme," *Les forces religieuses et la vie
politique.* Cahier 23 de la Fondation Nationale des Sciences Poli-
tiques. 1951.
Smend, R. "Protestantismus und Demokratie," *Krisis. Ein politisches
Manifest.* Weimar, 1932. Also in *Staatsrechtliche Abhandlungen.*
Berlin, 1955. Pp. 297 ff.
Sturzo, L. *Church and State.* London, 1939.
Talmon, J. L. *The Origins of Totalitarian Democracy.* London, 1952.
Thibaudet, A. *Les idées politiques de la France.* 1928.
Tischleder, P. *Die Staatslehre Leos XIII.* M.-Gladbach, 1925.
Tocqueville, A. de. *The Old Régime and the French Revolution.*
New York, 1955.
Toniolo, G. *Democrazia cristiana; concetti e indirizzi.* Vatican City,
1949.
Vaussard, M. *Histoire de la démocratie chrétienne (France, Belgique,
Italie).* 1956.
Weill, G. *Histoire de l'idée laique en France au XIXe siècle.* 1929.
Wimmer, A. (ed.). *Die Menschenrechte in christlicher Sicht,* Second
Supplement to *Herder-Korrespondenz.* Freiburg, 1953.

C) Chapter 1

1. SOURCES (NL-NATIONAL LIBRARY, PARIS)

Boisgelin, de. *Discours sur le rapport du comité ecclésiastique con-
cernant la constitution du clergé prononcé le 29 mai 1790.* (NL).
Bonneville, N. de. *De l'esprit des religions.* 1791.
Fauchet, C. *Oraison funèbre de Louis, duc d'Orléans.* 1786. (NL).
Fauchet, C. *De la religion nationale.* 1789.
Fauchet, C. *Trois discours sur la liberté française.* 1789. (NL).
Fauchet, C. *Lettre pastorale et la traduction de sa lettre de com-
munion adressée à N. S. P. le pape.* Bayeux, 1791. (NL).
Fauchet, C. *Lettre circulaire à tous les curés de son diocèse, à tous
les clubs et à toutes les sociétés du département.* Caen, 1791. (NL).
Fauchet, C. *Lettre pastorale aux pasteurs et aux fidèles du diocèse.*
Bayeux, 1792. (NL).

Fauchet, C. *Claude Fauchet au tribunal révolutionnaire et au public.* 1792 (NL).

Grégoire, H. *Légitimité du serment civique exigé des fonctionnaires ecclésiastiques.* 1791.

Grégoire, H. *Lettres pastorales (1791–1796).* (NL).

Grégoire, H. *Essai historique sur les libertés de l'église gallican.* 1818.

Lamourette, A.-A. *Instructions pastorales.* 1791. (NL).

Lamourette, A.-A. *Observations contre l'article XV du projet de décret du comité de législation sur les troubles religieux; prononcées le 21 novembre 1791 (Assemblée Législative).* (NL).

Rousseau, J.-J. *The Social Contract.* New York, 1947.

Rousseau, J.-J. *Lettres écrites de la Montagne (Oeuvres complètes de Jean-Jacques Rousseau),* 1832 ff., Vol. VIII.

Rousseau, J.-J. *Profession de foi du vicaire savoyard;* ed. by P.-M. Masson. Freiburg/Switzerland, 1914.

COLLECTIONS, JOURNALS

Archives parlementaires de 1787 à 1860, 1ère série (1787–1799). 1867–1892.

La Bouche de Fer; ed. by C. Fauchet and N. de Bonneville. 1791/92. (NL).

Bulletin de la Bouche de Fer. 1790. (NL).

Cercle Social. 1791/92. (NL).

La chronique du mois ou les cahiers patriotiques; ed. by N. de Bonneville. 1791–1793 (NL).

Journal chrétien, ou l'ami des moeurs, de la vérité et de la paix; ed. by P.-V. Chalvet). 1791–1793. (NL).

Recueil de documents relatifs à la convocation des États Généraux de 1789; ed. by A. Brette. Vol. I. 1894.

Recueil de documents relatifs aux séances des États Généraux, mai-juin 1789; prepared under the direction of G. Lefebvre and d'Anne Terroine, Vol. I: *Les préliminaires, la séance du 5 mai.* Paris, 1953.

Réimpression de l'ancien moniteur depuis la réunion des États-Généraux jusqu'au Consulat; ed. by L. Gallois. 1840–1847.

2. BOOKS

Aulard, A. *Le culte de la raison et de l'être suprême*. 1904.
Aulard, A. *Le christianisme et la révolution française*. 1925.
Barber, Elinor G. *The Bourgeoisie in 18th Century France*. Princeton, 1955.
Barruel, A. *Histoire du clergé pendant la révolution*. London, 1793.
Barruel, A. *Mémoires pour servir à l'histoire du jacobinisme*. Hamburg, 1800.
Bremond, H. *La vie chrétienne sous l'ancien régime* (*Histoire littéraire du sentiment religieux en France*, Vol. IX). 1932.
Brinton, C. *The Jacobins*. New York, 1930.
Brinton, C. *A Decade of Revolution*. New York-London, 1934.
Cassirer, E. *Die Philosophie der Aufklärung*. Tübingen, 1932.
Cros, H. "Claude Fauchet (1744-1793). Les idées politiques, économiques et sociales." Thesis, 1912.
Denys-Buirette, A. *Les questions religieuses dans les cahiers de 1789*. 1919.
Erdmann, K. D. *Das Verhältnis von Staat und Religion nach der Sozialphilosophie Rousseaus. Der Begriff der "religion civile."* Berlin, 1935.
Erdmann, K. D. *Volkssouveränität und Kirche. Studien über das Verhältnis von Staat und Religion in Frankreich vom Zusammentritt der Generalstände bis zum Schisma*. Cologne, 1949.
Ford, F. L. *Robe and Sword. The Regrouping of the French Aristocracy after Louis XIV*. Cambridge, Mass., 1953.
Gazier, A. *Études sur l'histoire religieuse de la révolution française*. 1877.
Göhring, M. *Geschichte der Grossen Revolution*. 2 vols. Tübingen, 1950/51.
Gorce, P. de la. *Histoire religieuse de la révolution française*. 1909 (Reprinted 1948).
Groethuysen, B. *The Bourgeois; Catholicism vs. Capitalism in Eighteenth-Century France*. New York, 1968.
Heinrichs, K. "Die politische Ideologie des französischen Klerus bei Beginn der grossen Revolution." Phil. Diss., Kiel, 1934.
Latreille, A. *L'église catholique et la révolution française*. 1946.

Leclercq, Dom. *L'église constitutionnelle.* 1934.
Lefebvre, G., R. Guyot, Ph. Sagnac. *La révolution française (Histoire générale;* ed. by L. Halphen and Ph. Sagnac, Vol. XII). 1938.
Le Harivel, Ph. *Nicolas de Bonneville, préromantique et révolutionnaire (1760–1828).* Strassburg, 1923.
Masson, P.-M. *La religion de Jean-Jacques Rousseau.* Thesis, 1916.
Mathiez, A. *L'origine des cultes révolutionnaires.* 1908.
Mathiez, A. *Le club des Cordeliers pendant la crise de Varennes et le massacre du Champ de Mars.* 1910.
Mathiez, A. *Rome et le clergé français sous la constituante.* 1928.
Mathiez, A. "L'église et la révolution française," *Revue des Cours et Conférences.* Vol. 32 (1931) and Vol. 33 (1932).
Meyer, J. de. *De Staatsidee bij de Fransche Philosofen op den Voravond van de Revolutie.* Antwerp, 1949.
Mornet, D. *Les origines intellectuelles de la révolution française.* 1933.
Orcibal, J. "L'idée d'Église chez les catholiques du XVIIIe siècle," *Relazioni del X Congresso Internazionale di Scienze Storiche.* Vol. IV. Florence, 1955.
Pouget, A. *Les idées religieuses et réformatrices de l'évêque constitutionel Grégoire.* 1905.
Préclin, E. *Les jansénistes du XVIIIe siècle et la constitution civile du clergé.* 1929.
Préclin, E. and E. Jarry. *Les luttes politiques et doctrinales aux XVIIe et XVIIIe siècles (Histoire de l'Église;* ed. by A. Fliche and V. Martin, Vol. 19). 1955.
Schinz, A. *La pensée de Jean-Jacques Rousseau.* 1929.
Sicard, A. *Le clergé de France pendant la révolution.* 3 vols. 1912 ff.
Tiersot, J. *Les fêtes et les chants de la révolution française.* 1908.
Wahl, A. *Vorgeschichte der Französischen Revolution.* 2 vols. Tübingen, 1905/1907.

D) Chapter 2
1. SOURCES

Bonald, A. de. *Oeuvres complètes;* ed. by Migne. 3 vols. 1859.
Bonald, A. de. *Oeuvres choisies;* ed. by L. de Montesquieu. 1908.

Bonald, A. de. *Théorie du pouvoir politique et religieux dans la société civile démontrée par le raisonnement et par l'histoire.* 1796.
Bonald, A. de. *Législation primitive considérée dans les derniers temps.* 1802.
Bonald, A. de. *Observations sur l'ouvrage ayant pour titre: Considérations sur les principaux événements de la révolution française,* par Mme. la baronne de Staël. 1818.
Lamennais, F. de. *Essai sur l'indifférence en maitière de religion.* 4 vols. 1817–1823.
Maistre, J. de. *Oeuvres complètes.* 14 vols. Lyon, 1884–1886.
Maistre, J. de. *Oeuvres.* 4 vols. 1851/52.
Maistre, J. de. *Considérations sur la France.* Lausanne, 1795.
Maistre, J. de. *Du pape.* Lyon, 1819.
Maistre, J. de. *Essai sur le principe générateur des constitutions politiques.* 1821.
Maistre, J. de. *De l'église gallicane dans ses rapports avec le souverain pontife.* Lyon, 1821.
Saint-Martin, L.-C. de. *Lettre à un ami, ou considérations politiques, philosophiques et religieuses sur la révolution française.* 1795.

2. BOOKS

Ahrens, L. *Lamennais und Deutschland. Studien zur Geschichte der französischen Restauration.* Münster, 1930.
Bagge, D. *Les idées politiques en France sous la restauration.* 1952.
Bayle, F. *Les idées politiques de Joseph de Maistre.* Paris, 1945.
Bertier de Sauvigny, G. de. *Un type d'ultra-royaliste: le comte Ferdinand de Bertier (1782–1864) et l'énigme de la Congrégation.* 1948.
Bertier de Sauvigny, G. de. *La restauration.* 1955.
Ferraz, M. *Traditionalisme et ultramontanisme (Histoire de la philosophie en France au XIXe siècle,* Vol. III). 1880.
Foucher, L. *La philosophie catholique en France au XIXe siècle, avant la renaissance thomiste et dans son rapport avec elle (1800–1880).* 1955.
Goyau, G. *La pensée religieuse de Joseph de Maistre.* 1922.
Johannet, R. *Joseph de Maistre.* 1932.
Lacroix, J. *Vocation personnelle et tradition nationale.* 1942.

Lubac, H. de. *The Drama of Atheist Humanism.* 1945.

Maréchal, Ch. *La dispute de l'essai sur l'indifférence.* 1925.

Merkle, S. "Die Anfänge französischer Laientheologie im 19. Jahrhundert," *Wiederbegegnung von Kirche und Kultur in Deutschland* (Festschrift für Karl Muth). Munich, 1929.

Moulinier, H. *de Bonald.* 1916.

Pouthas, Ch. "Histoire politique de la restauration" (Cours de Sorbonne, mimeographed).

Pouthas, Ch. "Le clergé sous la monarchie constitutionelle, 1814–1848." *Revue d'histoire de l'Eglise de France,* 29 (1943).

Rohden, P. R. *Joseph de Maistre als politischer Theoretiker.* Munich, 1929.

Spaemann, R. *Der Ursprung der Soziologie aus dem Geist der Restauration. Studien über L. G. A. de Bonald.* Munich, 1959.

Viatte, A. *Les sources occultes du romantisme.* 2 vols. 1928.

(For further literature on Lamennais see the next chapter listing.)

E) Chapter 3

1. SOURCES

Arnaud de l'Ariège, F. *Cercle de la démocratie chrétienne. Extrait des Statuts.* 1850. (NL).

Arnaud de l'Ariège, F. *La révolution et l'église.* 1869. (NL).

Buchez, Ph.-J.-B. *Introduction à la science de l'histoire ou science du développement de l'humanité.* 1833.

Buchez, Ph.-J.-B. *Essai d'un traité complet de philosophie du point de vue du catholicisme et du progrès.* 1838–1840.

Buchez, Ph.-J.-B. and P. C. Roux-Lavergne. *Histoire parlementaire de la Révolution française.* 40 vols. 1834–1838. (NL).

Feuguerray, H.-R. *La République et la Commune de Paris. Association démocratique des amis de la Constitution.* 1849.

Feuguerray, H.-R. *Essai sur les doctrines politiques de Saint-Thomas d'Aquin précédé d'une notice sur la vie et les écrits de l'auteur, par M. Buchez.* 1857.

Lacordaire, H. D. *Oeuvres.* 9 vols. 1872–1880.

Lamennais, F. de. *Oeuvres complètes.* 12 vols. 1836/37.

Lamennais, F. de. *De la religion considérée dans ses rapports avec l'ordre politique et civil.* 2 vols. 1825/26.

Lamennais, F. de. *Des progrès de la Révolution et de la guerre contre l'église.* 1829.

Lamennais, F. de. *Paroles d'un croyant.* 1834.

Lamennais, F. de. *Les affaires de Rome.* 1836.

Lamennais, F. de. *Le livre du peuple.* 1837.

Lamennais. F. de. *Du passé et de l'avenir du peuple.* 1841.

Lamennais, F. de. *Le prêtre et l'ami. Lettres inédites de Lamennais à la Baronne Cottu (1818–1854).* 1910.

Montalembert, Ch. de. *Oeuvres complètes.* 9 vols. 1861–1868.

Montalembert, Ch. de. *L'église libre dans l'état libre. Discours prononcés au Congrès Catholique de Malines.* 1863.

Montalembert, Ch. de. *Lettres de Montalembert à La Mennais;* ed. by G. Goyau. 1932.

Ozanam, A.-F. *Oeuvres complètes.* 11 vols. 1872.

Saint-Simon, H. de. *Le nouveau christianisme (Oeuvres complètes de Saint-Simon et d'Enfantin,* 1865 ff., Vol. XXIII).

JOURNALS

L'Ami de la religion (Editors: Picot, Affre, Dupanloup). 1830–1859. (NL).

L'Atelier (Editors: Corbon, Pascal, Chevé). 1840–1850. (NL).

L'Avenir (Editors: Lamennais, de Coux, Gerbet). 1830/31. (NL).

L'Européen (Editor: Buchez). 1831/32; 1835–1838. (NL).

La Revue Nationale (Editors: Buchez, Bastide, Ott). 1847/48. (NL).

L'Ère Nouvelle (Editors: Lacordaire, Maret, Ozanam, Arnaud de l'Ariège). 1848/49. (NL).

2. BOOKS

Aubert, R., J.-B. Duroselle, A. Jemolo. "Le libéralisme religieux au XIXe siècle," *Relazioni del X Congresso Internazionale di Scienze Storiche.* Vol. V. Florence, 1955.

Bastid, P. *Les doctrines et institutions de la Seconde République.* 2 vols. 1949.

Bazin, G. *Vie de Mgr. Maret.* 2 vols. 1882.

Boutard, Ch. *Lamennais, sa vie et ses doctrines.* 3 vols. 1905–1913.

Camus, L.-Y. *Frédéric Ozanam.* 1953.

Carcopino, C. *Les doctrines sociales de Lamennais.* 1942.

Carranza, A. R. *Ozanam et ses contemporains.* 1953.

Castella, G. *Buchez historien, sa théorie du progrès dans la philosophie de l'histoire.* Freiburg/Switzerland, 1909.

Castella, G. *Buchez.* 1911.

Celier, L. *Ozanam.* 1956.

Charléty, S. *Histoire du Saint-Simonisme.* 1896.

Cuvillier, A. P.-B. *Buchez et les origines du socialisme chrétien.* 1948.

Dolléans, E. *Histoire du mouvement ouvrier.* Vol. I. 1936.

Dudon, P. *Lamennais et le Saint-Siège.* 1911.

Duroselle, J.-B. "L'esprit de 1848," *1848 révolution créatrice.* 1948.

Duroselle, J.-B. "L'attitude politique et sociale des catholiques français en 1848." *Revue d'histoire de l'Église de France,* 34 (1948).

Duroselle, J.-B. "Arnaud de l'Ariège et la démocratie chrétienne (1848–1851)." Typescript. 1949.

Fesch, P. *Lacordaire journaliste (1830–1848).* Lyon, 1897.

Foisset, J. T. *Vie du R. P. Lacordaire.* 2 vols. 1870.

Geissberger, W. *Philippe-Joseph-Benjamin Buchez. Theoretiker einer christlichen Sozialökonomie und Pionier der Produktiv-Genossenschaften.* Winterthur, 1956.

Giraud, V. *La vie tragique de Lamennais.* 1933.

Goyau, G. *Ozanam.* 1925.

Guihaire, P. *Lacordaire et Ozanam.* 1933.

Gurian, W. "Lamennais," *Perspektiven III* (1953).

Haag, H. *Les origines du catholicisme libéral en Belgique (1789–1829).* Louvain, 1950.

Jürgensen, K. *Lamennais und die Gestaltung des belgischen Staates. Der liberale Katholizismus in der Verfassungsbewegung des 19. Jahrhunderts.* Wiesbaden, 1963.

Lallemand, P. de. *Montalembert et ses amis dans le romantisme (1830–1840).* 1927.

Lecanuet, R. P. *Montalembert.* 3 vols. 1900–1902.

Méjecaze, F. "Ozanam. Essai de synthèse des idées et des jugements littéraires." Thesis, 1932.

Mourre, M. *Lamennais ou l'hérésie des temps modernes.* 1955.
Mourret, F. *Le mouvement catholique en France de 1830 à 1850.* 1917.
Pocquet de Haut-Jussé, B.-A. *La Mennais. L'évolution de ses idées politiques jusqu'en 1832.* Rennes, 1955.
Renan, E. "Étude sur Lamennais," *Lamennais, Le livre du peuple.* 1872.
Rigaudias-Weiss, A. *Les enquêtes ouvrières en France entre 1820 et 1848.* 1931.
Rischke, M. *Ozanam.* Cologne, 1927.
Seiler, E. *Die Entwicklung berufsständischer Ideen in der katholisch-sozialen Bewegung Frankreichs.* Zurich, 1935.
Trannoy, A. "Le romantisme politique de Montalembert avant 1843." Thesis, 1942.
Trannoy, A. "Responsabilités de Montalembert en 1848." *Revue d'histoire de l'Eglise de France,* 35 (1949).
Vallery-Radot, R. *Lamennais ou le prêtre malgré lui.* 1931.
Villefosse, L. de. *Lamennais ou l'occasion manquée.* 1945.
Weill, G. *Histoire du catholicisme libéral en France.* 1909.

F) Chapter 4

1. SOURCES

Boissard, A. *Le syndicat mixte.* 1897.
Dabry, P. *Les catholiques républicains. Histoire et souvenir.* 1905.
De Clercq, V. *La doctrina sociale catholique en France depuis la révolution jusqu'à nos jours;* Vol. 1: *Les précurseurs,* Vol. 2: *Les contemporains.* 1905.
Dupanloup, Mgr. *La convention du 15 septembre et l'encyclique du 8 décembre.* 1865.
Féron-Vrau, P. *L'Association Catholique des Patrons du Nord.* n. d.
Ferrata, D. *Ma nonciature en France.* 1921.
Gayraud, H. *Les démocrates chrétiens.* 1898.
Harmel, L. *Manuel d'une corporation chrétienne.* Tours, 1879.
Langénieux, Card. *Les pèlerinages des ouvriers français à Rome et la question sociale.* n. d.

Lapeyre, P. *Le socialisme catholique ou christianisme intégral.* 3 vols. 1894 ff.

Le Querdec, Y. *Lettres d'un Curé de Campagne.* 1894.

Le Querdec, Y. *Lettres d'un Curé de Canton.* 1895.

Maumus, P. E.-V. *L'eglise et la démocratie. Histoire des questions sociales.* 1893.

Naudet, Abbé. *Le christianisme social (propriété, capital et travail).* 1898.

Mun, A. de. *Discours et écrits divers d'Albert de Mun avec des notices par Ch.* Geoffroy de Grandmaison. 1893 ff.

Mun, A. de. *Combats d'hier et d'aujourd'hui.* 1906–1911.

Mun, A. de. *Ma vocation sociale.* 1911.

Mun, A. de. *La pensée sociale d'Albert de Mun. Extraits receuillis et ordonnés par Ch.* Brossier. Marseille, 1929.

Piou, J. *Le ralliement.* 1928.

Valez, A. *Le socialisme catholique en France à l'heure actuelle.* Montauban, 1892.

JOURNALS AND NEWSPAPERS

La Justice Sociale. Bordeaux, 1893 ff.

Le Peuple. Lille, 1893 ff.

La Démocratie Chrétienne. Lille, 1894 ff.

La Vérité Sociale. Charleville, 1894 ff.

Le Monde. 1894 ff.

Le Peuple Français. 1894 ff.

Le Sillon. 1894 ff.

2. BOOKS

Accomb, E. M. *The French Laic Laws.* New York, 1941.

Ariès, N. *Le "Sillon" et le mouvement démocratique.* 1910.

Brugerette, J. *Le prêtre français et la société contemporaine.* 3 vols. 1933–1938.

Cornilleau, R. *L'Abbé Naudet.* n. d.

Dorigny, J. *L'Abbé Lemire, son oeuvre parlementaire.* 1914.

Eblé, M. *Les écoles catholiques d'économie politique et sociale en France.* 1905.

Fontanille, Henri. *L'oeuvre sociale d'Albert de Mun*. 1931.

Geck, L. H. A. *Die sozialen Arbeitsverhältnisse im Wandel der Zeit*. Berlin, 1931.

Goyau, G. *Autour du catholicisme social*. 1901.

Guitton, G. *Léon Harmel*. 2 vols. 1925.

Hoog, G. *Histoire du catholicisme social en France, de l'encyclique "Rerum Novarum" a l'encyclique "Quadragesimo Anno."* 1942.

Jarlot, G. *Le régime corporatif et les catholiques sociaux*. 1938.

Lecanuet, E. *La vie de l'église sous Léon XIII*. 1930.

Lestrat, G. *Les beaux temps du Sillon*. 1926.

Levasseur, E. *Questions ouvrières et industrielles en France sous la III/République*. 1907.

Maignen, Ch. *Maurice Maignen, Directeur du Cercle Montparnasse et les origines du mouvement social catholique en France (1822–1890)*. Luçon, 1927.

Moon, P. Th. *The Labor Problem and the Social Catholic Movement in France*. New York, 1921.

Rivain, J. *Un programme de restauration sociale. La Tour du Pin précurseur*. 1926.

Rollet, H. *L'action sociale des catholiques en France (1871–1901)*. 1947.

Rollet, H. *Albert de Mun et le parti catholique*. 1947.

Sangier, M. *Albert de Mun*. 1932.

Semichon, R. *Les idées sociales et politiques de La Tour du Pin*. 1936.

T'Serclaes, Mgr. de. *Le pape Léon XIII*. 3 vols. Lille, 1894 ff.

Turmann, M. *Le développement du catholicisme social depuis l'encyclique "Rerum Novarum,"* 1901.

Verdin, E. *Les origines du syndicalisme chrétien en France. La fondation du Syndicat des Employés du Commerce et de l'Industrie*. 1929.

Zamanski, J. *Nous, catholiques sociaux*. 1947.

Zirnheld, J. *Cinquante années de syndicalisme chrétien*. 1937.

INDEX OF NAMES

SUBJECT INDEX

A
Abbés démocrates, 266–269, 281, 296
Action française, 53, 59
Amis de la Vérité, 63, 208
Ancien régime, 59, 67, 72, 74, 105, 138, 144, 158, 165, 176, 198, 208, 240
Anschluss, 2
Anticlericalism, 27, 203, 239, 272n
Anti-individualism, of Christian democrats, 13–14
Association catholique, 259
Atelier, 63, 213
Atéliers nationals, 229
Au milieu des Sollicitudes (1892), 266, 275, 287
Avenir, 63, 191–196, 217, 219, 223, 227, 234, 286n, 290

B
Bastille, 108
Benedictine Order, 233
Boulanger adventure, 275
Bourbon, Restoration charter, 176n
Bourgeoisie (middle class), 34, 122, 212, 221, 285
  and church of *Ancien régime*, 90–97
  and Revolution of 1848, 229–231
"Buchezism," 210

C
Cahiers, 69, 99, 101, 261

Calvinism, 25, 154–155
Carbonaria, 207, 210
Cartesian philosophy, 165–166, 168–169
Catholic church,
  and Christian Democracy, 270–271
  and constitutional church, 124
  and democratic society, 288
  hierarchical concept of, 76n
  and Revolution of 1789, 98–107
Catholic emancipation, 236
Catholic politics, defined, 17–18
Catholic traditionalism, 58, 66, 141–142, 198, 221, 283–284
  De Bonald's view, 158–165
  and De Maistre, 146–158
  importance of Lamennais in, 146
  as political movement, 144–146
  as religious movement, 145–146
  theological view of, 165–175
Catholicism. See Liberal, Political, *and* Social Catholicism
Caucas system, Anglo-Saxon, 32
Cercle de la Démocratie catholique, 63
Cercle social, 63, 106–112, 126–130, 132–133, 136
Christian Democratic parties, 63
Christian Democratic Union of Central Europe (CDUCE), 3
Christian Democracy,
  in Austria, 2
  in Belgium, 2, 9, 180n, 273, 290–

321

research on, 48n, 71n
Saint-Martin's view, 152–153
Revolution of 1830, 45, 51, 143, 178,
   181, 195, 216, 227–228, 243, 290
Revolution of 1848, 32–33, 34, 43–46,
   51, 178, 181, 195, 197, 214, 216,
   223, 227–232, 239, 251, 283–284

S

St. Vincent Conference, of Ozanam,
   226
Second Empire, 51, 253
Second Republic, 230–231, 238, 285
Sens commun, 165, 171–173, 181, 185
   as revolutionary Catholicism, 199
Sillon, 5, 48, 53–54, 57, 281, 296
Singulari nos. See Encyclicals, papal
Social Catholicism, 247n, 261n, 263,
   269, 282, 293–296
   conservative school of, 245
   defined, 19–21
   and démocratie chrétienne, 231
   historical description of, 293–295
   indictment of, 56–57
   relation to Christian Democracy, 60–
      61
   Rollet's description of, 264
   and Thomistic philosophy, 199n
Socialism, 258, 280, 293–294
   Christian, 212, 214, 233, 255
   and Christian Democracy, 40–41
   Ozanam's distinction of, 246–247
   religious, 178n
"Sociological Catholicism," 180, 284
Sociology
   of Buchez, 209–210
   and Christian Democracy, 180–181
   Comte's, 52, 210
   and Démocratie chrétienne, 240–241
   of Lamennais, 183
   of party formation, 28–42

relation to Catholicism, 67
Solesmes, 233, 253n
Sozialkatechismus (Herder), 21
Staatskirchentum ("establishment"
   church), 196
Swiss Protestant People's Service, 6
Syllabus. See Encyclicals, papal

T

Théorie du pouvoir politique (Bonald),
   143, 159–160, 162
Third Reich, 27
Third Republic, 33, 52, 268, 271, 273,
   287, 293
Thomistic philosophy, 199n, 285n
Totalitarian democracy, 139, 282
Tridentine reforms, 89, 154
Trinitarian scheme, of De Bonald, 161–
   163

U

Ultramontanism, 52, 175, 243
   founder of, 158
Union movement,
   of Buchez, 245–246
   trade, 267, 281

V

Vatican I, 155
Vormarz, 29

W

Weimar Republic, 27
Working class, 231–232, 255–262, 269,
   271, 281
   Pilgrimage to Rome, 264–265, 276–
      278
Workmen's associations, 211, 246

Z

Zentrum, 5, 13, 47, 61, 273